Apartheid on Tuesday

Wendy Anne Lawson

© 2023 by Wendy Anne Lawson. All rights reserved.

No part of this book may be reproduced, except for a brief quotation, the source of which is fully acknowledged.

ISBN: 978-0-6481246-8-9

Cover photo: Port Alfred beach, Cape Province, South Africa, 1978.

Back cover photo: Sign in bus going up Kloof Street, Cape Town, 1972.

Table of Contents

Apartheid on Tuesday 1

Kwapitela and Compensation 144

District 6 151

Vrededorp (Pageview) 160

False Bay Station 168

Epilogue 170

Apartheid on Tuesday is not a memoir, it was written in 1972.

Some names have been changed.

In 1972 I gave some people false names to protect them from retribution by the apartheid government, and now I have given them back their real names, except where their profession means that privacy is an issue. In 2022 I have given false names to some others to protect them from being embarrassed by their own stupidity.

I came up with the title *Apartheid on Tuesday* on Tuesday 21 November 1972, on the way home from visiting the building with the four elevators.

Chapter 1

Saturday 22nd July 1972

Today I arrived home from Greece. Our plane stopped at Luanda on the way from Athens to Johannesburg, and the sun rose while we were on the ground. After take-off I gazed out of the window, and the terrain gradually changed from the rivers and forests of Angola to the desert of Botswana. We had a large marble statue on board, a gift from one tyrant to another. We knew about it because we had seen it being checked in at Athens airport while we were waiting in line with our luggage. Four men with a wooden crate on a trolley had shoved in front of us shouting "Make space, make space". They heaved the crate onto the scale, and the needle flipped to 200 pounds. It couldn't go any further as the scale only went up to 200 pounds. The check-in agent looked indecisive for a moment, then waved it through. One of the men proudly told us that there was a marble statue inside the crate - a gift from George Papadopoulos to John Vorster. The former is the head of the Greek Junta, the latter is the head of the apartheid regime.

The desert of Botswana changed to Transvaal bushveld, then down we went and landed in Sunny South Africa. The tourist pamphlets rave about the wonderful weather, but they don't mention that you won't get a tourist visa if your skin is dark.

As I walked across the tarmac from the plane to the building I was struck by the difference in the light. In the Greek Islands the light is white and clear, very beautiful. But the light in Africa is yellow and warm, also beautiful.

The security police inside the airport building tried to look nonchalant as we filed past them. They were doing a bad job of pretending that they were not watching us. They thought that we would not know that they were police because they were not wearing the dreaded grey uniform. They were out in force to survey our arrival because we were a charter flight of 156 students from the University of the Witwatersrand, and many of us had been involved in the June week of protests. They were probably most interested in Adam Klein, who was on our flight, and is particularly unpopular with the government at present.

The security police call themselves BOSS; Bureau of State Security. They think that wearing suits and ties makes them blend in, but they do not understand the nuances of style. They are not smart, in either sense of the word. For one thing, their suits don't fit well. They would have been less conspicuous if they had not all stood in the same way, dressed in the same way, in a long line, on the wrong side of passport control. There are always police in the building, but not usually security police. BOSS agents don't look as scary as the KGB, or the ESA in Greece, and although they do kill and torture people, they don't kill people like me.

The customs man asked me, "Do you have anything objectionable in your suitcase?"

"No", I said, and went through. I was not smuggling in any exciting contraband, dangerous firearms, or packets of heroin, but I did have a copy of a banned book, *The Strawberry Statement,* in my suitcase, which he would have considered objectionable.

After waiting for ages, then scouring the building, I found no sign of my mother. So I tried the telephone – a desperate move, considering what South African telephones are like. The first five coins fell into the Minister of Telecommunication's bottomless money pit, but the sixth one worked. When my mother heard my voice she said, "Where are you?" She was surprised to hear that my plane had landed on time, because earlier in the day she had phoned the airport and been told that our plane had been delayed by four hours. This kind of thing happens because of the job reservation laws. In South Africa whites get jobs because of the colour of their skin, not because of their ability.

Sunday 23rd July 1972

We had lunch at the Bryanston Country Club today. The club is for whites only, but only for posh whites who think that they are better than others. The club rules say that ladies may not wear slacks and men must wear ties. The black waiters wear white jackets and carry white cloths. When I was young my parents played tennis and bowls at the club, and I would spend hours playing in the veld, or swimming in the pool while the waiters looked on. I was usually the only one swimming, and the waiters would like it when I ordered a drink because it would give them something to do, instead of just standing there holding a tray. The fact that I could speak Zulu also cheered them up. Colonialists like to feel that there is always "staff" at their beck and call, and from the point of view of the staff it is better to be paid a pittance to do a stupid job than to die of starvation in the Bantustans.

According to the government there are four races, and everyone has to be classified into one of the races. Most of the population is classified as "Bantu", the rest are "White", "Coloured" or "Asian". Where a person lives and how much they can earn is determined by their classification. There are hundreds of acts of parliament that regulate what each race group is allowed to do.

The waiters at the club are all "Bantu", and the members are all "White". The whites get angry when someone points out the error of their ways. They forget their manners, even when they are at the Bryanston Country Club. Today the anger erupted because one of them called our waiter a boy, and I pointed out that a man who is aged over twenty-one is not a boy. In the midst of the tirade I was accused of being a liberal, a kaffirboetjie, and a communist. I am a liberal and a kaffirboetjie, but I'm not a communist. They don't even know what a communist is.

While I was in Greece I had been thinking that I should write a book about my encounters with apartheid, because so many of the fellow tourists that I met asked questions about it. I bought a copy of *The Strawberry Statement* from a tobacconist's kiosk in Constitution Square, and after reading it I thought I would also use the day-by-day method to tell my story. Being yelled at by those stupid people at the club today confirmed that I need to write about my experience of this insane society.

Monday 24th July 1972

The Whites who love apartheid are very touchy. They get angry at any remark that is "political". They can sit and complain about their servants for hours, and that is not political, but if I make a remark about how badly they treat their servants, that is "political". My friend Louisa says that they react like that because they have guilty consciences, but I think that some of them do not have consciences. I think that some of them get angry because they know that I and others like me want to bring about the end of apartheid, and they don't want that to happen.

There is a lot wrong with our society. Discrimination already existed in 1910, and after the four provinces were unified into the Union of South Africa, laws were introduced that made matters worse. When the Nats gained power in 1948 things got worse much faster. In their effort to make things better for the Whites they have passed laws that cause millions of people to live in dire poverty, and there are laws that make discrimination compulsory.

Although using the word "Bantu" is okay in anthropology, it is insulting when used the way the government uses it, so my friends and I refer to people who are classified "Bantu" as Blacks. Blacks are not citizens in South Africa, so they have to carry a "pass" at all times. "Coloureds" and "Asians" do not have to carry a pass, but there are lots of other laws that make life difficult for them.

The pass is a little book that says where the owner is allowed to be. A black person walking along the street can be stopped at any time by a white policeman who demands to look at their pass, and if permission to be in that area is not written there, they are arrested. After languishing in jail for a while they have a very short trial, and then they are sent to work on a farm for a month. They don't get paid for the work they do during that month. I once saw a pass offender be delivered to a farm in his Sunday best, and be sent straight away to clean a pigsty to teach him not to be a "cheeky kaffir".[1] It was because he was wearing a hand-me-down suit that he was regarded as a "cheeky kaffir".

Most black servants have a Sunday best. The Sunday best clothes are old fashioned and a bit worn out because they are second hand. Domestic servants get Sunday afternoons off, but only after lunch has been served, the dishes washed, and the kitchen cleaned. Then the servant is free to put on their Sunday best and leave the property. You see them sitting in groups on the grass on the pavements outside the white homes. They can go to church because the churches have services for Blacks on Sunday afternoons, but they can't go into any other building or to a park.

Servants also get Thursdays off. They have to serve breakfast and clean up, and then

---

1 Kaffir is a derogatory word for a black person.

they go off at 10 am. They can catch a bus into the city, or sit on the grass and chat with their friends. If they are married their husbands or wives are allowed to visit them, but are not allowed to stay overnight. If they go into the city on their day off they cannot go into anything like a cinema or a library because of the "whites only – net blankes" signs above the doors. They have to take their pass with them on their day off, otherwise if they are stopped by the police they will be arrested and then sent out to work as prison labour, unless their employer can find out where they are and pay some money to get them back.

Police vans drive up and down the streets looking for pass offenders. They stop people at random and demand to see the pass. Even if the person has the right stamp in their pass the police are often rude to them and sometimes hit them. A few weeks ago some UFOs were alleged to have been seen flying around above the Eastern Cape. The police even fired at them, hoping to achieve I don't know what. So now jokes are circulating about a spaceship landing and little green men climbing out and being arrested because they are in a whites only area without a pass.

The pass has to be signed by the employer every month to prove that the owner still has a job. Domestic servants have to work very long hours for very low pay. They have to call the woman of the house "Madam", and the man "Boss" or "Baas". A female servant is called "the maid" or "the girl", while a male servant is called "the garden boy" or "the house boy". You also get "cook boys", "flat boys", "rubbish boys", "garage boys", "ironing girls" and "nanny girls". A nanny has the task of bringing up white children from the cradle to school going age. That leaves white mothers with plenty of time on their hands to sit in chairs and complain about their servants and the United Nations. The white mothers do not have to do any housework, and most of them do not have jobs because their husbands earn a lot.

The maid servant's day starts when she brings tea or coffee to the family before breakfast, and finishes when the supper dishes have been washed. She has a rest period after lunch and does not necessarily work full-out all the time.

In Parkview where we live most white families have a woman who works inside the house and a man who works in the garden. When we moved here from Bryanston we brought two of our servants with us. Their passbooks had to be endorsed for the new area, and my mother went to the pass office with them so that they did not have to wait in the queue for three days. (A white person always goes to the front of the queue.) Our maid was Ester Luvuno, but she died on the day that I finished school. My mother decided that she was not going to replace her, and that our "garden boy", Ishmail Moabelo, would get a raise in wages and do kitchen work as well as the garden. So we wash our own clothes, make our own beds and cook

Ester in Bryanston.

our own food, but Ishmail washes the dishes and cleans the kitchen. He also holds the fort and looks after Lalli-dog whenever we are away. Ishmail's wife and children live in a rural area west of Potgietersrus. He usually spends three weeks of the year with them, but this year is different because he went home at the end of June to build another room onto his house.

When our neighbour's maid died she also was not replaced by another maid, and the "garden boy" started to do inside work as well as garden work. There isn't much garden work to do because the properties are only a quarter of an acre, so they sometimes manufacture work to do to stop themselves from being bored. The servant next door is called James Mpendu Zondi, and sometimes he prunes the hedge, then prunes it all over again two inches further back. On Thursdays he finishes the kitchen work at about 9 am, and his madam stands in the kitchen and watches him until 10 am. They both just stand there doing nothing for an hour. When the clock strikes 10 she says he can go. She has such power over him because the law prevents him from getting a better job. I know a lot about the servants in this neighbourhood because I speak Zulu and they trust me, but I don't know nearly as much as they know about each other and about the Whites.

Ishmail and Lalli-dog.

On the other side the neighbour's maid is called Maria. Looking at her face you can see that she has white ancestors, but she is classified "Bantu". She comes from Rustenberg, and has to leave her children there with her mother. Three of them have died because Maria cannot send enough money home to feed them properly. One white housewife in our suburb said about the death of Maria's children, "It's because they don't look after them." How is she supposed to look after them when she is forced to live a hundred miles away?

Past those neighbours is where David Gurney lives with his mother. They have a maid and they allow her husband to stay in her room at night. Last year there was a pass raid at night. When the police do pass raids at night they arrive at about 11 pm, and some police go to the front door to tell the white people what is happening, while others go to the servants' quarters at the back to catch any Blacks who don't have the right stamp in their pass. When David realised that there were police at the front door he dashed out

James Mpendu Zondi.

the back to warn the maid's husband to bolt into the lane, but he was too late. The police arrested the husband and they bashed him in the police van.

In our suburb of Parkview there are sanitary lanes down the middle of each block. In the old days carts used them to take away the sewage in buckets. Now the lanes are clean, and most of the garages come off the lane instead of coming off the street at the front. The doors can't be opened from the outside, so when I arrive home I drive up the lane to the back of our property, and then hoot so that Ishmail will come and open the garage doors. If Ishmail isn't there James comes from next door and opens the garage doors for me. When I was in Greece I was chatting with a Canadian guy about the servant situation in South Africa, and I mentioned this. He thought it was outrageous that the neighbour's servant could be at my beck and call. I told him that James really likes doing it because it relieves the boredom, but that didn't make the Canadian disapprove any less.

Ishmail often cleans the roof to give himself something to do, and he mows the lawn twice a week. Ishmail was paid R15 per month as a gardener, and now gets R20 because of the extra kitchen work. R20 is not even enough to buy a second-hand bicycle. The Whites can get away with paying such low wages because there are more people wanting jobs than there are jobs, and it is illegal for Blacks to get any of the other jobs that need to be done. Blacks are not allowed to come to the city until they have the right stamp in their pass, but they can't get the right stamp in their pass until they have come to the city and found a job. So they come to the city to look for a job, and if they find a job before they get caught by the police, they then have to work for a pittance.[2] The blacks who work deep down in the hot mines also only get paid R20 per month.

The double-decker buses that take Whites to the city from Parkview and the ones that take Blacks go along the same route, but the stops are in different places so that Whites don't have to stand near Blacks while waiting for a bus. To the north of Johannesburg

A Putco bus in 1982.

there is a black township called Alexandra where the people live in terrible conditions. The areas where Blacks live are called townships, not suburbs or towns. The Putco buses that carry the workers from Alexandra to the city are single-decker and painted blue.

The signs at white bus stops say "1st class", and at black bus stops they say "2nd class". On trains the black carriages are called "3rd class", because 1st and 2nd class are for Whites. So Blacks who catch buses are 2nd class, but those who catch trains

---

2 More than 2500 people were arrested each day for not having the right stamp in their pass.

are 3rd class.

Benches have "whites only" or "non-whites only" painted on the backrest, and post offices and government buildings have separate entrances and separate counters. Some shops have signs up, depending on the feelings of the owner, while discos, coffee bars and theatres have a more subtle "Right of Admission Reserved – Reg van Toegang Voorbehou," which really means "whites only".

Most Whites are unaware that the Blacks feel resentment about the way they are treated. They think that because the Blacks behave in a submissive way they are perfectly happy with the situation. If they learned to speak one of the black languages they would think differently. The servants around here know that I understand Zulu, so they are careful about what they say in front of me. But when I am surrounded by Blacks who don't know me, they speak freely amongst themselves. They assume that the Whites within hearing range can't understand what they are saying, because it is unusual for a white person to know the language. Zulu is the only black language that I understand, but it is spoken a lot around Johannesburg, even though Zululand is far away. It is often amusing to hear what they say about me and my friends, like when they are discussing our clothes. It is not funny when they are complaining about something bad that has recently been done to them by a white person. Usually there is a tone of indignation, but sometimes the hatred that is in their voices makes me shudder.

Wednesday 26th July 1972

Mr. Vaughn came round for dinner and created a fight as usual. I don't even have to say anything. Just the fact that he knows what I think makes him want to fight with me. It is people like him that are making it easier for the Russians to take over, but he accuses me of wanting the Russians to take over. I try to get him to see that the worse the Whites treat the Blacks the more likely it is that the Blacks will think that they would have a better time if the Russians took over. And preventing the Blacks from getting educated is even more dangerous, because uneducated people are more liable to believe that they would be happy under communism. The Russians are providing weapons to the terrorists north of the border because they want to get hold of South Africa's mineral wealth, and the more the Blacks are suppressed, the more likely it is that there will be a violent revolution.

One of the ways that blacks are suppressed is through job reservation. It is called "job reservation" because the good jobs are reserved for Whites. There are actually laws that prevent Blacks from getting good jobs. There is a long list of jobs that are only allowed to be done by Whites. On top of that it is also illegal for a white person to work in a job that has a person who is not white working above them. Companies can employ people who are not white, but they have to make sure that the job they do is of a lower status than the job that any white employee does. They also have to ensure that no white person gets instructions from a person who is not white.

Job reservation means that Whites don't necessarily get jobs because they have brains or ability; some get jobs solely because they have white skin. There are lots of government departments that employ white people to do almost nothing, and even then they do almost nothing rather badly. The government owns the railways, so trying to buy a train ticket can drive you mad because you are dealing with an incompetent person who knows that they are not going to lose their job no matter how badly they do it. Everything you try to do that involves officialdom is fraught with difficulty because most of the useless Whites get jobs working for the government. Things are much worse for Blacks. Officialdom is blatantly hostile towards them.

Thursday 27th July 1972

One of the things that Mr. Vaughn shouted at me yesterday was, "If you want to change the government you must do it through the ballot box." When I reminded him that the Nats have made it impossible for the government to be changed through the ballot box, he shouted, "The law is the law and you must obey the law." Funnily enough he does not believe that the law of the road applies to him.

There are three political parties in parliament; The National Party, the United Party and the Progressive Party. The National Party is the ruling party, and Mr. Vorster is the prime minister. They and their supporters are called the Nats. The United Party was the ruling party before the Nats came to power in 1948. The United Party is now the official opposition, but it doesn't do any opposing.

People who are classified white are the only ones who can vote, but even for those who can vote the system is unfair because of the way the Nats have laid out the boundaries of the voting constituencies. Constituencies that are predominantly English speaking have twice as many voters in them as the ones that are predominantly Afrikaans speaking.[3]

English speaking voters traditionally vote for the United Party, although many of them secretly vote for the Nats. If the United Party came to power they would not do away with apartheid. We would just have English apartheid instead of Afrikaans apartheid. You sometimes hear an English speaking person say, "It's not us. It's the Afrikaners." Meanwhile it is them.

The Progressive Party is anti-apartheid, and for the last 11 years it has had only one member in parliament, Helen Suzman. She has been in parliament for 20 years, and is outnumbered by one hundred and sixty six to one in the House of Assembly. Unlike the other politicians, she believes in human rights and equal opportunity, and is resolute in her fight for justice in this country. The Progressive Party and its supporters are called the Progs.

Helen Suzman represents one of the most affluent parts of Johannesburg. I sometimes wonder whether those rich people vote against apartheid because they have a lot to lose if there is a violent revolution, or because they feel confident that the Progressive Party will never get a majority. Whatever the reason, having Helen Suzman in parliament is wonderful, because she constantly reminds the Nats that what they are doing is wrong. They shout rude things at her when she is speaking, but they don't stop her from speaking. In parliament she can say things that would get other people jailed or banned. She has a team of researchers who supply her with facts and figures, and then she presents them in parliament. The Nats hate it, and some of them make it plain that

---

3 Afrikaans is a language derived from Dutch.

they hate her. She seems to be immune to jibes and insults, and she always has a sense of humour.

Another thing that makes sure that the Nats get voted in every time is that they control the radio waves. There is no TV in South Africa, so the radio is a very powerful instrument for propaganda. The Nats control all of the South African radio stations, and the ones from outside can only be picked up on shortwave. The Nats don't control the English language newspapers, but they do censor them, and they make threats against them.

The government department that runs radio broadcasting is called the South African Broadcasting Corporation (S.A.B.C.). It is controlled by a Control Board of nine members who are appointed by the state president. The news and other programmes are twisted in a subtle way to make it sound as though apartheid is moral, fair, and successful. A lot of listeners fall for it because it is so subtle. The radio keeps on saying that South Africa is a democracy, and that the government has been democratically elected, and a lot of white South Africans choose to believe it.

Friday 28th July 1972

In Greece we often met up with other English speaking travellers, and as soon as they heard that we were South Africans they would ask us whether we knew anything about the recent student unrest. I would start by showing them the little nail that had worked its way upwards from the sole of my sandal, and had bothered me as I ran away from the police. The Nats say that we provoked the police and that the demonstrations were organised by communists, but the demonstrations were really a spontaneous reaction to the terrible things that the Nats were doing.

It all started at a place called Turfloop. Turfloop is one of the new universities that the Nats have built so that they can pretend that they are being fair to the Blacks. About ten years ago the Nats passed a law which said that, except for Fort Hare, the existing universities would be for Whites only. The law also said that they would build new universities for the people who are not white. They have only built four universities, so now, including Fort Hare, there are five universities for 82.5% of the population, while the Whites, who are less than one fifth of the population, have 11 universities. The conditions at the new universities are not good, as is only to be expected when they are set up by a racist government.

Turfloop is in a rural area in the Northern Transvaal, and although it is for black students, it is run entirely by Whites. Even the vacation jobs are given to white students from other universities, and Blacks are not allowed to go into some of the shops on the campus. On the 29th of April there was a graduation ceremony at Turfloop, and Abraham Tiro made a speech that upset the white authorities. They were expecting him to say that he was grateful for his education, but instead he told the truth about the conditions at the university. He started off by quoting the Prime Minister, "No black man has landed in trouble for fighting for what is legally his," which of course is not true. Then he gently and eloquently described the hardships and racist indignities that the students have to endure. He ended off by saying, "In conclusion Mr. Chancellor, I say, let the Lord be praised, for the day shall come when all men shall be free to breathe the air of freedom, and when that day shall come, no man, no matter how many tanks he has, will reverse the course of events. God bless you all."

As punishment he was suspended from the university, and the next day the whole student body protested by staging a sit-in on the lawn. Every single one of them was suspended. It must have taken a lot of courage for the students to support Abraham Tiro, because they know that getting a qualification from that university is their only chance of getting a job that would pay better than starvation wages.

We white students are used to seeing Blacks suffer every day, it is just a part of life for us. However, we were stirred by the fact that eleven hundred and forty six fellow students had been suspended just because they had had the courage to support one student who had told the truth. There was a reaction among students at all the English speaking universities. The plan at Wits (University of the Witwatersrand) was to stage a one-day strike on the first of June. All of us who sympathised with the Turfloop students would attend a protest meeting on campus instead of going to lectures. I decided that I would take part in the strike.

The day before the strike was a public holiday, called Republic Day. It is eleven years since South Africa broke away from the British Commonwealth. There was a music festival on campus. Only two thousand people turned up, but it had a good atmosphere. There was no traffic noise because the city centre was empty, no thugs turned up "to teach us respect" for the republic, the music was good, and the vibe was peaceful.

The following day at 10 am I sat on the same lawn, this time as one of the strikers who sympathised with the students at Turfloop. The crowd looked the same, dressed in casual colourful clothing, but the feeling in the air was different. The smell of the air was different too, no joss sticks, and in place of the band stood Helen Suzman. She told us the facts about education in South Africa. Whites get their education free, while Blacks have to pay. So people who live below the poverty line have to pay, while the rich get free education. The government spends two hundred and fifty six rand a year on each white schoolchild, and nineteen rand a year on each black child who is fortunate enough to attend school. In Black primary schools the teacher to pupil ratio is one to sixty, and less than two percent of the teachers are qualified. Seventy percent of black children leave during the first four years, and only five percent reach high school. When she told us that only one in a thousand gets a matriculation, a gasp went up from the crowd. We had known that it was bad, but not that it was that bad.

Mrs. Suzman told us that Indians and Coloureds do not have to pay for attending school, but the facilities provided are inadequate. Three percent of Coloured children

Helen Suzman speaking at Wits University 1 June 1972. The original of this photo seems to no longer exist.

and two percent of Indian children reach matriculation. I was quite shocked by the figures. I had known that schools were overcrowded, but I had not realised how bad it was. I went home shaking my head and sighing. I did not realise that the strike was not the end of the protests.

The next day I went to university and attended lectures as usual. It was Friday the 2nd of June. That evening I heard on the S.A.B.C. news that the police had had to disperse some students who were demonstrating in Cape Town. It didn't sound like much and I carried on cooking.

The next afternoon when the newspaper arrived I discovered what had really happened in Cape Town. In reaction to the treatment of the students at Turfloop, some students from the University of Cape Town, which is a whites only university, had gathered on the steps of St. George's Cathedral in Wale Street, and had started addressing the passing crowd with loud hailers. They denounced the lack of education for Blacks, and they also held placards that expressed their views. The cathedral is in the middle of Cape Town city, really close to the Houses of Parliament. This protest was an "illegal meeting" because the students had not applied for permission to protest. If they had applied for permission, it would have been refused.

The police arrived and told the students to disperse. The students remained, so the police attacked. They charged with batons, hitting, dragging, pulling hair, kicking, and bludgeoning anyone they could get at. A journalist who witnessed the scene called it, "That unbelievable moment when the mass singing of the students turned to mass screaming." Some of the students tried to escape by running into the cathedral, but the police followed. The police hit them with batons inside the cathedral, even in front of the altar.

The Nats pride themselves on having made South Africa into a Christian state. The education they provide is called *Christian National Education*. Bible Study is a compulsory subject in schools, and the miniskirt is blamed for causing the drought, but they consider it quite moral to beat up students inside a church. Pamela Diamond, a Cape Town journalist, wrote, "I wonder if Mr. Lourens Muller, our Minister of Police, has met Mayor Daley of Chicago. They have a lot in common. They both have police forces which beat up students. There is only one difference, as far as I can see. Mayor Daley's bully boys did not go storming into a church and drag their victims from the altar by their hair and flog them through the nave, chase them around the christening font and pursue them between the pews – shouting obscenities all the while. All that was a refinement added by Mr. Muller's boys."

It was not only students who got hurt. Once the police had started they were having too much fun to know the difference between students and passers-by. They hit anybody they could lay hands on. One of the people who was attacked was a woman whose husband is a Nat, and who had spent the day at the parliamentary library translating government documents into French. On her way home she passed the demonstration. "What I saw has shocked me to the core and I would never have believed it if I had not seen it with my own eyes. A policeman was dragging a student across the sidewalk by his hair while a second and third hit and kicked him. It was more than I could take. I told them they were behaving like brutes and they told me to move away in spite of the fact that I was on public property." A policeman was about to strike her when she said, "You're young enough to be my son. Would you dare to hit me!" He left her but three others came up. "One ordered me away and pushed me off the sidewalk and when I objected to being pushed he raised his baton and hit me over the eye. I pushed him away and he told me he would lay a charge of assaulting a policeman against me for doing it." She was put in a police van with cut and bleeding students, taken to a police station, questioned, then put in a cell. "The police were abusive in their language when I retaliated to being treated so badly. They refused to address me as Mrs. Van Oudenhove and called me Yvonne until my husband arrived and had me released. I'm fifty years old and they refused to believe it when they asked me my age. One of them pointed at me when an officer came into the charge office and said, 'Dis die tannie wat ek geslaan het (That's the auntie that I hit)'."

Another of the passers-by who got assaulted was a pregnant woman. As they beat her she screamed, "I'm pregnant, I'm pregnant," and she vomited onto the pavement.

On Saturday night the S.A.B.C. were not so demure in their reporting as they had been the night before. They said nothing about the behaviour of the police, but instead tried to smear the reputation of the students. They said that the students inside the cathedral had been lounging on pews, that couples were kissing, and "the smoking of dagga is being investigated". For the next few days they kept on saying that the students had been doing these three things. The idea that the students might have smoked dagga (marijuana) in the church is ridiculous, but it worked as a smear tactic. The penalty for being caught with even a small amount of dagga is eight years in prison, so people who smoke dagga would not even take it with them when they go shopping, let alone when they are going to a protest. And they definitely would not light up and smoke when they are surrounded by police. It is not likely that the students would have been in the mood for kissing either. It is typical of the attitude of the Nats to believe that kissing inside a church is immoral, but that violently bashing someone inside a church is heroic.

I was furious when I found out what had actually happened in Cape Town, but I am furious about a lot of things that happen in South Africa, and am powerless to put things right. I might have felt less upset had I known that the attack in the cathedral had made headlines in the outside world. Important people were expressing outrage about it, including the Archbishop of Canterbury, who said, "The assault by policemen on students in St. George's Cathedral is a shocking sacrilege."

I came down with flu and spent a few days cooped up in bed. That gave me plenty of time to hear what the radio was saying about the students. I was still sick on Tuesday, but I was bored with being in bed, so I went to university. After lectures I heard that there was a protest next to Jan Smuts Avenue, but my car was parked on Yale Road on the other side of campus. I was aware of the fact that "student unrest" was "spreading all over the country", but I was sick physically, and suffered badly from that even worse disease, apathy. I went to the car and drove home. On Wednesday I was too sick to get up. The 6 o'clock news said, "This afternoon students of the Witwatersrand staged a placard protest on Jan Smuts Avenue, and they dropped their placards and ran away when police arrived on the scene."

On Thursday morning I arrived early for lectures, and found Glenda sitting outside the lecture theatre reading a newspaper. There was a square notice in the newspaper that had been put in by Professor Bozzoli, the vice-chancellor of Wits university. It said that because all gatherings of eleven or more people with a common intent or purpose out of doors had been banned, he was calling a mass meeting of all students in the gym.

"This business of eleven is ridiculous," said Glenda.

"I heard that yesterday there was another protest and they ran away when the police turned up," I said.

"We had to," said Glenda. "They chased us right up to those chains by the wooden hut, with batons."

"So you were there?"

"Yes. It was terrible. I've never run so fast in my life. Then when they went away we went back and stood on the pavement again, and they attacked us again."

I was surprised to hear that the students had gone back after running away, because I had believed what I had heard on the radio. I was also surprised to hear that they had not run away when the police arrived, they had only run away when the police attacked.

My lectures ended early so I caught a bus to the city to buy some sewing fabric. There was enough time for me to get back for the mass meeting in the gym. Mr. Ermert was on the bus on the way back. I know Mr. Ermert through the Archaeological Society. He was talking loudly about the bad behaviour of the police. The other people on the bus had agreeing expressions on their faces, some were nodding as he spoke. It didn't surprise me that such a well-educated and enlightened man as Mr. Ermert was opposed to police brutality and was willing to say so loudly, but that ordinary members of the white public were on the side of the students when the students were breaking the law was incredible. The radio had been telling the public that the students were dangerous and communistically inspired. Mr. Vorster's favourite word at this time was "hardcore". The S.A.B.C. frequently played his voice saying that a hardcore of communistically inspired students were inciting the rest to demonstrate in order to cause anarchy and to change the South African way of life. The propaganda obviously had not worked on the people on the bus.

I felt encouraged by Mr. Ermert's attitude as I walked across campus to the gym. It was already full so I had to stand on a side stairway. The gym was jam-packed with what I later found out was seven thousand people, and there were hundreds behind me who could not get beyond the first landing. I could not see the speakers because they were on a mezzanine floor above me, but I had a great view of the crowd. They were looking up at the speakers, and their faces were so grim, serious and determined; it made me smile. The only other time I had seen such a large group of people standing all squashed up together was in Trafalgar Square on New Year's Eve, but they had been full of joy and festivity.

This meeting was legal because it was indoors. Professor Bozzoli spoke first.

> The reason for the meeting is solemn enough, but it is also serious and tragic and critical to the highest degree. We are at a time of crisis – at a moment when the unhappy consequences of an act of 1959, the so called 'Extension' of Universities Act, are being experienced to the full throughout our country.

He then told us the history of Wits University, and the history of the introduction of racial segregation in all the universities, leading up to the present situation.

He continued;

> Yet the tension could be relieved tomorrow and a new era could be expected the day after if those in authority would demonstrate their wisdom and their real strength by having the education offered in Black and Brown universities studied now, by ascertaining the legitimate grievances of the students in them and taking steps to correct them, by conceding the truth known to all the rest of the world.
>
> We want no violence over any issue - we plead only for peace and wisdom. It is not a revolution in South Africa that we want, but I believe that one of the first steps to be taken to avoid a revolution is to bring about revolutionary changes in education. What I request is an examination, a diagnosis and a cure. ... Surely it is a procedure to be expected when there are signs of an illness within the educational system.

He told us that he had written to the prime minister asking for an investigation into the real conditions of education and the reasons for unrest, and that his brother-in-law was hand-delivering the letter to the prime minister while he was speaking.

The chairman of the University Council, Dr. F. G. Hill, spoke next. One of the things he said was,

> One wonders how educated and thinking people can seriously believe that communism and liberalism are linked when ... these concepts are diametrically opposed. Communism glorifies the state, liberalism the individual.

When Adam Klein, president of the Student's Representative Council, spoke, he refuted the idea that we students had been incited to demonstrate by agitators, and showed how the protests had been provoked by the injustices that the Nats meted out. He called the word 'unspontaneous' "that new naughty word in the Nationalist vocabulary." The Nats have been using it a lot recently.

Last to speak was Professor Ellison Kahn, Dean of the Faculty of Law. He read out the proclamation of the Minister of Justice which banned gatherings of eleven or more people. Have you ever seen seven thousand glum people burst out laughing at once? Professor Kahn attempted to analyse the proclamation, ending off with,

> So here we have this inept government notice of doubtful validity, professing, on the face of it, to ban more meetings than the governing act permits, and barely understandable even to a lawyer who knows his way around this melancholy corner of the law.
>
> I do not suggest that any of you do anything to test the validity of this government notice. Indeed, I beg you not to do so. You may be acting illegally. And in any event, legal niceties are no immediate answer to a blow administered by a truncheon-happy constable who may have removed his identity number, or a person wielding a truncheon but not

clad in police uniform and who, for all we know is not a member of the force at all but is simply masquerading as one.

At what a sad state of affairs we have arrived. Law and order. Freedom of speech. 'the right of the people peacefully to assemble' to discuss or signify grievances. Democracy? Shame!

Then they read out the telegrams that had been sent from universities around the world. They were from Holland, Canada, Britain, America, all over. If those far away students could have heard the applause their messages received they would have known how much they were appreciated. There was also a telegram from Peter Hain. It made me feel warmer to know that while we, way down on the tip of Africa, took our stand against the iniquitous injustice of apartheid, people far away were thinking of us. By the end of the meeting the glumness had left, but the seriousness remained. The unity in that crowd was remarkable. I felt uplifted and warm.

A newspaper photo of the meeting in the gym retrieved from microfishe.

This day I had come by bus, so after the meeting I walked towards Jan Smuts Avenue to catch the bus home. I saw a group of people standing under the trees by the fire hydrant. I changed course and went to join them. Some of them were holding placards which read, "Free education for all." Others stood on the lawn behind.[4] I saw a friend and started chatting with him. I only noticed my bus as it left the stop. "I'll catch the next one," I thought. With Johannesburg's erratic bus service you never know when the next one will be, but I thought that I would see it approaching along Ameshoff Street and be able to run fast enough from where I was.

---

4 This lawn is now covered by the Oppenheimer Life Sciences Building

The crowd was growing. I decided to stay. I was hungry. The bus stop is outside the door of a café. I stood and looked at the café, thinking that I would go and buy something to eat in a minute. My feet never took me there. Some of the cars going past hooted short, sharp hoots to show their support for what we were doing. People were leaning out of the windows and shouting things like, "Right on" and "Good for you." The public were quite obviously on our side. An old lady with white hair went past. It was a good thing that she was the only one on the road at that time as her car was going zig zag zig across the two lanes as she had one hand on the hooter and the other giving a thumbs-up sign.

There were a few police on the other side of Jan Smuts Avenue. A boy came around giving out pieces of white cloth. He said, "When you get into teargas put this around your face and run." Then he gave me one of the pepper casters collected from the canteen and said, "When a police dog attacks you throw pepper into its eyes. Don't run, it'll tear you apart, just throw pepper at it."

"Whaaat?" I said, but he had moved on to others. I kept the cloth in my bag, and the pepper in my pocket with my hand on it, in case an Alsatian[5] materialised in front of me. When a small white car with three police and a dog in it went past, a groan went up from the students.

I saw my classmate Helen on the lawn and worked my way back through the crowd to chat with her. A chap with a loud hailer climbed onto the fire hydrant[6] and told us that the police were on their way, and that we must all move back and sit down on the lawn, which we did. Then the police vans arrived and a mass of grey uniforms jumped out of them. Helen put her head on my shoulder and said, "Oooh" in an agonised tone, then she sat up straight and tried to look composed. We were scared. The Nats later accused us of provoking the police for the fun of it. This was not my idea of fun.

In my bag I had a valuable book that was out of print. I told Helen that I was just going to put it away, and ran to the library, shoved my bag and jacket into a locker and ran back, keeping the pepper on me. Everybody was still sitting on the lawn, the police were on the other side of Jan Smuts Avenue. There were strange vibes around, tension, and yet everybody was relaxed. Suddenly the grey shirts jumped into their vans and drove off. We all stood up smiling. Apparently some people had been negotiating with the brigadier, and he had said that he would allow the demonstration to continue if we remained on university property.

The concrete pavement along Jan Smuts Avenue is public property, but the flower bed that stretches along next to the pavement from either side of the fire hydrant is on university property. Aloes and succulents are planted in the flower bed, and little paths have been made between the plants because students take a short cut through it every day as the gate is in an inconvenient position. After a while some students walked through the flower bed onto the pavement. The brigadier raised his loudhailer and said, "Please, you promised." There were shouts from the mass of students behind, and after being called all sorts of names the wayward students skulked back onto university property.

Then a student got onto the fire hydrant with a small branch in his hand. While

---

5 German Shepherd.
6 The fire hydrant was a large concrete structure with a flat top.

waving it about he shouted that we should all get weapons to defend ourselves against the police. The crowd shouted him down and he got off the hydrant.[7] The message was passed around that we must use the principle of passive resistance, because that is more effective.

The hooting from passing cars continued. Soon after four o'clock somebody who had been listening to the radio lifted the loudhailer and said, "The S.A.B.C. has just announced that you have all gone home." We laughed and cheered, "Yay for the S.A.B.C." There were only about four hundred of us standing there by that time, but we were not transparent.

The atmosphere was amazing. There was such a sense of hope and purpose. It was easy to speak to complete strangers. Some students were sitting cross-legged on the lawn studying for exams, and the fact that they came here to study instead of doing it in the usual places showed their determination to express their feelings about the injustice of the education system. Two guys were discussing photography. I joined in the conversation. One of them said, "You see that girl? Yesterday she was lying on her back and some fuzz were hitting her in the stomach. Then a boy picked her up and ran off with her," he laughed, "It was all very chivalrous, and the BBC television cameras were trained on it, got the whole thing."

I heard more stories about what had been happening. I learned that people had been arrested every day that week, and released on bail when somebody had offered to pay. I was told that they either could get fined or imprisoned for demonstrating when the emergency regulations in the Riotous Assemblies Act were in operation. Someone suggested through the loudhailer that we should make a definite time for the protest to end so that our numbers would not merely diminish until there was no one left. We decided upon 6 pm. Some students collected the pepper casters to take back to the canteen, but I was told that I could keep the cloth.

I saw my friend Roger and we started reminiscing about the facilities that we had had at high school that were a total waste of money, like the Mettler balances that never got used. We also talked about the Whites who whine that it would be unfair for money to be spent on black schools because Whites pay most of the taxes. That is so stupid because if Blacks were paid proper wages for the jobs that they do, then the Blacks would pay more taxes.

It is bad enough that the Nats force people to go to separate schools, but they make it even worse by wasting money on white schools and not spending enough money on black schools. At our school we had an overhead projector in every classroom for the teachers who don't like writing on blackboards, while the black schools don't even have blackboards. There were little rooms behind the science laboratories that were filled with all sorts of exciting gadgets that were never used. One that I liked was a projector for microscope slides. In the strongrooms there were hundreds of books lying on shelves that had not been opened for years. I used to open the covers and read

---

7 This was Craig Williamson, who, unbeknownst to most of us, was actually a spy and agitator working for the security police. Among his activities in later years were the killings of Ruth First, Jeannette Schoon, and Katryn Schoon. In 1996 the commander of an apartheid-era police hit squad testified that Williamson had been involved in the 1986 murder of the Swedish Prime Minister, Olof Palme.

the date that they were last taken out while waiting for various teachers to organise what we were to carry.[8] We had a gymnasium, a swimming pool and a library with thousands of books, all of which did get used, but the government could easily afford things like that for black schools as well. South Africa is a very wealthy country.

When it started getting dark I said that I had to go home, but Roger said he would give me a lift so that I could stay until 6 pm. When I got home my mother opened the door with a big grin, "I was wondering whether you had been arrested or not, and," with an even bigger grin, "I was wondering if you had been arrested, whether I was going to go and bail you out or not."

"But the S.A.B.C. said we had all gone home at 4 o'clock."

"Yes, I heard that," she said.

It had been a pleasant afternoon once the police had gone. I found myself thinking about the ramifications of the education system while I was doing the evening chores. It was in the middle of my mind. When Ishmail came in to wash the dishes I started telling him that the police had beaten up students here and in Cape Town. "Yebo, mina yasi", he interrupted. I asked him how he knew. "We all know," he replied.

When I told him that I had been at a protest he was shocked. "You musin' go there. Yena funa shaya wena."[9] He agreed that there are not enough schools for Blacks, but he did not agree that I should put myself in danger.

On Friday morning the dominant topic of conversation at university was how tactful Brigadier Schroeder had been. One girl was getting quite carried away about how much she admired him for avoiding violence. After lectures I headed towards Jan Smuts Avenue. I passed Helen sitting with some friends on the lawn outside the canteen. "Come along," I said. She was in no hurry to move; the sun was rich on the winter grass. She promised to come along later.

A small crowd had gathered around the fire hydrant by the time I arrived, and it grew quickly. Because of the peaceful end to the demonstration on the day before there was no one offering pepper casters or gas masks. People were still talking about Brigadier Schroeder's tact and preference for non-violence. I saw David holding a placard on the pavement, and I went and stood beside him. Someone had got wind of the fact that we were soon to be paid a visit by the police. We were a big group. The row of students extended right along the pavement in front of the lawn, and there were thousands of people on the grass behind us.

On the traffic island in the middle of Jan Smuts Avenue clustered the journalists, ready and waiting with their cameras. I counted them. Fourteen. There were a few plain-clothes policemen standing around too. One looked like a caricature of a plain-clothes policeman. I chose the journalist who was nearest to him, zipped across the two lanes when there was no traffic, and said to the cameraman, "I just want to warn you that you journalists are breaking the law because you are gathering in a group of more than eleven. You had better watch out because the police will be here soon."

He said, "Ha, ha, ha, thank you, thank you," in a Scandinavian sort of accent, and backed away looking embarrassed. I smiled at the caricature plain-clothes policeman,

---

8 I was unaware that the Nats ensured that books that were discarded by white schools were burned so that they could not be given to black schools.

9 Zulu was not his mother tongue. He was saying that the police want to hurt the students.

but his stony face stared straight in front, not amused. I think I was the last person to cross the road in safety.

I went back to standing next to David. A police photographer went down the line taking photos of us. He had a weird looking square camera and stood very close to us to take them. He moved along three people at a time, and was slow. No exposure change was necessary, but he seemed to need a long think between each click and wind-on. Some students put their hands up in a peace sign when they were being photographed. A while after he had passed us I saw another friend further down the line and went and spoke with him. When the fuzzman came by I was photographed again. Jokes started to fly about how the fuzz would look at the photos at John Vorster Square (police headquarters) and say, "Look, here's twins." Security police are not credited with having much intelligence.

The number of plain-clothes police on the traffic island was increasing. They looked comical, all wearing dark suits, short haircuts, and scowls. The thing that really set them off was their shirts. The most violent colours, with ties to match, blared out of that V-shaped area below their faces. Perhaps they thought that wearing bright colours made them less conspicuous than they would have been in conservative white shirts.

Passing cars were hooting as they had done the day before. Professor Philip Tobias drove past very slowly, hooting long and loud. A cheer went up from those of us who recognised him. Someone told me that you could get three years imprisonment for standing on the pavement, because it is public property. Three years. I saw three years stretching out ahead of me. I thought of all the travelling and experiences that could fill three years, and I moved onto the lawn. A student was holding a walkie-talkie. He informed us that the police were coming from the direction of the Civic Theatre. "This is almost like war," said someone near me.

Well, they came, hundreds of them. All in plain clothes. And all with dark suits and bright shirts. But once they had arrived they just stood there, on the traffic island, looking at us, unsmiling, like a brightly decorated wall of granite. Their stance was stiff. I was later to learn that this was because they had batons hidden under their suit jackets, which they had to prevent from falling on the ground by standing up straight and pressing their arms to their bodies.

I saw Helen and had a few words with her. The journalists and the police were not the only groups who were breaking the law along with us. There were at least a hundred people standing on the opposite pavement, outside the brewery. Some had climbed onto the wall of the brewery so as to have a better view of the attack when it came. They were mostly R.A.U. students, (pronounced row as in rowdy, not the kind you do in a boat,) recognisable by their clothes and haircuts. The Rand Afrikaans University does not allow girls to wear slacks, or boys to grow their hair below the tops of their ears. There is only a brewery between the two campuses, but the two ideologies are worlds apart. They were shouting abuse at us and throwing rude signs. We gave peace signs back.

We were discussing what we would do if the police charged. Some said they would run, others said they would stand. I knew that I would run. I thought of that girl who had been hit in the stomach, and the thought made me sick. I was frightened of the pain of being hit on my arms or legs, but the thought of a blow on my stomach or head terrified me.

I noticed Zorba sitting on the lawn with his study notes. We often have conversations in which he says that trying to change South Africa is a waste of time because the forces of evil are too strong, so partying is a better activity. I asked him why he was here and he shrugged his shoulders. "I just had to come," he said.

There were no longer only plain-clothes police on the traffic island. Floods of grey uniforms had joined them. The brigadier announced through his loudhailer that we must disperse, and that the police were going to make us disperse if we did not. He said he was very sorry, he did not want to do it, but the order had come from above. He told us that he was going to announce the order to disperse three times in both official languages, and if we had not dispersed by then the police would charge. Some people started moving back, keeping an eye on the road. I was already at the back. I saw a pile of pamphlets lying on the lawn. I did not know what they were, but I picked them up, thinking what a waste of ink it would be if the police got them.

The brigadier was still announcing his spieël in a clear voice when the wall of police fell forward into the road. I saw the faster ones reach halfway, and then I was running, running up the grass and across the cement towards the Great Hall. Nothing but the sound of running footsteps filled my ears. I did not see who was running beside me, I did not look. I dumped the too heavy pamphlets on the low wall outside Biology block. People sped past me as my action slowed me down, their footsteps sounded strange.

Shouts and cries were coming from behind us. I kept running. I always wear Indian sandals, and the right sandal of my current pair has a little blunt nail that has worked its way up from the sole and pokes into my foot. When I walk or run normally it doesn't hurt, but running at speed made it jab into me every time I put my foot down. My primary thought was to get away from that falling-forward wall of dark clothed men. I ran down between the library and Biology block. It was a long way to have run, but I was intent on not getting bashed. When I emerged from the gap between the two buildings, panting students were slowly walking back to Jan Smuts Avenue. The pamphlets had gone. I asked about them, and somebody said he had seen a policeman walking off with them. So they had come up that far! I was pleased I had kept running. Some people had made the mistake of running into Physics Block for cover, but the police had followed them and dragged them down the stairs and out of the building.

The NUSAS (National Union of South African Students) blokes were asking anyone who had a friend missing to report his or her name at the fire hydrant. The list of names came to 44. The brigadier announced through his loudhailer that those arrested were not going to be released on bail. We were horrified. Now I was even more afraid of being arrested than of being bashed.

My friend Patrick came running over the lawn towards me shouting, "Have you seen Geoff? Have you seen Geoff?" I did not know who Geoff was. He ran to the person with the list of names, very upset, and eventually they established, after much running about, that Geoff was nowhere to be found, and added his name to the list.

I had no intention of going onto the pavement. I was scared enough being on the lawn. But no matter how scared I was, I was not going to go away. Perhaps it was because I knew I was right. I knew that the government could afford to educate everyone in South Africa, and I knew that they were wrong for wanting to bash us for saying that we knew it.

Suddenly everyone started running again. I ran, far. When we stopped we did not know what it was all about. A false alarm, we thought. We moved forward again. I tried to remove that nail from my shoe, but it would not budge.

Time passed.

There were four plain clothes police, short haired and wearing suits, sitting on the lawn to the right of the main body of students, holding up some placards which had been made by students. I don't know why they were sitting on the lawn holding up anti-government placards. Surely they did not think we would mistake them for students. Other plain-clothes police were drifting about through the crowd, listening to what we were saying. Some had tried to disguise themselves as students and were going around asking for dagga. These people have a dagga complex. They are convinced that wherever you find long-haired kaffirboetjies you are going to find dagga. They dress the way they think that hippies dress, and they try to talk the way they think that hippies talk. They stick out like sore thumbs. One of these individuals was not only trying to get us to sell him some dagga, he was also trying to get us to march off university property, "So we can all have a nice fight". He said that we were cowards for not doing it. "It would be much more exciting to march and have a big fight with the police." And in between all of this he kept on asking us for dagga. He didn't seem to realise that we knew he was not a student.[10]

Most of the police who were infiltrating the crowd between attacks were doing so peacefully, and we did not mind them. But Professor Bozzoli did mind them. He asked all people who were not students to leave university property. Then he crossed the road and spoke to the brigadier, who repeated the request through his loudhailer.

I wandered back towards Biology Block. Some black watchmen, dressed in their brown uniforms, were conversing in Zulu with a student whom I recognised as the leader of a black dancing group.[11] The student is so fluent in Zulu that I could not understand the conversation, so I asked him how the watchmen were feeling about what was going on. "They say they don't like fighting, and we should all go home because we'll get injured."

"Augh," I groaned, "And we're doing it for their good, or at least their children's good."

Suddenly people were running, so I ran too. There had been no announcement of a charge, but I was not going to ask any questions, I just ran. What was happening was that the police standing on the traffic island would decide which person they did not like the look of, then three or four of them would dash across the road and grab that person and bundle him or her into a police van. The students did not know if they were coming for them or the person next to them, so a whole group would rush back, and the people behind would rush back too, and the ones behind those who could not see what was happening would turn and run. Once they had their backs to the scene they could not see that the others had stopped running, and there would be a general flight of all the students at the rear of the demonstration. I would only stop when there were no longer hundreds of footsteps thundering past me.

My running was becoming slower and tireder every time. I was unfit because I had

---

10 We thought we could detect the police spies, but the most vicious and dangerous one of all, Craig Williamson, had successfully conned thousands of us.
11 The student was Johnny Clegg.

been sick. By this time I hardly ever went nearer the front than the top of the lawn. One time when we ran for no reason, and stopped, we laughed at ourselves as we started walking back. Professor Bozzoli misunderstood the cause of our laughter. "This is not a joke," he called from afar. "You are not playing games. You don't realise what kind of men you are dealing with. They'll stop at nothing. You don't realise what types they are. This is not a game."

I talked to a lot of people, all scaredy cats like myself, hanging on at the back. One boy told me that he had never done anything in the way of protest before, "And even if I never do anything again, at least I'll know that I was here today, and for that I'll be able to live with myself for the rest of my life."

The day was darkening. Patrick said he would give me a lift home. It was peak hour so the traffic was slow as we drove down Jan Smuts Avenue. As we rounded the bend below the brewery we both caught our breath. A long line of police vans was slowly creeping up the hill towards the students who were still at the demonstration. "My God, we've got to warn them," said Patrick, and there we sat, in the slow traffic, knowing what was in store for the students, and not being able to do a thing about it. I counted the square grey vans. There were ten. I could see through the mesh air vents that all but the second last one were full of dark figures. There was something sinister about that snake of vans creeping up the hill that made my flesh crawl. "It looks just like something out of a film about Russia," said Patrick.

When we eventually reached Empire Road we turned left and the traffic was moving a bit faster. Before we got to the Yale Road turn off Patrick took a short cut over some sand, and then we zoomed up Yale Road as fast as the Beetle could go. We parked below the SRC office and ran up the hill to the demonstration. My lungs hurt because I was unfit.

Of course the police had already arrived, and they had charged, more students had been arrested, and more bashed. A young man was limping along the concrete towards us, supported by a friend. With one hand he was awkwardly clutching at his back.

The tension of the afternoon had burst, not into hysteria, but into electric fear. More people had moved towards the back, but there were still the brave ones at the front, still prepared to run the risk of being arrested even though they knew they could not be bailed out.

There was teargas drifting about. Suddenly men in suits poured out of a lecture theatre, gasping and holding handkerchiefs up to their faces. They were part-time students who had been attending lectures after work. The fuzz had thrown teargas into their lecture theatre.

Patrick had been upset by Geoff's arrest, and more so by the frustration of the slow-moving traffic, not that it would have made any difference if we had got back in time to warn the students. Then he saw a girl he knew stumbling along with eyes streaming. He rushed towards her shouting, "Sandy, Sandy," but ran straight into a cloud of teargas. He staggered back, eyes pouring, and she went down the steps and leaned in misery against the wall of Biology Block. Sandy told me later that she had not been affected by teargas, she was just shocked. Patrick stood on the low wall, eyes streaming, crying out, "I hate them, I hate them, I hate them."

A girl said, "You mustn't hate them. You can only be stronger than them if you love them." Then there was talk of the police using guns if we did not go home.

"They couldn't," said one girl, aghast.

"Couldn't they?" I asked.

"No. Never. They would never get away with it. The public would never allow it. They couldn't!"

"Mmm. Remember what happened at Kent State."

She did not remember, so I reminded her. "Then perhaps they could," she said.

"And what will you do if they fire at us?"

"Run," said another chap.

"Can you run faster than a bullet?" I asked.

More time in space existed, the air was still electrified. Then suddenly there was running again, and we were in the wrong place. We had moved to in front of the hut, and the only way to escape was behind Physics Block. There was no safety in Gate House, we knew that. I felt safer in the open air, but there was no escape here, cornered between buildings with no wide view of the situation. Seeing the side door of Physics Block we dashed in, into the heart of the building, other footsteps sounded dangerous, were they fuzz or friend? Then the footsteps stopped running, they were scared of us too. We came to a flight of stairs and I dashed up, calling over my shoulder to Patrick, "If they are fuzz come with me into the ladies. They won't follow us in there."

"If they'll follow you into a church they'll follow you anywhere," he replied.

I didn't have the stamina to laugh, just to smile wryly, and keep on running. After more confusion and running and fear we found an unlocked door. Some other students had already found this sanctuary, and were standing at the window. They looked round as we burst in and told us to shut the door. At last I felt safe. I felt that no policeman would come this far into the building and open this particular door.

We were in a laboratory. I wandered around, fiddling with the trinkets that are the product of our western civilization. I turned a gas tap quickly on and off to hear that familiar hiss. I felt pleased with my decision to study literature, not science. That was my last thought before I wandered over to the window, pulled myself onto the windowsill and looked out. In those few moments I changed.

The twilight did not decrease visibility, it merely made the scene unreal, as though the air in between was not real air but a transparent medium filled with dusky pigment, with a celluloidic performance taking place on the other side of the medium. Although it appeared unreal, I knew it was happening. The baton arms were swinging, onto heads, onto arms, onto backs. Four against one, three against one. People were being dragged along the ground by their hair, screaming. I realised that this had been happening all afternoon, and all week, and that by this brutality they were trying to defend their other iniquities. All the pieces of anger that had accumulated within me during my life with apartheid came together. They melted and fused and expanded, filling the entire volume of my body. The heat was so calm and firm that it has not cooled down.

The police retreated with as many victims as they could take with them, and this was our chance to get out of the building. Professor Bozzoli and Professor Ellison Kahn were running about asking the students to come to the steps of the Great Hall. Prof. Kahn was clutching a huge book. We all trooped along to the steps and sat looking upwards at the two men. Prof. Kahn told us that the police have the legal right to shoot us dead, and he read out the law that gives them that right.[12] Then Professor Bozzoli asked us to go home. "It is getting dark now and these men will be able to infiltrate amongst you without your being able to detect them. You must not let this happen. You do not realise what kind of men these are, they will stop at nothing. I fear for you my children. I cannot impress upon you the importance of your ending this demonstration before one of you gets seriously injured." There was a short discussion, and we all agreed that we should go home because the darker it became the more dangerous it became. We decided to meet in the Great Hall at 10 am the next day. "And please," said Professor Bozzoli, "Don't go home by way of Jan Smuts Avenue, use the Yale Road exit rather."

A student at the back jumped up and shouted, "Yale road not jail road." We laughed, and began to disperse.

Patrick and I went to the car and left via Yale Road. He was still visibly trembling when I said goodbye to him at my front door. Cooking supper was difficult. Conditioned reflexes seemed to have left me. I fumbled over words while trying to tell Ishmail what had happened. I was quite calm, I just had difficulty in speaking. He seemed to understand though. "Yebo, mina yasi," he said, "Lo police, yena skelms." ("Yes, I know. The police, they are skelms.")

Later, lying in bed, with my eyes open or closed, I still saw the baton arms swinging. Then I would want to run, run, run, into the building, people running in all directions, no direction in it, just to flee. People running in my head, across the lawn, down an echoing corridor, frightened of everyone, every footstep, fear everywhere. There would be stairs to climb, never ending, still climbing, so frightened, so steep, the silhouette of a young man stopping, cupping his hands around his mouth and shouting at the police, then running on, but the sound that came out was not the sound I had actually heard that afternoon, it was a wail of pain. Then I would shake myself to try to get rid of it, so that I could sleep. And it would subside, and I would close my eyes, and the baton arm would start swinging slowly downwards, then others faster, at the real life speed, onto bodies, a replay of what I had seen through the window. Then from the back of my mind they would come running, more footsteps, and fear. The image of the arm with the baton slowly descending kept with me till sleep.

I awoke feeling stiff, but as soon as I moved I realised that this was no ordinary stiffness. So much running in an unfit state had affected my muscles so that even the pressure of my jeans on my thighs hurt.

I went to the meeting in the Great Hall. There were about a thousand of us. It was a long meeting, with much discussion. Advocate Maisels was one of the speakers, and he asked us to refrain from further demonstrations and to turn our attention to other means

---

12 In 2016 I read Prof. Bozzoli's memoir, and in the part about June Week I was startled to read, "By this time police helicopters were hovering low overhead, with clearly armed men on board and something had to be done to cool things down." (p 191, *A Vice-Chancellor Remembers,* ISBN 0-620-19369-7.) It jolted me into the memory of those terrifying low-flying helicopters, so menacing in the dusk. I had actually seen a gun in the hand of a man in one of the helicopters. It was obvious at the time that the helicopters were what made Prof. Bozzoli and Prof. Kahn panic about the possibility of us being shot at, and beseeching us to come to the Great Hall steps. I have pondered why I did not mention the helicopters when I wrote my account of June Week, and I really don't know the answer.

of expressing our desire for justice, because we would not be able to achieve much "in jail with a broken head". A petition to the prime minister was started. As I walked out of the dim hall and foyer into the blare of the bright winter sun reflecting off concrete, I knew that June Week was over, but that the spirit of June Week would not be over until justice prevailed.

Later that day my mother and I went to visit the Moores. I groaned as I lowered myself onto their sitting room floor. "She's stiff from running away from the police," explained my mother.

"Don't tell me that you've been involved in all this," said Mr. Moore, shocked. He did not say it in a disapproving way. Like much of the white public he had been appalled by the police violence, but it was a shock to him to discover that someone he knew, quite an ordinary person, had been involved. He had thought it was only unwashed students who took part in demonstrations.

The day went by. My head was still filled with images of violence and fear for the people in jail. The CNA scooter came up the road and the "scooter boy" threw *The Star* over the gate. It showed pictures of the police attacking the students. The names of all the people who had been arrested were there in small print. Each name that I knew sent a feeling of horror through me. My nerves just needed an excuse to snap. It was when I came to Helen's name that I began to cry.

Mr. Vaughn came for dinner. I was trembling slightly all the time, and had trouble breathing. I said something about the attack, something very mild, and he raised his hand and pointed a finger at me, saying, with utter contempt in his face and voice, "You are suffering from mass hysteria."

"No, I am not. I am suffering from shock." My mouth took over. I described to him what I had seen, and what it felt like to be a witness to such brutality. I do not recall my words, but they must have been effective because when I stopped from lack of breath the expression on his face had changed from contempt to surprise.

"Oh. Oh. I'm sorry. I didn't mean that in a criticising sort of way." It had not occurred to him to look at a newspaper. He had only heard about "student unrest" on the radio, and he had believed what the S.A.B.C. had said.

The Sunday papers also printed pictures of the police bashing students. They showed quite clearly that students on the ground were being kicked and beaten with batons by three or four policemen at the same time. Journalists

No bail for 66

(From Page 1)

weary parents left the Supreme Court. All they knew was that their children would not be charged before Monday and there was no chance of bail.

At one stage during the night one student walked into the charge office at John Vorster Square carrying a placard saying "Release the Innocents."

He was promptly locked up.

According to student sources, these are the students arrested yesterday: Robin van der Plank (Anglican chaplan), Marika Sboros, Gavin Gardy, Bernard Hess, Charles Mendelow, Craig Williamson, Maureen Caplan, Daphne Jacobson, Gillian Hall, Alana Dishy, Christopher Martin, Simon Conradie, Bruce Davies, Alan Mabin, Peter Daniels, David Walker, Stephen Mendel, Kim du Toit, Stephen Lipan, Stanley Goldstein, Stevan Barber.

Colin Lamont, Seymour Kantor, Malcolm Rosenfeld, Carol Fischer, Monty Ho, Derek Brown, Robyn Shenker, Mervyn Musnitsky, Dave Wolpe, Geoff Shuttleworth, Andrew Love, Russell Grinker, Evan Oxenhaf, Allan Levine, Ricky Burnett, Ralph Kahn, Maurice Smithers, Jasper Mortimer, Gavin Keevy, Alan Simpson, Basil Payne, Anton Johnston, Judy Favish, Glenda Milne, John Weaver, Brenda Callan, Leonard Sherman.

Lindy Sifrin, Jenny Cunningham, Felicity Lewis, Pat Horn, Sally Cunliffe, Jenny van Biljon, Lyn Bays, Anne Martins, Margaret Fish, Dehlia Rezek, Renia Jameson, Stan Been, Marcia Rollnick, Helen Sideris, John Brown, Roy Cuckow, Stephen Barker and Chris Wood.

Miss Caroline Clark, of the Sunday Times, and Mr Larry Butchins, of the Sunday Tribune, were also arrested.

The Star, 10 June 1972.

at the scene of the demonstration had also been attacked, and two had been arrested. They were released on Saturday afternoon, after having been charged with impersonating a policeman, which is quite funny because one of them is a woman. The Nats were not pleased with the newspapers for printing photos of students being bashed. They accused the newspapers of committing that most foul of crimes, "Blackening the name of South Africa overseas". They don't get it that it is the police violence that blackens the name of South Africa, not the newspapers.

When an opposition Member of Parliament said that the police action in St. Georges Cathedral had caused South Africa a great deal of harm, the Prime Minister said that he did not agree. "Right thinking people all over the world are sick and tired of this sort of behaviour by students. If the police had not acted in this way then I personally would have been disappointed in them."

Before June Week I had not realised that the Nats use news bulletins for propaganda purposes. There are some programmes on the radio that are quite obviously biased, including a three minute propaganda piece called *Current Affairs* which comes on after the news. The fact that the news bulletins so blatantly lied about the student demonstrations and police behaviour made me wonder what else they lie about in the "news". They said things like, "The police behaved tolerantly under extreme provocation," and, "There is reason to believe that there are planted communist agitators in certain universities." The news readers also use their tone of voice to convey their message. They manage to keep emotion out of their voices when floods drown hundreds of people, or when children are killed in an accident, but a strong tone of disapproval comes through when they are speaking about protesting students.

Protests about the lack of education for Blacks had taken place at every English speaking white university. *Current Affairs* spent its time telling the public that student protesters were a threat to national security, that they were communistically inspired, that their aims were anarchy and destruction, that they should be getting on with their studies instead of making a nuisance of themselves, that the situation had "necessitated police action", and that the police were a band of noble young men who had been greatly provoked. But despite all of this, most of the white population knew that the police had behaved savagely for no good reason. *Current Affairs* also attacked the newspapers for trying to "damage South Africa's reputation abroad".

Some individuals who spoke out in support of the students were threatened in public, others in private. One night during June week there was a public protest meeting in Cape Town City Hall at which Helen Suzman, Sonny Leon, Paul Pretorius, Dr. Marius Barnard, and the Dean of Cape Town, the Very Reverend E. L. King, spoke in support of the students. Dr. Marius Barnard is a heart surgeon at Groote Schuur Hospital, which is a government hospital. When it became known that he was going to speak at the protest meeting he was sent a letter telling him that he would be fired if he spoke, but he went ahead and spoke anyway. He expressed his disapproval of racial discrimination in education, asked the students to continue to be non-violent, and suggested alternatives to demonstrating. He told a journalist that he had agreed to speak at the meeting because even after the police turned violent, the students continued to protest peacefully. This could have turned out to be just another example of state reprisal against an individual, but Dr. Marius Barnard, heart surgeon, happens to be the brother of Dr. Chris Barnard, heart surgeon. Chris Barnard is a jewel in the crown of the South African ego because his action in performing the world's first heart transplant rocketed South Africa's name to fame, instead of to notoriety, as most events in South Africa do. Dr. Chris Barnard said, "If they sack my brother Marius for taking part in the protest meeting in Cape Town City Hall on Tuesday night, I'll close up shop and leave with him."

Some Nat made a petulant speech saying that South Africa would not miss the Barnard brothers, but the truth is that the Nats would miss the Barnard brothers as much as the heart patients at Groote Schuur would miss them, so Marius' job was safe.

Mr. Vorster's "proof" that the demonstrations had been "unspontaneous" was that they had occurred at all the English speaking universities at the same time. Perhaps he is stupid enough to believe that. It is obvious to normal people that the demonstrations occurred at the same time because they were a spontaneous reaction to the treatment of the students at Turfloop. The reaction got bigger because of the attack in the cathedral, and the demonstrations ended because the university authorities asked the students to protest in a less dangerous way. Mr. Vorster said that there is a lack of discipline at English speaking universities, and they would not be allowed to "promote the aims of communism and terrorism". He said that if people wanted to change South Africa they must do it through the ballot box, which is what Mr. Vaughn was repeating when he said it to me.

The students who had been arrested were released from John Vorster Square on Sunday night and had to appear in court on Monday morning. In class I felt the absence of Helen very strongly. We took good notes for her to borrow. I told Louisa that I felt bad that I had encouraged Helen to go to the demonstration, and that she had been arrested while I had not. In her usual understanding way Louisa reassured me that Helen would have gone anyway, and she felt sure that the sentence would not be too heavy.

There was a mass meeting at lunch time, with Professor Philip Tobias and Reverend Peter Storey being the main speakers. Reverend Storey talked about the way freedom of speech is being progressively suppressed, and that when the law is "misused to become opinion enforcement," the law will be the casualty. He said that he would call a mass meeting of the Methodist Church, and that we should all try to inform people through our churches and clubs what was happening in South Africa.

I know Professor Tobias because he sometimes comes on the archaeological excursions that we go on. He is Professor of Anatomy at the medical school and has a keen interest in palaeontology. Apart from being brainy he also has a moral backbone. He said that he would like to;

> ... criticise very severely the Prime Minister and other members of his cabinet for their appalling reaction to the cause for which the students have been protesting. Instead of instituting an enquiry into the expulsion from a university of its entire student body, an action unprecedented in the history of higher education in South Africa, we are promised by the Prime Minister that there will be an enquiry into discipline at the university next year.
>
> Instead of instituting an enquiry into the manifestly undue and unwarranted violence employed by the police in Cape Town on Friday June 2, they have promised an enquiry into rumours of dagga smoking and other

alleged misdemeanours in the precincts of the cathedral. Instead of frank recognition that thousands upon thousands of protesting students, black and white, may have legitimate grievances, may be genuinely motivated by a desire to see the educational system in South Africa vastly improved, we are told that the Prime Minister has the impression that the English-speaking universities are being ruled by a small group of leftists, and there is an implied threat to expel foreign students.

Having said that, I want, with all the persuasion I can muster, to implore you to keep your further protests within the law. A student out of jail is a more effective member of our community than one in the cells. A student with an intact skull can do more than one with a broken head. ... Legal protest may take many forms. ... petition, huisbesoek, the writing up of this episode for all the world and for posterity to read. ... Let the past not inglorious weeks not be forgotten. ... You are keeping alive a flickering light whose glow extends far beyond the academic community, far beyond this republic to the four corners of the world, wherever man cherishes freedom. You are writing a new and glorious page in the history of the struggle for freedom of thought. Every line you write on that page is indelible, so pause and consider every word before writing it; weigh it carefully; strengthen the justice of your cause by maintaining the legality of your future protest.

After the meeting I wandered onto the library lawn to sit in the sun with my friends. My pen had disappeared so I asked Glenda to loan me hers. I took out some paper and started writing. Petitions and huisbesoek are all very well, but I had decided on the third suggestion, "the writing up of this episode, the chronicling of it for all the world and for posterity to read".

The next morning Helen was in class as the court case had been remanded for two weeks. She had not been badly injured. "Well, how was it?" I asked.

"Well, it wasn't so bad. It was quite an experience actually. It was awful. I've never known such a terrible time. But it wasn't so bad actually. It was quite an experience." We laughed at her inconsistency. She had had to sleep on the floor without a mattress, but at least they had all been together, with boys and girls separate of course, so they had been able to keep up each other's morale.

The SRC at Wits produced a leaflet entitled "Education" giving the facts about education in South Africa and explaining the reasons for the protests. "Our issue is not police brutality but education." For a few days I went into the city after lectures to help distribute it to the public.

Someone put up photos of the police attack in the foyer of the canteen. One was a photo of police running up the lawn towards students, and there among them was my neighbour, Johan, with his police identity number missing from his chest. "Wow! I know him. He lives next door to me," I said in shock.

"Where do you live that things like that live next door to you?" said a contemptuous male voice next to me.

"No, no, he's nice. I mean he's alright. So he was there! I can't believe it." In my mind I could not equate the two images; Johan and the police bashing students.

On Friday evening Johan came around to return our ladder. After he had put it in the garage he asked, "What do you think of all this student business?" I told him what I thought. "Yes but you don't realise that communists are trying to take over in South Africa," he replied.

"I do realise that. And the students are not communists."

"No, not all of them. But some are." We stood there arguing. My mother kept putting her head out of the kitchen door and reminding me that I needed to get dressed for my date. Johan believes that the reason why the protests started on more than one campus is that they were inspired by a few communists.

"Those girls who got beaten up must not complain that they got hit, because they knew that if they stood there they would get hit just the same as the boys."

"Look, I don't see the difference between a girl and a boy being beaten. It's just as bad either way. But why do police go particularly for girls, and why do three police hit one girl when she is lying on the ground?"

"Yes, I agree they shouldn't do that." He continued, "It wasn't the ideas of the demonstrators that we were fighting against, it was the illegality".

"Then why didn't they break up all the people on the other side of the road? And if they're so worried about illegality, why do they take their police numbers off and put them in their pockets?"

"Yes, I agree, they shouldn't do that." I didn't let on that I knew that he had taken his off. I asked him why the police had used such violence if all the police wanted was for the students to disperse. Aha, now he had something to tell me. "After the students had left on Thursday the security police searched the grounds where they had been and found a whole lot of weapons. Sticks and iron bars and broken bottles."

"That's nonsense," I said. "Who told you that?"

"A security policeman," he said, in a tone that implied that clinched that it was true.

"But there weren't such things. That's nonsense."

"There were. They found them."

"You know why they say they found them on Thursday and not some other day? Because Thursday is the only day that ended peacefully. They could not invent the lie about any other day because if there had been weapons on Wednesday or Friday they would have been used and seen. That's why they invented the lie for Thursday."

"But they did have. They had bottles wrapped in paper, and iron bars …."[13]

"Nonsense."

"And pepper," he said, as though pepper were napalm.

"Ah, yes, there was pepper. I had some myself. But that was for the dogs, not for the police, though I don't think I really would have been able to throw it at the poor dog

---

13 This is really interesting in light of the fact that Craig Williamson was working undercover for the security police, and he had tried to incite the students to violence against the police on that Thursday by climbing onto the fire hydrant and brandishing a small branch. He was hoping to give his masters the right to say that we had been violent. The branch that he had waved about while standing on the fire hydrant was the only weapon that had been there that day.

when it's not its fault." This was the first time that Johan realised that I had been there. When I saw the look on his face it struck me how ridiculous the whole idea of violence is. They can beat people they don't know, but what would he have done if he had found me standing in front of him?

It's funny that they want to discredit the students by lying that they are violent, but they don't see their own violence as something that would tarnish their reputations.

There were exceptions. In Cape Town some of the higher-ranking police tried to prevent excessive violence by shouting at their men, "Push them, don't hit them," and Colonel Crous had prevented one from throwing a middle aged woman down some steps.

On the peaceful Thursday at Wits some of the Rand Afrikaans University students had been planning to kidnap some of us, cut our hair, and beat us up. This is their traditional way of dealing with "hippies". But Brigadier Schroeder had heard about it and put a quick stop to it.

However, there was one person of very high rank in society who did not have the same feelings about violence. He was the Prime Minister, who said, "I associate myself fully with the police and I am on their side". He said that the same thing would be done as often as necessary. An opposition Member of Parliament said, "As an Afrikaner it is my tradition not to desecrate churches, and Mr. Vorster, as an Afrikaner and a church-goer, should apologise to the Anglican Church for what they have done". In response Nat MPs shouted out, "Never, never," and Mr. Koornhof, the Minister of Sport, accused the opposition MP of being an agitator. When I was travelling in Greece the thing that Canadians, Americans, British, Australians, and New Zealanders mentioned most often about South Africa was the police bashing people inside the cathedral.

The Nats say that the first police attack on white students at St. George's was caused by student provocation. Yet the police had a practice run on the lawn outside the Houses of Parliament before the attack. An officer demonstrated how to do a baton charge, then the group of police ran across the lawn swinging batons in the air. They did this just before they left for St. George's cathedral, which is nearby. This shows that the police attack was "unspontaneous".

During the following week there were more protests on the steps of the cathedral and thousands of people crowded the streets in support. The police hit some people and threw teargas, but they did not go into the cathedral again. Three of the people who were arrested were high ranking church men. When one was arrested, his wife objected, and she was arrested too. When the wife of another church man went to the police station later to pay bail for her husband, she was picked up and physically thrown out of the door. Then she was told she wasn't allowed to be on the sidewalk because it was police property.

On the Wednesday hundreds of police suddenly turned up on the campus of the University of Cape Town and started attacking people. The campus is on the side of Table Mountain, with hundreds of wide granite steps, called Jammie steps, going up the middle of it. There are student residences on either side of the lower part of the steps. When the police turned up on campus they told all the people sitting on Jammie steps to go home, which is a bit silly as that is their home. There are always people sitting on Jammie steps. The police then attacked the students and anyone else who was nearby. Three policemen attacked two Coloured janitors who were leaving work at 5 pm on their bicycles. The police knew they were not students. One of the janitors was bashed so badly that he was unconscious and had to be taken to Groote Schuur Hospital.

During term time my school friend Lydia lives in Fuller residence next to Jammie steps. She sent me a letter with a newspaper cutting about the attack at St. George's Cathedral. In the newspaper picture she had circled the heads of people I know. One of them was my friend Gail, but I did not recognize her until I was told that it was her. I found it hard to believe that the features on Gail's face could move into such a position. I know the horror of seeing vicious brutality; how much worse it must have been to be the victim of vicious brutality.

Jammie steps during uni recess.

Lydia wrote;

> The happenings of the past week have been absolutely amazing to live through. I never thought I'd experience anything like it in my life. I just cannot describe the atmosphere in Fuller on Saturday. It was frightening because we felt as though we were sitting on the brink of a volcano and we didn't know when it would erupt. I'll never forget Jammie steps being absolutely packed with people and everyone was so united it was incredible. ... I went to a mass meeting at lunch time and they read out a whole lot of telegrams – was quite incredible – from student bodies all over the world, including Wales, Denmark, the U.K., – and from Peter Hain! (with love).

She told me that she had stopped taking part in the protests because;

> It had started on Thursday and Friday as a protest against black education (or lack of it), but when the police went wild on Friday, something which I deplore as much as anyone else, the whole focus of the protesting shifted onto the injustices of their action. ... The thing is Wendy, black education has been almost forgotten and now all they're protesting against is injustice against themselves. So many people on Monday had hardly thought about the whole thing and were just filled with indignation at the injustices we suffered. They would never get nearly so emotional if it was Blacks, as it always has been up to now.

I think she is right that if the police had not attacked white students at St. Georges, the demonstrations would not have escalated in the way that they did. But at Wits at least the focus did remain on the issue of education. The fact that they used violence to try to stop us from saying that the lack of education was wrong just made us more determined to say it.

The staff of the University of Cape Town issued a statement saying that they supported the action taken by the students, that they condemned the use of violence by the police, and that the students had acted with maturity and great restraint. Seven hundred staff members signed it. The university also suspended lectures for a day so that the students could conduct a publicity and petition campaign in and around Cape Town. Lydia decided to go petitioning on that day.

> We went to Milnerton and unfortunately, Wends, I can't tell you all the details, but I was so pleased I went because I really spoke to people. Spent up to 15 minutes with some people. Although a lot of them would not sign because they are too scared and for business reasons (we went into shops mostly) at least we could tell them what the situation actually is with black education and they couldn't help but see our point. I nearly fainted, the very first shop I went into, there was a varsity student working there and I ended up talking to him and his mother. The next thing, I looked up and he said "Oh look they've come to fetch you already" – there was a police van with four policemen stopped directly outside the shop. I nearly fainted, especially as one was talking into a microphone and the other got out and walked into the shop. Anyway all he wanted was a side view mirror, but I can promise you, I hid that petition very fast.

> On Thursday I came back from case work and was dropped on De Waal drive from where I walked. You can just imagine how I felt when I found about 30 police vans absolutely packed with police in Rugby Rd, the road below Fuller. The whole atmosphere was very ominous. When I got to the steps I saw crowds sitting near Jammie. The next thing I knew police and batons and dogs were just streaming past me and around me. A lot of students left when they were told to do so, but the others stayed, and apparently they ended up in two lines – the police facing the students, and were chatting and joking together. Anyway, ten minutes after the said final minute the truncheons started flying again. All I know is that I could never put myself into such a position because I know that I would not be able to turn the other cheek if a policeman got stuck into me. And it was a rather grim reminder (excuse the cliché, but everything we say is clichéd anyway,) when I walked down the steps this morning and saw a whole lot of dried drops of blood.

Johan's father is a news writer for the S.A.B.C. He told me that if people hear the same thing said over and over again, they begin to believe it is true. That was the principle that Goebbels used, he said, and that is the principle that the communists use when they are brainwashing the students. Actually it is the principle that the S.A.B.C. uses.

The S.A.B.C. kept on saying that communist agitators were behind the protests, that the government was spending a lot on black education, that "the students had shown no respect for a house of God", that the police had been sorely provoked and had acted with restraint, and that "complaints that dagga was being smoked were being probed".

They kept on using the phrase "student riots" when there had not been any student riots, and they kept on saying that there was a subversive plot trying to overthrow the government. They even produced an hour-long radio programme on black education in which they said that the Blacks have got it good and the government is doing so much for them.

They contradict themselves when they then go on to say that the government cannot afford to educate the Blacks. That is complete nonsense. The real reason why they don't want to educate the Blacks is that they don't want them to have the power that education would give them. They don't want them to be able to do anything other than cleaning houses or working in factories and mines. They don't want to lose their cheap labour force, and they want to preserve the luxurious lives that they live, being waited on by servants.

They use the public's fear of communism as a lever against the students. But surely the most effective way of combating communism would be to educate the Blacks so that they will know what the realities of communism are. It is much easier for communists to convince ignorant people that communism is the perfect system with total freedom and equality than it is to convince educated people who can read and write. This to me is the greatest irony of the whole sick situation.

Chapter 2

Tuesday 1st August 1972

This morning I had the educational experience of spending a few hours in an office in the city, waiting for a document that was supposed to arrive early. There was a lot of chatter going on, and very little work being done. The main topic of conversation was how they were going to get a cup of tea at eleven when only one "tea girl" had turned up to serve the whole building. The trains from Soweto had not run, so the firm was in dire straits as regards black employees. The woman in charge of the office had a leg in plaster, and she had the lowest drawer of her desk open with her leg propped up on it. She was deeply concerned about the prospect of not getting tea at eleven. The electricity supply was not working too well either, and the lights kept on turning on and off. The intercom telephones ran off the same electricity supply as the lights, so every time the lights came on she would lunge across her desk and grab the yellow phone, with her leg still balanced on the drawer, and start frantically dialling the kitchen. It was all to no avail as there was no one in the kitchen to answer the phone. When the tea eventually did arrive, brought in by a young black woman, the woman with the leg on the drawer said to her, "Die ministers is nou gefired, en nou kom die treine nie". ("The ministers are now fired and now the trains don't come.") That got a laugh from the Whites, but the black woman did not react. There was a cabinet reshuffle yesterday, and our erudite lady seems to think there is a connection between the gefiring of ministers and the lack of trains from Soweto.

When it was time for a second cuppa there was not enough milk, so I was sent down to the kitchen on a lower floor to get more. The trains had arrived and the kitchen was filled with black women. I wanted to ask them what time they normally have to catch the train in Soweto, but the atmosphere was so heavy and their attitude so hostile that I was scared off. I know that they have to leave home very early to get to work on time. Soweto is only 14 miles from the city centre, but it is like another world. A million people are crowded together in a small area, with tiny little houses. They don't have electricity, so the smog from their coal fires blows over the white suburbs, and the Whites complain about it. There is a special railway line to Soweto to make sure that the workforce that keeps Johannesburg going can get to work. The workers from Soweto get off at Park Station, which has separate entrances for Blacks and Whites.

There is a swish modern building for the Whites, with shops and waiting rooms and a high roof, but non-Whites have to enter through a narrow entrance, and their part of the station is dark and dingy. I've been into it illegally quite a few times. When you go through the entrance you get swept along because the crowd is so thick. At rush hour there are more people using the black side than the white side, and they have less space – much less space.

Most trains have separate carriages for Whites and non-Whites, but there are no white carriages on the trains to Soweto. Whites are not allowed to go to Soweto without a special permit, but you can get a glimpse of Soweto from the mainline train that goes to Cape Town. If you are looking out of the window about five minutes after leaving Johannesburg you can see the roofs of little houses all squashed together. The view only lasts for a few seconds, and it only shows a small bit of Soweto.

Taken from the train in the few seconds that Soweto was visible.

Taken from the train on a different day with a telephoto lens.

People who live in Soweto have to stay indoors at night because it is too dangerous to go out. Poverty breeds crime and the main danger is the tsotsies. Tsotsies are young black criminals who rob people with home-made weapons. They also come into the city and even into the white suburbs. You can see who they are by their attitude and their clothes. They wear soft shoes that don't make a sound on the pavement, their trousers are baggy, hanging low on their hips, they swagger as they walk, and when they run they are gone in a flash of tan-soled sand-shoes. They can make more money out of stealing one watch than by working a forty-hour week, so it is an attractive occupation for a young black man.

When the police cruise around the white suburbs at night looking for Blacks to arrest they don't find the tsotsies who are hiding in the shadows. They only find the Blacks who are walking normally along the pavement.

Once the panic about the tea was over the next big issue in the office was *The Neighbour* and *The Key*. The woman with the leg in plaster had paid her servant last night, and this morning she could see from her back door that the servant's room was empty and the door was standing open. As there was a blanket, a mat, and a clock in the room, she wanted the door to be locked. She could not go down the steps to the room with her leg in plaster, so her plan was to phone her neighbour from the office to ask her to lock the door. She dialled her neighbour's number many times, still with her leg balanced on the drawer, but the phone lines don't work too well in South Africa because of job reservation. When the telephone eventually co-operated, everyone in the office was treated to a long session about the disappearance of the servant. "I just don't understand it. She was a good girl, and I told her I was going to buy her a primus stove. She was a good girl, and we got on well. I just don't understand them."

"Them" means all Blacks.

She did not seem grateful that the servant had not taken the blanket, the mat, and the clock with her when she did her midnight flit. A cheap alarm clock is worth more than half a month's pay, so it would have been a great temptation.

Saturday 5th August 1972

Mr. Vaughn was ranting today as usual and I made him crosser by mentioning the Coloureds who are being moved out of Newclare. The Nats say that they are putting all the Coloureds whose houses they demolish into nice new flats, but that is not true because there are hundreds of families out in the cold. Charities have provided tents for them to live in, but it gets very cold at night during these winter months because of Johannesburg's high altitude. I don't know if the Nats lie about it because they have guilty consciences or because they want everyone to believe that they are good guys, but Mr. Vaughn certainly has no conscience about it. He says that it is just fine that all these people are sleeping out in the cold. If they had paler skins he would not think it was fine.

There are many laws that make life horrible for people who are classified "Coloured" under the *Registration of Population Act*, but the laws are not as bad as they are for the Blacks. Coloureds and Indians do not have to carry a pass, and they are allowed to start a business, but only in an area that has been designated for them under the *Group*

Areas Act. Indians are classified as "Asian", and so are the few Chinese people who live in South Africa. The Nats are such hypocrites that they have classified Japanese businessmen as "honorary Whites". Some countries are imposing sanctions against South Africa, but Japan is trading with us more and more. There are no Japanese people living in South Africa, but there are lots of visiting Japanese businessmen. The Nats want them to be able to stay in white hotels and eat in white restaurants, so they have classified them as "honorary Whites". But Chinese people who are born here cannot go into the hotels and restaurants.

A person is classified "White" when they are "pure" going back four generations. So if a person's great grandmother was half Coloured, he is classified as Coloured. Of course DNA goes back further than four generations, and black genes can show up unexpectedly. When a white person has a few black genes that show up in their hair and eyelashes, genteel white people say, "He has a touch of the tar brush". A "white" person who has this embarrassing ancestral mistake written on his hair and skin is able to vote and live and work as a White.

When a child is born with a slosh of the tar brush instead of a touch, strange things begin to occur. Investigations are launched, and judgment is passed as to whether the child should be classified White or reclassified as Coloured. Depending on who the parents are, one of them might be reclassified too. If that happens it then becomes illegal for that person to be married to their spouse. The spouse will have to also become reclassified Coloured, or else get divorced. A spouse who becomes "Coloured" forfeits the right to vote, and a whole lot of other rights too. Sometimes a couple who have been classified white give birth to a really dark-skinned child, and in some cases they get rid of the child.

The overseas media often reports about families being broken up by reclassification, and White South Africans feel angry with them for reporting it.

Friday 11th August 1972

At lunch time today I went to a lecture by Paul Pretorius, the head of NUSAS, in the Great Hall. He told us that groups that criticise the government are currently being "investigated" by a thing called "The Select Committee", and that this committee is soon going to present its findings. He expects that the intimidation of individuals is going to get stronger once the report comes out.[14] He is calm and collected about it, but it makes me nervous. He said that although repression is going to increase, we must be committed to bringing about change in ways that are well thought out, because whatever the Nats do, they will never succeed in silencing everyone.

The government continually accuses NUSAS of subversion, but as Paul pointed out, all the activities of NUSAS are open to the public. Paul says that the government

---

14 Paul Pretorius was banned on 27 February 1973, proving that his prediction of an increase in oppression was correct. Neville Curtis, Paula Ensor, Phillippe Le Roux, Chris Wood, Sheila Lapinsky, Richard Turner and Clive Keegan were banned on the same day. Three days later Steve Biko, Barney Pityana, Bokwe Mafuna, Drake Koka, Saths Cooper, Jerry Modisane, Strini Moodley and Harry Nengwekhulu were also banned. Once they were banned it became illegal for anyone to repeat what they said, including anything that they had said in the past.

is using methods outside of the law to attack NUSAS, because it knows that it could never prove its accusations against NUSAS in a court of law.[15] I wish that I could make people see what the government is doing.

We will defy - Pretorius

If the government took action against NUSAS and thus curtailed the right of students to meet together to express their views and make decisions, NUSAS would be forced to ignore such action and to bear the consequences thereof, Paul Pretorius, NUSAS President, said in the Great Hall last Friday. Mr Pretorius was speaking in Civil Rights Week.

Mr Pretorius began his address by reporting back on NUSAS Congress. He mentioned that the Congress took place at a time when attacks against students were at their height. The Congress had realised that infighting was a 'luxury that we could not afford'. He stressed that the most important result of the Congress was the emergence of a broad base of student unity.

On the topic of Civil Rights, Mr Pretorius began by replying to the Minister of Police and the Minister of National Education pointing out that students were aware that much intimidatory action had been taken against them, and that the Ministers concerned had 'strange notions of subversion and conspiracies — but we know that you have not found us guilty in a court of law of the things you openly accuse us of every day.' Students were also aware of the Select Committee, and of the fact that 'as soon as we begin to exercise our rights effectively you use force and violence against us.

Mr Pretorius then went on to discuss the possibility of action against NUSAS. The fundamental rights of students to work for the common good of their country was being threatened. But NUSAS would not allow itself to join the ranks of those organisations which had been 'bullied out of existence'. 'We will, in short, continue to meet, to organise and to act on a national level. 'This is no hysterical outcry; it is just that we are mindful of the record of your government's actions We are concerned with the future; we have weighed up the situation carefully and have decided that we shall not back down. If we are true to ourselves, we have no other choice.'

As far as action was concerned, Mr Pretorius stressed the need for students to think deeply about the issues involved and how they could act in the circumstances. He stressed the need for students to think in terms of detailed planning and thought. There had been large — scale involvement and enthusiasm during the June protests, but now everything had returned to normal and the campus was once again dead. This could not be allowed to happen.

'We are not playing a game — we must commit ourselves to well-thought out action — not to just reacting as we did in June.'

He called on all students who were concerned about the future of student rights in South Africa, and particularly about the Select Committee, to begin organising among themselves. The resources of the National Union were open to all groups who had a plan of action which they wished to implement.

Wits Student, 18 August 1972.

---

15 If Mr. Donker had agreed to publish this book in 1973, he would have had to leave blank spaces in place of what Paul Pretorius said.

After his talk those who were "really interested" were asked to come up front for discussion. About a hundred people came. There is a rumour that a new ban is being put on demonstrations in Cape Town. The group wants to protest about it if the rumour is true.

There are also plans for a "laugh campaign" here and in Cape Town. In Cape Town they are planning to go along to the S.A.B.C. building, pretend to raise it from the ground and move it a few feet to the left. An idea for Johannesburg is that Wits students could go to the S.A.B.C. building and stand along one side of it as if we were holding it up, and tell the newspaper journalists, "The S.A.B.C. is so slanted that we're afraid it is going to fall over soon."

Ralph Judah ended the meeting by saying that we should meet tomorrow at 2.30 in the SRC office.

Saturday 12th August 1972

Our numbers had dwindled to only eight today, probably because it is a Saturday and people are not on campus. The ban on demonstrations in Cape Town was just an expired ban being reinstated. So there is no reason to protest. No reason, except for the contract labour system, job reservation, black wages, the Alexandra Hostels, starvation in resettlement areas, political censorship, delimitation,[16] the deportation of foreigners who dare to criticise, the Blacks who die "accidentally" in prison, the Broederbond, families broken up by the *Immorality Act*, detention without trial, lack of black education, government monopoly of the S.A.B.C., the forced takeover of LM Radio, the migrant labour system, and the pass laws.

So there we sat, trying to think of a way to deal with all these things. Ralph Judah says that at least a laugh campaign would make some people take note of the issues, and maybe even laugh at themselves. It is so hard to make the white population aware of the need for change. They don't realise that by ignoring the situation they are only going to harm themselves in the long run. When you try to tell Whites that they will eventually suffer because of the way things are going, they either get angry or they tell you that you are overemotional and too idealistic. What can we do? With the S.A.B.C. pouring out its Nat propaganda, what hope have we of countering it? They use schools to indoctrinate white children, but if we were to hand out pamphlets in schools, apart from the fact that we would be arrested, the children would be told that they must not listen to us because we are trying to indoctrinate them. It is hopeless.

Then I started thinking about how the government would have viewed our little meeting, had they known about it.[17] They would have regarded us as a dangerous group of revolutionaries; a bunch of morally perverted kaffirboetjies, attempting to commit that most unpardonable of crimes; changing the status quo. They would call us "communistic". They have the power to call us anything, when all we want is democracy.

Most of the Whites that I mix with believe that South Africa is a democracy. When I say that it is not they get angry and become adamant that it is. More than 80 % of the

---

16 Gerrymandering
17 I was so naïve. Craig Williamson was one of the eight at this meeting.

population does not have the right to vote, yet they can't see that that means it is not a democracy. They are also not bothered by the unfair way that the voting constituencies are laid out. In a democracy people cannot be convicted of a crime unless they have been found guilty by a court of law. In South Africa it is illegal to be a communist, but if someone is suspected of being a communist, they don't get put on trial to see whether they are guilty. They can be banned or detained without the courts having any say about it.

The Suppression of Communism Act states;

> if ... the Minister is satisfied that any person ...
> 1. advocates, advises, defends or encourages the achievement of any of the objects of communism or any act or omission which is calculated to further the achievement of any such object, or
> 2. is likely to advocate, advise or defend or encourage the achievement of any such object or any act or omission; or
> 3. engages in activities which are furthering or may further the achievement of any such object:

they can be banned or detained without trial. The Minister does not even have to think that a person is doing something which may further communism, he need only be satisfied that a person is *likely* to do something which *may* further communism. One of the aims of communism is having a state-owned railway. South Africa has a state-owned railway, so the Minister of Transport should be banned.

The Nats use this vague law to silence anyone that they don't like, and sometimes people who are in detention without trial die under suspicious circumstances. White people who like apartheid say that it is a good law because it stops the communists from taking over. They deny that in practice the law is abused, and that people who are not communists get detained or banned. At least once a week I hear someone say, "We don't have to worry about the government. They know what they are doing." They certainly do know what they are doing. They have made it possible to silence any person whom they think is a threat to their power.

People get banned for speaking out against apartheid or for doing something that helps Blacks, like building a school or a clinic. More than a thousand people have been banned. The newspapers are allowed to report that they have been banned, but they are not allowed to report how the person feels about being banned, nor anything that the person has said in the past. Anything that a person has written automatically becomes banned once the person is banned.

Banning orders are imposed for a period of five years. The details are not always the same. Some people are put under house arrest, while others are just restricted to a municipal area. Some are allowed to be in the company of only one person at a time, but they can get special permission to have four other people in the room when they get married. Others have to remain solitary except for being allowed to see their parents. Some can go shopping, but cannot go to a cinema or party, and must report to a police station at a certain time every week.

Anyone who quotes a banned person is guilty of a crime, so serving someone with a banning order is a very effective way of silencing criticism.

One of the more recent bannings was placed on Father Cosmos Desmond, a Franciscan priest who wrote a book called *The Discarded People*. The book describes the living conditions of Blacks who have been moved to resettlement areas. Those who remove people from their homes and dump them in an area where there is no food or work or clean water are the ones who increase the risk of communism, not the person who draws attention to what has been done. It is as if the Nats have learnt nothing from history.

The trouble is that most of the white public don't care. They don't care about what has happened to Father Cosmos Desmond, nor about the children who are dying in resettlement areas, nor about what it means for their own long-term safety. After Father Cosmos Desmond was banned, the Deputy Minister of Bantu Administration visited Sada, one of the dumping grounds that Father Desmond had written about. He was appalled to see the dreadful conditions in which the people lived, and said that something must be done to ease their misery. But he did not arrange for anything to be done to ease their misery.

I go around telling white people that the banning of Father Cosmos Desmond shows that the government is acting to silence criticism and to protect its own power, rather than to suppress communism. They usually reply with something like, "Oh, but they wouldn't ban him for nothing. He must have done something wrong."

It is because of the Bantustan policy that people are forced to live in resettlement areas where conditions are terrible. The Nats call the Bantustan policy "the logical conclusion of separate development." The idea is for every tribe to have a "homeland" which will one day be an independent state. Small patches of the country have been designated as Bantustans, and the Blacks are being moved from their homes into these patches. They have to leave their animals and their crops behind, and there are no job opportunities. When everyone has been moved the Whites will be the only people living in South Africa, and the United Nations will no longer be able to say that Whites are a minority. Everyone will be happy. The Zulus will be in their homeland, the Xhosas in theirs, the Vendas in theirs, the Coloureds in … oh wait, there is not going to be a homeland for the Coloureds. The Coloureds are not going to vanish off the face of the earth, no matter how forcefully the Nats ignore reality. And millions of Blacks who are born in the townships do not feel that they belong to any particular tribe. Some have parents from different tribes, and they speak two languages at home. They don't want to be moved to a faraway place that the Nats describe as their "homeland". I wonder if, when the Blacks are all neatly packed off into Bantustans, white suburbia will start washing its own dishes, making its own beds, scrubbing its own floors, and hanging up its own clothes. Will the gold and the coal and the platinum jump automatically from underground to the surface, and will the factories and farms run themselves?

On Tuesday night the film *The Dumping Grounds*, which was made for British TV, was shown at Wits. It was legal to show it, but the security police zoomed in and confiscated the film. They don't want people to see the deadly effects of their evil Bantustan policy.

Lots of people criticise the Bantustan policy without getting banned. What Father Cosmos Desmond did was to expose the reality of its consequences.

Whites have been stealing land and cattle from Blacks since long before the Bantustan Policy, and even long before the Land Act of 1913, and although millions of people have been dispossessed so far, the Nats still intend to "resettle" many more.

Sunday 13th August 1972

When we lived in Bryanston I had lots of wonderful trees to climb, but they were left behind when we moved to Parkview seven years ago. I soon discovered that boundary walls provide a substitute means of elevation, as well as an opportunity to see what is going on next door. The walls along the sides of the property are eight feet high and two bricks wide, and the wall along the front is four feet high and one brick wide. I used to run along the tops of the walls, leaping over the space at the front gate, giving all adults who were not used to such country behaviour near heart failure.

The front gate.

At the back of the property the garage and servants' quarters back onto the sanitary lane. The garage roof is a good spot for observing the neighbourhood, and for watching the weavers build their nests in the pepper tree. When we bought the house there were two tiny rooms for domestic servants, and a slightly bigger store room next to the garage, with no window. My dad got Ishmail to put a doorway through the wall between the two smaller rooms, and to convert one of the doors to a window. Then Ester could put her bed in one part and a small table but no chairs in the other part. Ishmail got the bigger room with no window. At the end of the servant's quarters there is a little room with a flushing toilet, but there is no running water for washing, so my dad got Ishmail to put basins with hot and cold taps in the rooms. There is no bath or shower.

The house and the servant's quarters were built in 1911. You would think that these days things would be different, but when new houses are built they still make the servant's quarters tiny. In Parkview there are still servant's quarters that lack electricity, and the servants have to use candles at night. There is no consideration for the comfort of servants.

James the gardener next door is paid R20 per month. One month he asked his madam for an advance of $5 for a family crisis, and he got it. During that month the madam was driving back to Parkview from Rosebank along Jan Smuts Ave, with James in the back seat, when she passed out at the top of that steep hill in Parkwood, and the car sped down the hill. James jumped over the seat into the front, grabbed the steering wheel, put his foot on the brake pedal and brought the car safely to a halt. He always had to sit in the back when she took him out in the car, and he had figured out what the gears and the pedals are for by watching her drive. He was hoping that she would reward him for saving her life by not deducting R5 from his pay at the end of the month, but at the end of the month she paid him R15.

Monday 14th August 1972

Johan came to supper tonight. After eating we moved into the lounge and started talking about June Week. He still believes that the security police found weapons on the campus after Thursday's peaceful demonstration. No amount of my telling him the truth will convince him otherwise.

He explained to me how communism works. "First of all there's the centre with all the branches going off." He held up his hand like a spider, pointing at the fingers as he spoke of the branches. "Then the branches divide and get thinner, but they are still controlled by the centre. Then at the very end of the branches are the people like you students, who don't realise that you are being controlled by communism."

I replied, "And what you don't realise is that you are being controlled in the same way. First of all there's the government at the centre, and then the branches. You are at the very end of the branches, and you don't realise that you are being used by the government for their own ends."

He did not agree. Then I asked him about violence; "Don't you think it's wrong to beat people up when you are only supposed to arrest them? Don't you think it is wrong for four men to beat up one girl?"

"Wendy, I don't think."

I waited for him to qualify this statement. I mean, you do not say a thing like that without qualifying it. Nothing was forthcoming, so I said, "You mean you just obey?"

"Yes."

"And if my mother told me to go and beat up old Mrs. Jeffries?"

"You wouldn't do it," he said vehemently.

"But then why do you do it?" I asked.

He pondered for a moment.

"No, Wendy, you don't realise what these communists are trying to do."

"I do realise what the communists are trying to do. We all do. That's one reason why we think Blacks should be given an education, because educated people are less likely to favour communism."

He does not understand that the Nats are more like the communists than the liberals are.

Friday 18th August 1972

Only forty two of the students who were arrested during June Week are still on trial. The rest of them have either had the charges against them dropped or have been found not guilty. Those who are still on trial are allowed to take their text books into the court room and read them while the trial is in progress. They say that they feel encouraged by seeing other students in the public gallery, and have asked for more students to come and show solidarity in this way. A separate trial has been started for the two journalists who were arrested at the demonstration.

The lawyers for the students have succeeded in making the police admit that many of the students were sitting down on the lawn when they were arrested. When Brigadier Schroeder was questioned, he said that the students who went onto the lawn after he had warned them to disperse had satisfactorily obeyed his command.

One thing that the lawyers have not been able to get any of the police to admit is that the plain clothes police had batons with them on the day, even though the court has been shown photos of plain clothes police bashing students with batons.

Saturday 19th August 1972

Last night my mom and I went to a talk by Hugh Tracey. He travels around the wild parts of South Africa recording traditional African music. With intrepid resolve he is determined to capture the "real" music before it disappears. He showed us slides of people playing the instruments that we were listening to. Some of the instruments were made out of modern things, like petrol tins, but they still played the traditional music on them. He also played some records of the "township music", the type of music that I hear coming from Ishmail's radio. Hugh Tracey calls it "degenerate" and "monotonous", but I rather like it. I also like the traditional music that he played for us, and I think it is wonderful that he is recording it for posterity. He had some LPs for sale with the music he has recorded. I wanted to buy one but my mother wouldn't let me.

Ishmail has an FM radio which picks up a station that transmits in his own language. He only gets paid R20 per month, so it must have been a really cheap radio for him to be able to buy it. The Nats don't want Blacks to hear radio stations that broadcast from outside of South Africa, so they have come up with a clever ruse to prevent them from being able to hear anything that is not in line with Nat philosophy. They have flooded the market with cheap FM radios, and they broadcast in the various African languages from FM transmitters all over South Africa. They call it Radio Bantu. FM signals can only travel for sixty miles, so these cheap radios can't pick up broadcasts from the BBC and Radio Moscow, which transmit on shortwave from Zambia. The Nats view the BBC with the same suspicion as they view Radio Moscow.

There is a radio station in Mozambique called LM Radio which transmits on short wave. Although it is based in Mozambique it broadcasts in English, not in Portuguese. It plays pop music for South African teenagers, and it advertises South African products. It used to play the best pop music, including songs that are banned in South Africa. The Nats did not like that so they sent a deputation to Mozambique to tell the owner of LM Radio that he had to sell the station to the S.A.B.C., "or else". They did not even try to

Wits Student — Friday 18 August 1972

Students on trial

Students on trial at the Magistrate's Court on charges under the Riotous Assemblies Act have appealed to fellow students to support them by attending the trial. Yesterday the trial entered its second week, and is expected to continue for some time.

Thus far, about fifteen state witnesses have been called, and many have been subjected to rigorous cross-examination. After calling a police photographer and Brig. H.J.Schroder the state then began calling each policeman who had effected an arrest individually. Approximately twelve policemen had been called at the time of going to press. Approximately thirty have still to be called.

CHARGES

Since the beginning of the trial, charges against 6 students have been dropped, and four of the accused have been found not guilty and acquitted. There are now forty-two accused remaining on trial. Twenty-three have been discharged and two newspaper reporters charged with impersonating the police, will appear in a separate trial.

EVIDENCE

A feature of the evidence of the police witnesses is the fact that all of them have denied that the plain clothes police were carrying batons on the day of the arrest. Pictures have been produced which, the defence allege, show members of the CID in plain clothes wielding batons on the day in question. One plain clothes policeman admitted having a piece of sjambok with him on the day.

Many police witnesses have testified to the fact that accused had walked back from the rockery at the edge of Jan Smuts Avenue and sat down some way away. Under cross-examination, Brig. Schroder has said that he would have considered sitting down after his warning to be a satisfactory dispersal.

SUPPORT

Students on trial spend most of their time studying. They have been forbidden to read or play chess by the magistrate, but are allowed to read setworks and textbooks. Many of them have mentioned the fact that they find it hard to concentrate continually on the trial. They have commented on the fact that they are greatly encouraged by seeing fellow-students in the public galleries. They appealed to more students to show solidarity with them in this way.

This is the article in the student newspaper, *Wits Student*, that prompted me to write the entry of 18 August. They have spelled Schroeder wrongly. The head that I have encircled is that of Craig Williamson.

cover-up the way that they did it. They are so sure of themselves because they know that they can get away with it. As soon as the S.A.B.C. took control of LM Radio they started playing shallow, repetitive pop songs instead of the good music.

Four years ago Lydia and I had the big thrill of being taken on a tour of the radio station by none other than Darryl Jooste, our favourite DJ. We were staying with Lydia's Auntie Athena in Lourenco Marques, and she knew someone who could organise the visit for us. We loved LM Radio, and now it no longer exists, or at least it exists in name, but it is no longer worth listening to. There is no music station for us now because everything is controlled by the S.A.B.C.

Before they branched into FM the S.A.B.C. had only three radio stations, The English, The Afrikaans, and Springbok Radio, all on medium wave. There is no TV in South Africa. If you want to see TV you have to go to Rhodesia or South West Africa.

Some of the Nat propaganda on the radio is blatant, but most of it is subtle. It is not like Peking Radio which gives Mao's thoughts and nothing else. The S.A.B.C. tries to give the impression that they are airing different opinions by staging "interviews", but the person being interviewed is always a government supporter, and the interviewer feeds them questions which are designed to give them an opportunity to spout government opinion.

In the "news" they quote Bantustan leaders who say things like, "Separate development is the answer to South Africa's problems," or "Bantustans prove that Mr. Vorster is sincere in what he says," but they don't quote the ones who criticise the Bantustan policy. A Nat recently stood up in parliament and said that the Coloureds were definitely not the result of the white settlers mixing with indigenous people. The S.A.B.C. repeated his statement in the "news", not in a tone to show what an idiot he is, but in a tone which indicated that it is a fact and that we must believe it. It sometimes quotes Helen Suzman when it can take her words out of context to make her sound like a radical. When an overseas anti-apartheider is mentioned, the news will go something like, "Mr. Jones was referring to so-called racial discrimination in South Africa," or, "... a meeting will be held about what he termed as a system repressive to Blacks". When they want to justify banning someone they say something like, "He was siding with the subversive forces that are trying to destroy the South African way of life by blackening the name of South Africa overseas."

The Nats have the gall to say that the reason why they do not allow political parties to buy radio time is because they do not want politics over the air. Meanwhile they dish out politics all the time. I don't know how often they tell direct lies in the news bulletins. When they told the lie on the news that all the students had gone home despite there still being hundreds of us at the demonstration, I was there, so I know about that one. They probably tell many lies like that and there is no way of knowing what is not true.

English language newspapers are able to report a lot of what is going on. Afrikaans language newspapers support apartheid, so they deliberately do not tell their readers what is going on. Many English speaking Whites hate the newspapers because they report things that make them feel uncomfortable. *The Star* and the *Daily Mail* are the two English language newspapers in Johannesburg, and the *Daily Mail* is more inclined to attack the government.

Last year The Nats held grandiose events at the Rand Stadium to celebrate the tenth anniversary of the Republic, and Wits students distributed pamphlets that pointed out that there was no reason to celebrate. My friend Peter James and some other students were handing out pamphlets when a man walked up to one of the girls, grabbed her pamphlets, and started punching her. The police stood by and watched, but Peter and two other guys rushed to her rescue. The police then arrested the three boys and refused to take the name of the man who had punched the girl in the first place. The boys were taken to Booysens Police Station, made to fill in forms, and then released. They were never charged with anything. This incident was reported in the English language newspapers, including how the police did nothing when the girl was assaulted. The

Nats are annoyed by the English language newspapers, and they continually threaten that they are going to "curb the irresponsibility of the press".

Tuesday 22nd August 1972.

Mrs. Thompson came for lunch today. She is a member of The Black Sash, but we know her through the Archaeological Society. The Black Sash is a woman's organisation that protests against injustices and tries to help the victims of injustice. When they protest in public they have to do it one at a time, because two protestors would be classified as a riot. There is often a Black Sash lady standing at the beginning of Jan Smuts Ave, with a wide black sash over one shoulder and around her waist, holding a placard that says something about what the government is doing. It is a good spot because most of the traffic leaving the city for the Northern Suburbs passes by and has to see her.

They run advice offices in the cities to help Blacks who are having trouble with officialdom. The officials in the pass offices are lazy and incompetent, and sometimes corrupt. One of the Black Sash offices is near the pass office in Albert Street. There are always long queues of Blacks waiting outside the pass office in Albert Street.

The police harass Mrs. Thompson because she is a member of The Black Sash. When she goes out they often follow close behind her in their big police car. One night she was driving home from an anti-apartheid meeting, with a police car following her, when she stopped at a red traffic light, and a drunk black woman lurched head first off the pavement into the side of the car and broke her neck. The police laid a charge of manslaughter against Mrs. Thompson, even though they had seen how it had happened because they had been right behind her.

She is 74 years old, but in their opinion that is no excuse for wanting peaceful change. They started a court case against her, and each time she appeared the police asked for an adjournment for one ridiculous reason after another. The police made her go to a whole lot of different places to have her fingerprints taken over and over again. When she got fed up with the way they were wasting her time she hired a lawyer, and the lawyer said something in court that made the magistrate close the case. The dent from the blow was on the side of her car, so the police would never have been able to convict her. Their harassment did succeed in making her nervous and jittery, but it did not make her change her opinion that apartheid is wrong.

At the moment she is taking part in a campaign that The Black Sash is running against the Alexandra Hostels. Most black townships are cleverly positioned so that you don't see them from a road, but the edge of Alexandra Township can be seen as you drive along Louis Botha Avenue. The land slopes away from the road so that you can only see the houses that are nearest to Louis Botha Ave. Alexandra Township was built a long time ago and the houses are made out of proper bricks. The trouble is that nowadays there are far too many people living in each house, and shacks made of corrugated iron fill the space between the houses. The *Group Areas Act* has forced thousands of people to be squashed into a small area. The houses were originally owned by Blacks, but the *Land Act* meant that the houses were stolen from their owners, and now the descendants of those owners have to pay rent to the apartheid bureaucracy.

The original houses were well built in 1912, and some were purchased by blacks. A year later the law prohibiting blacks from owning land was introduced. People coming to Johannesburg in the hope of finding work caused a huge increase in population, but no more houses were built. There were nine people living in that enclosed veranda. The women in the picture are carrying jerry cans to collect water from the communal tap.

Alexandra Township is part of the municipality of Sandton. The white people in Sandton are richer than the people in Bel Air in California, yet the municipality does not provide sanitation nor electricity to Alexandria, and the water supply just goes to a few taps in the street. Like everywhere else in South Africa the wages paid to parents are not enough for them to feed their children enough calories, but because some white people run a charity called *The African Children's Feeding Scheme* the children in Alexandra are better fed than the children in Soweto and in rural townships.

The roads were unsealed despite being in one of the wealthiest municipalities in the world.

A family of four lived in this little room. On Sundays they would sit in the sun on the car seat. I took this and the other photos of Alexandra in 1981, accompanied by a resident who knew how I could avoid being arrested if we were spotted by patrolling police. It was illegal for a white person to enter Alexandra without a permit.

The Alexandra hostels have been built because the government has come up with an evil plan to make black workers disappear from the white suburbs at night. They call it the "white by night" policy. They want black workers to be easily available as labour for white Johannesburg, without having them sleep over in the white suburbs. They don't want domestic servants to be living in the back yards of white people's properties, so they have decided that they are going to get them all to sleep in hostels in Alexandra. Parkview had not yet been proclaimed "white by night", but when it is, Ishmail will have to go too.

The Nats bulldozed a whole lot of the old brick houses, and the people who had lived in them were sent off to the slums of Tembisa and Meadowlands, and their children had to go to the Bantustans. In place of the houses that were bulldozed they have built two huge hostels, one for men and one for women. They are said to be for "single" people only, but the people who have to live in them are not single. The Nats feel no shame about separating married couples because they do not see Blacks as human beings, they see them as units of labour.

Even though the hostels are huge, you can't see them from Louis Botha Avenue. They are built to hold three thousand people each, but they have only one entrance, so many people would be trapped inside if there was a fire. The rooms in the hostels are very small and they either have two, four, six, or eight beds. In the women's hostel there are also forty single rooms, but there is no such luxury in the men's hostel. No visitors are allowed into the rooms. There is a lounge for visitors, but children under 12 years old are not allowed to visit their parents.

There are fourteen people per toilet, fourteen people per bath or shower, and fourteen to each hand basin. There is no hot water on Sundays, which is the only day on which they can wash their clothes, and there is nowhere to hang the laundry. On weekdays the hot water runs out before everyone has a chance to wash.

In the kitchen there are five people to each gas ring. The small dining room must also be used in turns because they are not allowed to take food into the rooms. There are sinks for washing the cooking utensils, but there is nowhere to hang towels. After travelling in overcrowded buses to work and home again, they get back to an overcrowded hostel where they have to line up to cook their food, and they cannot have a quiet moment to themselves. There are no fridges, so they have to buy their food every day on their way home from work.

There is no heating in the hostel. It is a concrete building with concrete floors. There is no electrical socket in the room, so they cannot use their own heaters. Johannesburg gets very cold at night during the winter because of the high altitude. There is one overhead light bulb per room, and with no socket they cannot use their own bedside lamp. The windows in the men's hostel are so high that the occupants cannot see out of them. Each person has a steel cabinet about 20 inches square for keeping all their belongings; their clothes, shoes, cooking utensils, pass, – the lot. They have to lock everything away or else it will be stolen while they are out or asleep. There is nowhere to sit except on the bed. Mrs. Thompson has done a tour of the hostels with The Black Sash.

The Mens Hostel. The Nats planned to demolish all the houses in Alexandra and replace them with 25 hostels, but Pastor Sam Buti and his supporters prevented more than two from being built.

The corridors are 4' 6" wide. At intervals there are sliding doors which can close across the corridors when a remote button is pressed. Their purpose is to shut the hostels off into sections if there is a riot. Mrs. Thompson says, "It shows that they are expecting those living conditions to cause trouble".

The Black Sash, the Progressive Party, and the churches got together and formed *The Citizen's Hostel Action Committee*. They set up petition tables in public places and put up posters all over Johannesburg saying, "Silence means consent. Say NO to the Alexandra Hostels", "Build homes not hostels", and "House people don't herd them". More than thirty thousand people signed the petition. The Action Committee also asked the government to convert the hostels into flatlets for families. The English language newspapers publicised the campaign, but the Nats say they are going to demolish all the houses in Alexandra and build more hostels. The Nats could easily afford to build enough little homes for the Blacks to live in, and there is lots of empty space around Alexandra in which to put them.

There was lots of empty space around Alexandra Township. One of the Alexandra hostels can be seen in the top picture. The tall building in the second picture is on a distant rise, and is the municipal centre of Sandton.

The Black Sash was founded to try to prevent Coloureds from being taken off the voters roll. Before 1910 Coloureds who owned land were allowed to vote in the Cape Colony. In 1910 the Cape Colony became one of the four provinces in the Union of

South Africa, and the new constitution said that land-owning Coloureds in the Cape Province could continue to vote. The Nats did not like this, but they couldn't change it easily because the constitution said that things in the constitution could only be changed if two thirds of the parliament and the senate voted in favour of the change. Another thing that the constitution said was that English and Afrikaans would both be official languages. When the Nats were scheming to take Coloured voters off the roll in the Cape it made English speaking Whites feel worried that they might also try to remove English as an official language. So The Black Sash got a lot of support from English women. Then the Nats got up to their trickery. The constitution did allow them to change the size of the senate, so they created more seats and put a whole lot of Nats in them, which meant that they got enough votes to say that Coloureds could no longer vote.

After The Black Sash had failed to stop Coloureds from being taken off the voters roll it turned its attention to other forms of injustice, and the number of supporters decreased. Some irate English speaking women even turned up at Black Sash offices and handed back their membership.

Sheena Duncan from The Black Sash lives nearby, and last year she turned up at a Civil Defence meeting for housewives in Parkview. She brought up the topic of how badly servants are treated, and some of the housewives are still talking about how much they hate her.

Wednesday 23rd August 1972

There is great fury in Parkview because Peter Hain has been found not guilty in a British court. "Has the world gone mad, letting that good for nothing vandal get off scot free?"

"The only reason that he was acquitted was that it was a multiracial jury, so of course you couldn't expect a true verdict."

They think that digging holes in a cricket pitch is immoral, but causing children to die from starvation is not immoral. Peter Hain has been trying to stop whites-only rugby and cricket teams from playing in England, sometimes by damaging the fields on which they are about to play.

"Imagine allowing somebody to spoil the pleasure of thousands of people. There are thousands of people who would really have loved to have seen those cricket games. That one man should be allowed to spoil the pleasure of those thousands of people is absolutely criminal!" Spoiling the lives of millions of people by forcing them to live in dire poverty is of course not considered criminal.

The S.A.B.C. spends its time telling us that Peter Hain is a typical young hooligan, that he is bitter because he no longer lives in South Africa, and that he is intent on doing as much damage to his former country as possible by "trying to blacken the name of South Africa overseas".

The S.A.B.C. uses a tone of moral indignation when it mentions campaigns to prevent all-white South African teams from playing overseas. They call the campaigns a "vicious vendetta", and they repeat over and over again that boycotting South Africa is "bringing politics into sport". They are such hypocrites that they do not consider imposing apartheid on sport as bringing politics into sport. In South Africa whites are forbidden by law to play sport with people of any other racial classification, and very few people with other classifications have amenities for playing sport.

I often hear grumbling Whites use the phrase "bringing politics into sport", which shows how effective the radio propaganda is. If you point out that selecting teams on the basis of race is bringing politics into sport, they just look at you blankly. To them apartheid in sport is not politics, it is just normal. They do not consider the suffering of seventeen and a half million victims of apartheid to be a valid reason for the boycotts.

Saying that you agree with the idea of boycotting South African sport causes far more anger than saying that black wages are too low. One night while I was still at school Mr. Vaughn was here, and he was feeling tetchy because a cricket tour of England had been cancelled. When my date came to pick me up Mr. Vaughn asked him, "What do you think about Peter Hain?"

My date replied, "I think it's wonderful that one person can achieve so much". Mr. Vaughn exploded with anger and shouted at my date that he was a traitor and sick in the head.

Chapter 3

Thursday 24th August 1972

I was planning to attend court today to see how Helen's trial is going, but instead I'm off to Cape Town. I'm on the milk train which takes two nights and a day to get there. The Karoo is flashing by the window, with miles of blue sky above. I could have taken a train that leaves at 2 pm one day and arrives in Cape Town at 10 am the next, but I prefer the milk train because you get a whole day of looking out at the Karoo, and I love the Karoo. This really is the milk train because it stops to pick up milk. The farmers leave the milk next to the line in huge silver urns. Or at least their employees leave the urns next to the railway line. There is a posh train called the *Blue Train* which some people like. I hate going on it because you can't open the windows and you can't smell the veld and the soot from the engine.

A thick cloud of black smoke is volupting into the blue sky. There is a lot of blue sky. Every now and then a huge stone blockhouse flashes by. They were built during the Boer War. Sometimes you see a meerkat perched upright on an anthill, staring at the train as if wondering what to do about it, but I haven't seen one today.

I'm excited about going to Cape Town. Cape Town is wonderful, and there are two people there that I am particularly keen on seeing. One is of course my school friend Lydia, the other is Stephen, whom I met on a Union Castle ship when we sailed from Cape Town to Southampton two years ago. It took a while to make friends with him because he was depressed and withdrawn. His family's cabin was near ours, so I often passed him in the passageway. He always looked down when I smiled at him. I was right in thinking he was lonely, but wrong in thinking that he was an Indian.

When he eventually decided to talk to me we sat in deck chairs at the back of the ship with our feet on the rails watching the wake get left behind, and for hours his story flooded out. Most of the feelings he described were self-evident, but it was good for him to talk and unburden himself. He told me his family history – quite a mixture. He has black genes which come from a half French half St. Helena ancestor. He also has German, British and other European ancestry. His one grandparent was this, another that, while another was half this and half that. "So what am I?" he asked despondently.

"A human being," I suggested. The look of gratitude on his face was gratifying in one way and sickening in another. He had never before been made to feel like a human being by a white person. All of his relations are classified Coloured, but some of them look white and they can go wherever they like, even to white restaurants and white nightclubs, without it being detected that they are there illegally.

His parents decided that because he was so dark he would have a better future in England. At sixteen years he was as sad about leaving his friends and family as he was about the life he had been forced to live in South Africa. His mother was going to stay with him in England for six months, then return to South Africa. When she spotted us chatting at the back of the ship she came up and said, "Oh, Stephen, I'm so pleased to see that you've made a friend at last. I was so worried about you, I told you you shouldn't have stayed there hanging around the cabin all the time."

After our talk he stopped avoiding me and the other Whites on the ship. All the young people would be on deck together then split up going down to the cabins. As our cabins were near each other, Stephen and I would be together when we passed the purser's office. Stephen looked older than 15, so the snooty Union Castle officers would raise their eyebrows every time we passed, much to our amusement.

His mother's suitcase with all her dresses in it had been mistakenly put in the hold, and when she reported it to the purser's office she was literally told to go to hell. When my mother heard about this she marched off to the purser's office, where she was politely told that once something had been put in the hold, it could not be retrieved. On Christmas Eve everyone was dolled up to look glamorous, but Stephen's mother was wearing the same dress that she had worn throughout the whole voyage. When I wished her a happy Christmas at midnight she burst into tears and ran down to her cabin. Towards the end of the cruise I spoke with a white woman whose luggage had also been accidentally put in the hold, and had been fetched for her as soon as she asked for it. This was a British ship with British staff.

When they had been in England for three months we received a letter from his mother saying, "It is true that there are many facilities, you do not have to be afraid. It is wonderful to be free,

Stephen took this photo of me outside the art gallery. The LP I am holding is the music from the stage production of "Hair". Stephen had bought it in London for me as it was banned in South Africa.

55

to go in, and where you want to be, not having to draw back or pass by. The places are all very beautiful wherever you go, and I appreciate it all, but our family is a very close unit, and I think Stephen missed his brothers too much, and we had to wait for a permit from Home Office to gain admittance to a school. By the time it did come, we had decided to return together."

Stephen's letters were scrawly and moody. He bitterly said that I had changed his opinion of the "superior race". The Nats have made it impossible for Coloureds and Whites to meet socially, so it is not surprising that many Coloureds think that all Whites are like the Nats. He and his mother returned to South Africa in August, and I visited them in Cape Town in November. On the second day that I was in Cape Town I met up with Stephen in the Gardens. We behaved as if we were still on Southampton Docks, then we remembered. I was vaguely aware of staring faces as we walked through the park. When we sat down I forgot to look and see whether the bench we were sitting on was marked whites only or non-whites only. We reminisced like old age pensioners, then Stephen suggested we visit the art gallery as that is the only place we can both go in.

After that we went to his home. To get there we caught a double-decker bus that was a white downstairs and non-white upstairs specimen. One day they will put examples of these in museums.[18] In Johannesburg the buses are either all white or all non-white, but in Cape Town you get four different arrangements. You get all white buses and all non-white buses. Then you also get double-decker buses and single-decker buses that anyone can get on, but you have to be careful where you sit. The double-decker buses are white downstairs and non-white upstairs. You never get non-white downstairs and white upstairs buses. The single-decker buses are even more bizarre. They have an X hanging above the third seat from the front, and a Y hanging above the second seat from the back. Only Whites can sit in front of the X, but they are not allowed to sit behind the Y, while anyone may sit in between.

A sign inside a Cape Town bus. Some passengers scowled at me when I took this photo, others gawped.

---

18 When I made that off-the-cuff remark about the buses appearing in museums in the future, I was thinking that apartheid museums would be established a hundred years in the future, not during my life time.

In the area where Stephen's family lives the houses are small and close together, not because the inhabitants are poor, but because there is no other housing available.[19] The children have to share a bedroom, but they each have their own car. It is legal for me to visit an area that has been designated as "Coloured" under the Group Areas Act, and it would even be legal for me to sleep over at their house. The condition would be that I would have to have my own room, and the door between my room and the rest of the house would be shut. The law specifically states that the door must not be a bamboo curtain.

His mother was pleased to see me. She told me all about their time in London. She also kept saying, "We are not Coloureds, we are St. Helena people." She never uses the word "Coloured" in front of small children.

Friday 25th August 1972

The train arrived early in Cape Town, and then I caught the suburban train to Rondebosch. There were no taxis, so I had to make my way up the steep mountainside to the university on foot. Squirrels were frisking about in the trees, even in the trees on the island in the middle of the freeway. Halfway up an old lady helped me with my luggage. She asked me why I have a reel of copper wire with me, and I told her that I make hippie jewellery. That didn't make her give up on me.

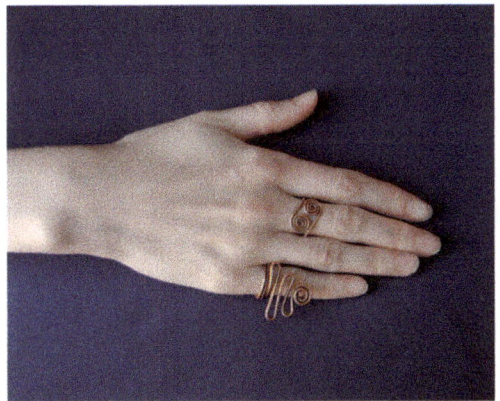 

Hippie copper rings I made.

When I got to the university I went to the residence where Lydia stays, dragged my luggage into her room, got into her bed and pulled the blanket over my head. I woke up a few hours later when she opened the door. Her eyes first hit the luggage on the floor, then rose to where mine peered at her over the blanket. I had been promising her that I would be visiting Cape Town "soon" for so many weeks that she had stopped believing it. After the recovery there was the reunion, then the explanation, then I went to get some lunch.

There were notices at the top of Jammie steps announcing a mass meeting to discuss

---

19 The houses in Kensington were built in the 1920s.

the arrest of Geoff Budlender. Yesterday while I was on the train things were happening here in Cape Town. Students had been handing out pamphlets when one of them was arrested. He was Geoff Budlender, the president of the University of Cape Town SRC. The other students then told the police that although they had also done nothing wrong, they were just as guilty as Geoff, and they demanded to be arrested too. They were not arrested, which shows that the police have a particular grudge against Geoff.

I went along to the mass meeting. First of all Steve Jooste recounted the events of yesterday. He spoke well, making us laugh at the stupid things the police had said. Then a chap with a beard gave a long speech. He was very earnest, and said the usual things about our society needing reform. He described how, while he was handing out pamphlets yesterday, he had argued with a woman who came out with the common excuse that Whites pay all the taxes. He had said to her, "The tragedy of this is that you are a good woman, and it is people like you who could save our country, but you will not see it." He had told her how the gate keeper at Auschwitz had been put on trial at Nuremberg even though he had not personally killed anybody.

I spent the afternoon with Lydia, then set off for the Muizenberg youth hostel. The lady who runs the hostel thought that I was strange for expecting to be able to sleep in a bed for the night. She said that she was closed for the winter and I must go to the Camps Bay youth hostel. I pointed out that the Camps Bay youth hostel is on the other side of the mountain and it was already dark. She relented and said I could stay for one night, but I would get no bedding. I've got my own bedding, so I'm in a room for 100, with 99 empty beds. The silence is strange. I can imagine the bustle when it is full in the summertime.

The Cape of Good Hope. That is what they called it three hundred years ago. The Cape of Good Hope. The Fairest Cape in all the World. Surely there is hope for a city where squirrels play beside the freeway and old ladies help you with your luggage?

Saturday 26th August. 1972

Lydia and I went into town in the morning. I sold some jewellery and bought some jeans at "The Market", which is a whole lot of cubicle shops inside a big room.

Then I caught a white downstairs non-white upstairs bus to Stephen's house, and his mother gave me a huge lunch. As I was approaching the house a little boy called

Hippie copper chokers I made.

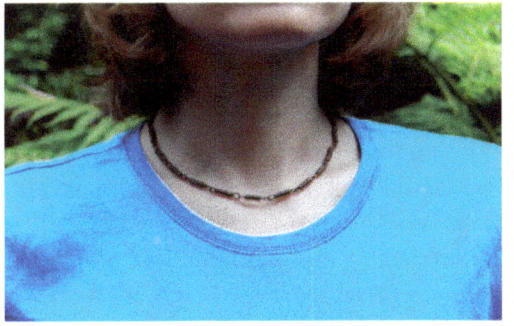 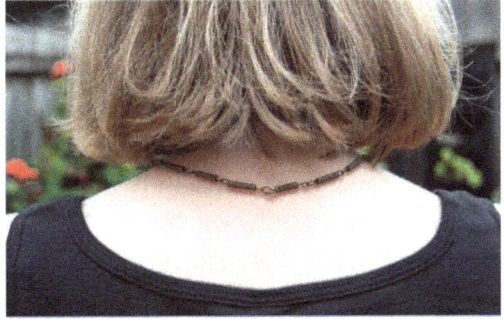

Hippie copper necklace I made on a knitting needle.

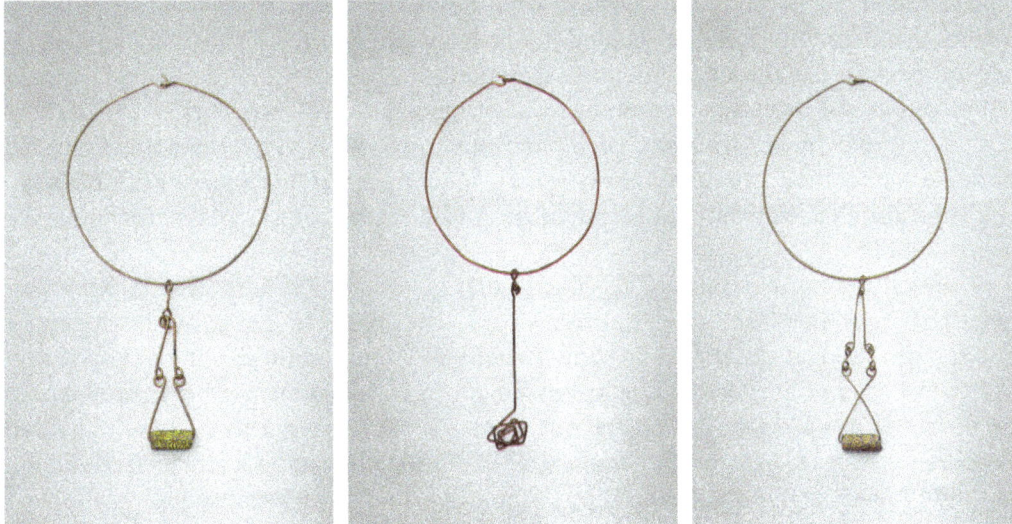

Hippie copper chokers, two with goulamine beads.

out, "Hello Wendy, hello Wendy." Little Peter had grown so much since last year that I only recognised him by his voice. Perhaps when little Peter and all the other little boys playing in the street are big men they will not be so friendly towards Whites. The Whites should think about that instead of thinking about the luxurious lives that they live now.

After lunch Stephen and I went to visit his girlfriend Temba. Temba is the Xhosa word for hope. Her mother is Coloured and her father is German. When the *Immorality Act* was brought in her father had to get himself reclassified as Coloured in order to stay married to his wife. His skin is whiter than mine. In theory he cannot go through a door labelled "whites only", but in reality, if he did go through a door labelled "whites only", no one would know that he was breaking the law.

Cape Town has to be different, so unlike the rest of South Africa, it rains in the winter. It started pouring, and we sat in Temba's warm kitchen, drinking coffee and eating sour figs. It was nice to be with adults who spoke about interesting things instead of the latest boredoms of the stock exchange and how bad the United Nations is. Her father told me about democracy in Germany and a writer called Gunther Grass.

The Nats are not satisfied with labelling people as Coloureds; they have invented sixteen subdivisions of Coloured too. To add insult to injury they have classified Temba as "Other Coloured".

Stephen's brother drove me to the Camps Bay youth hostel. We were in no danger of being arrested under the *Immorality Act* because his girlfriend was also in the car. When I got out of the car he said, "You're not going to have much of a Saturday night. If your pigmentation was a little bit stronger we would be able to take you with us, but, being as weak as it is, you can't come."

"It's not weak, it's just scattered," I said in defence of my pigmentation, which led me to wondering how long it would be before they reclassified all people with freckles, and whether or not they would grant us a homeland.

There were two girls already in sleeping bags when I came into the room. One is an Australian, the other is an American who met her Indonesian husband working on a kibbutz in Israel. In London she and her husband applied for a visa to come here. It was refused. In Israel they applied again, separately, because they thought the mixed marriage must be what the government did not like. She was granted a visa, but he was not. They came down Africa and he applied again in Rhodesia, but did not get one. So now she is travelling around South Africa while her husband waits for her in Rhodesia. I'm surprised that they thought he might get a visa when there would be no hotels for him to stay in.

I started telling her some of the things that go on around here. She kept putting her hands over her face, wriggling with repulsion, and retracting into her sleeping bag saying, "Sick, sick." I told her how I could not go out with Stephen's brother and his girlfriend, not because it would be socially unacceptable, but because it would be illegal. When I got to the part about Temba's father having to become classified Coloured in order to stay married to his wife she could not handle it any longer, and did not want to hear any more. Some Whites say that I am "sick" because I do not believe that Whites are superior to other people.

Sunday 27th August 1972

I went hospital visiting with Lydia at Groote Schuur. The neurology wards are the most depressing. Some of the patients speak a different kind of Afrikaans, so fast and disjointed that I can't understand them. I just nodded and smiled and they seemed happy.

Groote Schuur is an enormous hospital. There are whites only wards, but the Whites don't have a section of the hospital all to themselves. The non-Whites are separated into a variety of ethnic wards, except for the non-white children, who are all together. The order of the wards along the passages is all mixed up, so that white wards are in between non-white wards. This is different to Johannesburg, where there are completely separate hospitals for the different racial classifications.

Saturday 2nd September 1972

I spent the morning with Lydia and then Stephen fetched me from Fuller Hall at midday. After five we drove over Kloof Nek to Camps Bay, and I asked him in for coffee to meet all the cool people in the hostel. One of the Americans who is here was at Woodstock. I went to my room to dump my bag, and when I returned his expression had changed. He said he didn't want any coffee. The warden had seen him through the window and sent her husband to chase him off. "Don't worry," said Stephen, "I'm used to it." He was trying to make me feel better, but the fact that it happens to him often made me feel worse.

After he had driven off, the hostel warden's husband, who had started cleaning his car, looked down the embankment at me and said quietly, "I want to talk to you." I climbed up, and he started, "Now look, this is not a question of your point of view, nor is it a question of my point of view, but the facts are that no Coloured is allowed on these premises." It is very much a question of his point of view. It is neither against the law of the land, nor the law of the youth hostels association, for Stephen to come into the kitchen and drink coffee.

Monday 4th September 1972

The Camps Bay youth hostel is about halfway down a deep ravine called The Glen, which is inhabited by all sorts of Cape natural life. The Glen runs down from Kloof Nek between Table Mountain and Lion's Head to Camps Bay, and there is only one other building in it. From the veranda you can look down at the Atlantic Ocean way below and at the majestic Twelve Apostles to the left. Squirrels scamper through the pine trees, taking long leaps from branch to branch. The pine trees are the same species as the ones on Palatine Hill in Rome. I've never seen them anywhere else. Tiny exquisite flowers sparkle in the early morning when you leave the hostel. At sunset the sea turns pink and Camps Bay houses reflect an orangey pink and the twelve mountain heads stepping into the bay change to soft orange and everything close by is green green green and flowers.

Cape wildflowers just south of the hostel. The mountain is one of the Twelve Apostles.

This evening there was a downpour, and now the bank of nasturtiums behind the hostel is sparkling with raindrops. Each individual leaf is huge because of the fertile soil, and the round flat leaves each hold one large, shiny ball of rain. The air is warm despite the rain, and the scent of wet earth hits you as you walk out of the kitchen door and see the sparkling bank of colour reflecting the hostel lights.

The Palatine pines in The Glen, with Camps Bay and the Twelve Apostles behind. Sandy Bay is between the last Apostle and the mountain in the distance. 2015.

Thursday 7th September 1972

One of the people staying in the hostel is an American called Ron who says he is part Cherokee Indian. You can tell by looking at his face that he is part American Indian, but the border guards obviously couldn't tell or they would not have let him in. He has travelled overland from Cairo with a haversack and a guitar, and now he wants to work in South Africa for four months before setting off for India. We South Africans can't get visas to go to most countries in Africa. We can only go to Rhodesia, Mozambique, Botswana, Malawi, Angola, Lesotho and Swaziland.[20]

He was offered a job as a fireman, but he felt it wasn't worth their training him as he is only going to be here for four months. One attractive sounding offer, which looked as though it entailed sitting on a beach all day, turned out to be driving from beach to beach in a motor car, dressed in a uniform, checking that no one was playing ball games on a Sunday. It is illegal to play ball games on a beach on a Sunday. For some jobs he needed to be able to speak Afrikaans, but the thing that really got in his way was job reservation. In America he could get a job doing any manual work, but in South Africa someone who is classified white has to do "qualified" work, because Blacks have to do all the "unqualified" work, and there are no manual jobs left over.

After the first day of looking for work he cut off his hair, swapped a shirt and

---

20 At this time Namibia was occupied by South Africa, and a visit there was not regarded as leaving the country.

borrowed a tie. I have accompanied him on some of his traipsings because it is interesting going into the firms and offices. He likes me coming along because I know my way around, and he says I look so virtuous that I create a good impression!?!

Today we caught a bus to Epping where he had a job interview, and we were the only two on the bus. The bus driver went off the bus route to take us to where we wanted to be. If he had been white he would not have done that. After the interview it started to rain, and I realised that we were in the vicinity of Stephen's house. We found our way there, and Stephen's mom helped us to dry out. Ron made a phone call, and came back into the kitchen beaming. He has a job. Tomorrow he will move out of the youth hostel, and we won't be entertained by his mimicking ability any more. When he mimics the birds in the Glen it takes a few tries for him to get it right, then they answer him. He also copies the songs of the frogs at night, but they do not answer, they just snap into stunned silence. He says he can do it because of the Cherokee genes. I asked him which ancestor was Cherokee, and sure enough, he is way more than one sixteenth Cherokee. I told him that he would be classified non-white if he was South African. "I don't care," he said, "They can make me go in another door at the post office if they like. I don't care."

"You would care if you had been born here. It's more than going in a different door at the post office, and being looked down on by Whites. You wouldn't have been educated unless your parents were rich. You wouldn't be able to travel about. You wouldn't be able to use the facilities that you pay taxes for, and you wouldn't have the freedom of mind that you have."

On Tuesday while he was job searching he wanted to have tea and scones in the grounds of the Mount Nelson Hotel. I liked the idea because I hadn't done that since I was seven years old. The Mount Nelson Hotel is a very posh outpost of the British Empire. Tables and chairs are set out on the lawn, quite far from the building, and waitresses with lace aprons come to serve you.

While Ron and I were waiting for our order to arrive he was looking at job adverts in the paper. "Male Indian driver wanted for heavy duty. Sober habits. Between

The entrance to the Mount Nelson Hotel.

25 and 49 years old." Or, "Coloured girl wanted for laundry work. No chancers."

"Wow" said Ron, in America you're not even allowed to advertise for whether you want males or females, let alone what race you want."

A second waitress came up to our table and asked us what we want. "The other lady already took our order," said Ron.

"Do you know why she smiled like that?" I asked, when she had gone away.

"No."

"Because you called her friend a lady, not a girl."

Last night in the kitchen I heard him say to another traveller, "I used to think that I came from the worst country on earth, but now that I've been to South Africa, I know that I come from the second worst country on earth."

My mother has a favourite story about having tea and scones in the garden at the Mount Nelson Hotel. In 1947 she and my dad travelled by train to Cape Town, and she had with her a little brown paper bag that contained some of the diamonds that were to be given to the British Royal family at a ball in the town hall. Another train that supposedly brought the diamonds from Johannesburg to Cape Town had travelled with an armed guard, but there were no diamonds on that train. Jan Smuts had arranged for them to be taken to Cape Town by people like my mother who would not attract attention. In case her handbag was snatched she carried the diamonds separately in the little brown paper bag. From the train they went straight to the Mount Nelson Hotel to hand over the diamonds to her boss, Mr. Kadinsky. They settled down for tea and scones at one of the tables on the lawn, and she put the paper bag on the ground next to the chair. When the waiter came to take their order he accidentally kicked the little brown paper bag. My mother often says, "I wish I could have told him he had just kicked the crown jewels."

The diamonds ready to be presented to George, Liz, Lizzie, and Margaret in 1947.

Saturday 9th September 1972

There's an Australian called Tim staying in the youth hostel who is on his way to England. He can work there for two years because Australia is still part of the Commonwealth. He and I decided to go to Hout Bay today, but en route we were waylaid by the beauty of Llandudno. The road to Hout Bay runs along the feet of the majestic Twelve Apostles, with the sparkling sea below, and if you turn right before crossing the nek to Hout Bay, you go steeply downhill to Llandudno, through a village of stylish houses, to a beach with lovely fine sand, big round boulders, and a huge beautiful mountain towering over it.

Tim heading down the steps from the Camps Bay youth hostel to the road that runs next to the sea.

Half an hour's walk from Llandudno it gets even better. There is a beach with no road access that bears the corny name of "Sandy Bay." As Tim and I walked from Llandudno to Sandy Bay he raved continuously about the beautiful scenery. When he apologised for his enthusiasm I told him it really bugs me that most people don't rave about such exquisite scenery. Most of the time Tim has been singing Neil Young's *Heart of Gold*, because we heard it the other day in a record shop.

We sat on the sand and looked and talked. I don't like swimming on the Atlantic side of the Peninsula because the current comes up from the South Pole and is freezing cold. We saw a man bury three beer cans at the edge of the waves. When he came back to collect them the tide had moved in, and his landmarking system had failed. He and Tim searched within a twenty-foot radius, but I knew where the beer was, and dug rapidly while the cold splashes of Atlantic waves were getting higher and higher. When I produced the beer cans it was proclaimed as the greatest deed of the century. It's funny how men love beer.

Then we saw the seal. There were two surfers, one in a rubber wet suit with a board, the other with a natural wet suit and no board. The seal was the better surfer; its shiny brown body cutting the clear green wave, then keeping ahead when the white foam roared down. Whenever the human surfer flipped back over the wave it turned and shot back with him, then cavorted in the waves further out, impatiently waiting for him to paddle back so that they could catch another wave together.

Tim took this photo of me at Sandy Bay. He had given me the red jumper a few days earlier.

Back at the hostel everyone in the kitchen was still talking about the terrorist attack at the Munich Olympics. I had been the one to break the awful news to them two days ago, and I had been surprised by the strong reaction. This casual, laughing bunch of hard-boiled travellers changed into a bunch of angry, distraught, sensitive individuals. Every time someone who did not yet know about it came into the kitchen and was told, there would be another round of cursings and exclamations.

I have been trying to tell myself that if those eleven people had been killed on a kibbutz there would not have been the outcry that there is, so I should not get too upset just because they were athletes at the Olympic Games. Tonight an Israeli guy who always has a wistful look on his face, and speaks very little, was sitting opposite me at the kitchen table. It was late when the kitchen emptied, but he still sat there, while

I made copper jewellery. For the first time he spoke without being spoken to, and the wistful look intensified into a heart-rending expression. "Well," he said, "Today is our New Year, and it is a very sad day." I could not say anything and I nearly started crying.

Monday 11th September 1972.

On Saturday night three churches here in Cape Town were attacked because of their anti-apartheid stance. This kind of thing happens a lot. Red paint was smeared on the Methodist church in Buitenkant Street, and the sign outside St. Georges Cathedral was spattered with paint. The hall of St. Thomas church in Rondebosch was broken into and set on fire. The Christian Institute had held its annual meeting in the hall a few hours earlier, which is probably what provoked the attacks. The Christian Institute believes in human rights and it speaks out against apartheid. Funnily enough the police never manage to catch the perpetrators when vandalism and arson are directed against people who speak out.

St. Thomas Anglican Church, Rondebosch, built in 1864.

Tuesday 12th September 1972.

Hermanus beach is always lovely, but today it was lovely in a different way. There were no other humans on the beach because of a gale force wind, so I had the miles of sand all to myself. The waves were crashing mightily, and the blue mountains in the distance shimmered behind a haze of salt. Seagulls staggered against the wind, but the little sandpipers darted about as if nothing was different. The wind whipped up the sand so fast that it made little cuts on my ankles. I collected shells for making necklaces.

The only other object as big as myself on the beach was a post with two notices on it. The notice that was parallel to the shoreline said, "This beach for the use of whites only", and it had an arrow painted on it pointing to the west. The other notice, which was at 90 degrees to the shoreline, said, "Hermanus Municipal Boundary." So this means that the beach to the east of the post is not whites only, as it is not part of the Hermanus municipality. The wind was blowing grains of sand out of the whites only part of the beach into the other part of the beach, as if nature did not realise how important it is for the grains of sand to retain their purity.

The Nats manage to have complete control over people, but what are they going to do about nature? Surely if Whites can be contaminated by being on the same beach as Coloureds, they will be contaminated by swimming in the same water. Supposing a drop of water flows from a black beach to a white beach after having been touched by a black person, and then touches a white person. Surely white purity will be threatened?

Thursday 14th September 1972

I sat up late with Ben last night. He is an Australian who grew up in Rhodesia. We talked for hours about our travels around the world and our personal histories. He hasn't always had a nice time. In 1965 he was drafted into the Rhodesian army. He asked to carry a camera instead of a gun, and was given the job of accompanying the Rhodesian soldiers and sending back information and photographs of the terrorist attacks. Reports trickled through the bush that something had happened to a farm near the border, so Ben and some soldiers were dropped in the area by helicopter. It took three days to find the farm. They smelt it before they saw it. In the lounge they found the remains of a few people, but they were not quite sure which bits belonged to which person. A man sitting in a chair had had his head cut off with a panga (machete), and it had flown through the air and wedged into the second shelf of a bookcase. In the bedroom were the remains of three children. There were blobs of baby all over the walls. Half a baby's face was on the mirror, and some fingers on the floor. They found the mother tied to the washing line outside.

The black servants had been similarly dealt with in their own quarters. It was Ben's job to photograph the scene and send the film to Salisbury. He never saw any of the pictures he took, but he does not need a photograph to remind him of what he saw at seventeen years of age. He saw other atrocities too, but this one was the worst. He says that most South Africans do not believe him when he tells them about it. He thinks that they do not want to hear about his experiences in the Rhodesian army because they know that this is what is in their future.

I get the same reaction when I try to tell Whites about the war that is going on in Mozambique. They are very concerned about the war that is going on in Vietnam, but they do not want to believe that the war in Mozambique is serious. One lady said that I was "ridiculous" for comparing the war in Mozambique to the war in Vietnam. "Vietnam is a full-scale war. Mozambique is child's play in comparison." When I am in Mozambique I listen to what the soldiers and soon-to-be-soldiers have to say, but this lady thinks that they are all lying.

People believe that atrocities like My Lai and the Charles Manson murders actually happened because they were reported in the press, but they do not believe that atrocities could happen to them. Sometimes they actually laugh out loud when I tell them that they have something to worry about on their own borders.

The terrorists have Russian weapons and they get money from Russia, which wants to take over South Africa because of its great mineral wealth and its strategic position.

The Whites are content with living the easy life with Blacks doing all the work, and they just ignore the fact that they are going to lose it all if they make the Blacks think that the Russians would give them a better deal.

Saturday 16th September 1972

I am on top of Table Mountain, sitting on a rock at the edge looking over the city and the bay. It is a clear, warm, windy day. The water in the docks is twinkling like a million distant windscreens catching the sun. Cape Town looks like a toy city with toy cars moving up and down Adderley Street. I can see the dock where you sail for England, and the train station where you arrive from Johannesburg. I can also see the place where the laws are made, the church where students were beaten up, the theatre that Coloureds paid for but are not allowed to go into, and the place from which thousands of Coloureds are being moved. I can also see Robben Island in the middle of Table Bay.

Last year when I came to Cape Town by train there was a girl in my compartment who was returning from Pretoria University to her home on Robben Island, where her father is a jailer. She said that it is a lovely place to live because the sea is so clean for swimming, and it is so easy to catch crayfish that they eat crayfish nearly every day. When I asked her if she ever sees any of the prisoners, she said, "No, they're not a problem."

In the distance I can see the winelands, where the farmers pay their workers with wine instead of with money. It's a great system for the farmers because the workers live long enough to produce the next generation before they die from cirrhosis of the liver. Workers are born on the farm and have no option but to work for that farmer. They live in hovels and the children don't go to school. It is called the dop system.

The Cape Flats are flat and they stretch all the way from Table Mountain to the Hottentots Holland Mountains. The Nats want only Whites to live on the slopes of this mountain, so they are moving all the Coloureds from the suburb of District 6 onto the Cape Flats.

A lizard is peering at me from the next rock. There is a suspicious look in his eye. The spring flowers are out. I wonder if the spring flowers are out on Robben Island. Most of the roofs on the island are red. This mountain is high. The edge where I am sitting must be a 400-foot drop. A pied crow is circling below me. A stream going downwards is catching the sun like mica.

Near the cable car station there is a relief map of the peninsula, and around it are arrows pointing to other cities, with their distance. Durban and Hanoi are in the same direction, so are Johannesburg and Delhi, and Lusaka and Tehran. Honolulu is eleven thousand miles away, straight over the South Pole.

Sunday 17th September 1972

Today I went to Bloubergstrand with Hans who has been in the hostel for a few days, because I had told him that you get the classic photo of Table Mountain from there. The air was not as clear as yesterday, so the mountain shimmered behind the haze, but at least we could see the famous mountain with Devil's Peak to the left of it and Lion's Head to the right of it. We sunbathed on the dunes, and seagulls dived to investigate us. The sand on the beach is made of tiny chips of colourful shell. I have been to many places in the world, but I agree with the old-time sailors who called this the *Fairest Cape in all the World*.

I took these four photos despite being displeased with the light conditions.

Monday 18th September 1972

Tim sailed for Italy today and eight of us went to see him off. I went into the docks in a fiat with two short haired guys. We slowed down at customs and the guy driving said, "Nothing to declare," and we were waved through. We found Tim's ship and eventually found Tim. Then we lolled on deck chairs and looked over the flat harbour water while the sun went down. The mountain grew more and more beautiful as the evening grew darker. The harbour lights dissolved into the water like in an Impressionist painting.

When the foghorn blew we knew that we had to leave. It was hard saying goodbye to Tim when we have all had so much fun together.

As the ship moved out of the harbour we ran along the quay waving at Tim. Because of his long hair his silhouette was discernible for a long time.

I left the docks in a Combi driven by two long-haired Australians. There were four of us on the floor in the back, and when we got to customs the officer opened the side door and glared at each one of us in turn. Then he scowled at the dulcet tones of Neil

Young emanating from the tape player. He doesn't know anything about Neil Young, he just finds the style of music offensive and communistic. If he suspected us of having dagga, he was not going to find it by squinting into the dark depths of the Combi like that.

Tuesday 19th September 1972

    I was sitting on the floor of my room packing my bag for the day when a voice at the door said, "Is there a girl called Wendy staying in the hostel?" I looked up, but although there was something familiar about the figure, I could not see him properly against the light. Once outside I found that it was Kevin, someone whom I had met at Stephen's house last year. His car had broken down on the glen road, and he remembered that Stephen had said that I was staying in the Camps Bay youth hostel.

    "I'm glad you came round the front and didn't ask at reception," I told him, remembering how they had treated Stephen. I had been planning to catch busses from Kloof Nek to Sea Point, but Kevin said he would give me a lift once his car was fixed. When we got to his car he started wrapping insulation tape around some wires, and people driving past us gaped. Then it started to drizzle, so I got in the car, and Kevin was convinced that we were going to be arrested. There were some wires that he could not reach, so we coasted as far into Clifton as we could, and then started walking. I wanted to hitch a lift to get to Sea Point in time, but Kevin was nervous that doing that we would really be arrested. The white man who picked us up spoke with a British accent, and did not even remark on the fact that we were of different colours, let alone arrest us.

The spot where Kevin's car broke down. Photo taken in 2015.

After having tea and scones with my godparents at the Arthur's Seat Hotel in Sea Point I went into the city and bought stamps from the stamp machines at the main post office. As I headed from the post office to the OK Bazaars the fruit sellers seemed to be noisier than usual. I could not figure out if they were shouting for a reason, or if it was the usual "eight for ten cents" with a few lines of jingle in between. Then I saw Coloured children running and ducking behind cars. A man with an open box of bananas ran into the flower market not caring about the bunches that he dropped. Then I saw a police car and three huge fuzz with rows of medals on their chests standing disconsolately by a hastily deserted makeshift stall. Their quarry had got away. One kicked an empty carton half-heartedly, the other two were leaning towards each other, conversing seriously, as if they were planning some great manoeuvre against Rommel. Their raid had fallen flat.

As I entered the OK Bazaars a child with a wedge of brown paper packets tucked into the back of his pants dodged past me. He dived beneath the underwear counter and hauled out a box of beautiful avocado pears. The drama was over and they were setting up shop again.

When I came out they were singing, "Eight for ten cents" again, and I bought some guavas. I asked what had happened.

"Ag, merrem, the police they jus' chasing us aroun'. They don' want us making a hones' living. They want us to go steal and get us in the jail. Only then they satisfied. Thank you very much merrem."

Later on I just missed a bus so I caught the one behind it. It was only when I was on it that I realised that it was a "non-whites only" bus. I did not know whether to get off or to wait to be thrown off. The conductor took my money, but said nothing. I would not say that he was pleased to see me, nor were the two people sitting opposite me. They must have been thinking "Oh yeah, if we had got onto a white bus by mistake we would have been kicked off, not left alone like she is."

Wednesday 20th September 1972

Last night somebody had acquired a *Welcome to Sunny South Africa* pamphlet put out by the Minister of Information, and was reading it aloud in the hostel kitchen. The greatest roar of laughter was caused by the part that said, "South Africa is well known for its political stability." The thing that the travellers remark on the most is the touchiness of Whites when they dare to criticise. The ones who have been here long enough have learnt that when the inevitable question is asked, "Well, what do you think of South Africa?" they must answer something like, "The climate is wonderful," or, "The scenery is magnificent", or else they will be in for a lecture on why apartheid is the correct system. They have been told that the Whites are too poor to educate the Blacks, that the Blacks leave school so young because they don't want to be educated, and that there is no point in educating Blacks because they are too stupid.

One girl told me that she responded with, "But Blacks in my country are educated," and the South African yelled at her, "How dare you criticise this country when you don't live here. It's all you foreigners who cause all the trouble for us."

They have also been told that the Blacks have lots of land of their own in the

Bantustans, that Blacks don't need money, and that Blacks don't know how to vote. If they keep their opinion to themselves while they are being lectured, the lecture ends with, "You will go back to your country and tell them what it is like here, won't you?"

"Yes, I will," they say.

The travellers do not even get to see the terrible poverty in the townships and the rural areas, and they do not know that it is all supported by violence and oppression, yet what they see in the cities is enough to make them aghast. When I told them that the government breaks a million eggs a day, has a pipeline going into the sea to get rid of excess milk, and destroys tons of oranges every year, they were bewildered.

The tourists did not see the poverty in Cape Town itself because it was always out of sight from the main roads.

White South Africans concentrate on trying to convince foreigners that there is nothing wrong with apartheid; no poverty, no repression, no injustice. But when all else fails they resort to the principle of four wrongs make a right.

"Look at England with its poor standard of living. South Africa is much better."

"Look at America with its race riots in New York. How dare they criticise us?"

"Look at the way the Australians killed 90% of the Aborigines."

If you respond to this kind of argument with facts and figures they get angry. If you point out that only Whites have a high standard of living, they will scream at you that there are three millionaires in Soweto. If you say that the majority of people in Soweto live below the bread line, they will tell you that New York is smoggy and slummy.

Our charming warden, the one who told her husband to chase Stephen off the property, cornered some Australians one evening and told them, in her British accent, why South Africa is the only country worth living in. They just stood there saying "Mmm" "Mmm" "Mmm" while she spoke. Perhaps she thinks they will go back to Australia and tell everyone there to emigrate here, but they will really go back and tell everyone about her.

The travellers in the hostel are amused by the fact that atheists are not allowed to immigrate here. Despite so much intolerance in other spheres, there is complete religious freedom, but they don't want any more atheists. There are mosques, synagogues, churches, ashrams and anything else that anyone wants to set up, but Blacks are not allowed to go into Dutch Reformed Churches. Even a servant who wishes to attend a master's funeral cannot go into the church. Blacks are only allowed in to clean the floors and pews when no one is using the church. The Nats call South

Africa a Christian state.

Every Sunday night the guys who have cars or motor bikes grumble because there is "nothing to do". The rest of us are content to stay in the hostel and hang out and play ping pong. The Calvinists make the rules so there are no cinemas or nightclubs open on a Sunday.

One Australian guy says it freaks him out the way the police drive around in paddy wagons instead of in cars. This is so that they have room for all the pass offenders that they plan to capture, but I think this guy is scared that they might turn their attention to rounding up long haired Australian surfers.

Long haired Australian surfers at the Camps Bay youth hostel.

A typical police van (what the Australian called a paddy wagon) outside a police station in the Transvaal. Note the fence between the whites only and non-whites only pathways. I took this photo in 1980 after it had become illegal to take photos of police or police stations. The individuals confined inside this police van were not destined for a good experience.

One night a guy in the hostel kitchen was staggered by what he had seen happen that day. He had been on a "whites only" downstairs "non-whites only" upstairs bus. They came to a bus stop at which there waited three Coloureds and a White. There was room for one upstairs, but the downstairs section was almost empty. So the bus picked up one Coloured and one White and drove off leaving two Coloureds standing in the rain.

Everyone in the hostel kitchen was exclaiming that such a thing could happen, and one said to me, "You don't seem at all surprised."

I said, "No, it happens all the time."

"You mean this sort of thing happens every day?"

They will go back home and tell people what it is like here, and the Whites who say that Blacks have thick skulls and small brains will be talked about as much as the separate buses and separate entrances.

Last year when I was walking around with Stephen I learned what it is to be stared at. Mostly the expressions on the faces of the starers were just looks of surprise, but sometimes they were looks of disapproval. It was not only Whites who stared, everyone did. It began to be quite amusing. Whenever I caught the train back to Rondebosch we would stand talking outside the station door which has the signs "Whites only" and "No dogs allowed" on it. The stream of white commuters on their way home would rush past us and through the doorway, every single one of them looking back and gaping.

Here in Cape Town Coloureds ride on the same suburban trains as Whites, but they have separate carriages. Each carriage has a green sign on it with "whites only" on one side and "non-whites only" on the other. The sign can be flipped over to show whatever is required for a particular journey. It means that Coloureds and Whites can travel in the same carriage, but not at the same time. Whites go into the beautiful station building, with its shops and restaurants, while Coloureds go through a side door straight onto the platform.

Stephen said that his cousin in London could spot a South African Coloured who was new to London because they would step back to look for signs above the door before going in to a pub or restaurant.

The Minister of Information and all his pretty little pamphlets about South Africa being heaven on earth for all races do not succeed in convincing the young travellers. A lot of taxpayer's money is spent on trying to project a good image of South Africa, but these efforts are undermined by their experience of reality.

Soon after I arrived in Cape Town there was a report in the newspaper about a woman who needed a Caesarean, but had to wait for two hours because the doctor on duty was Coloured. All of the nurses on duty were White, so they could not work under a Coloured doctor, and the doctor could not do a Caesarean without help from nurses. He had to call a white doctor, who took two hours to arrive. The doctor told the newspaper that having to sit and listen to the woman's cries of pain for two hours was the most terrible thing for him to endure.

The travellers in the youth hostel find it hard to believe that this really happened. No amount of glossy pamphlets will make them think that South Africa is a normal place.

Saturday 23rd September 1972

I caught a Coloured bus on purpose today because there are no white buses going to Maitland. I was going to see Roy, who is one of Stephen's friends. I have not seen him since last year, so we had a lot to talk about.

On the wall near the front door of Roy's house there is a framed photograph of Rev. Peter Storey holding up a board which reads, "All who pass remember with shame the many thousands of families who were forced to leave their homes because of the colour of their skins. Father forgive us." The photo is addressed to Roy's parents and signed by the Reverend. His protest was about the forced removal of the residents of District 6.

After a lavish lunch Roy's brother drove a bunch of us to Strandfontein to egg on some friends of theirs who were walking for charity. Strandfontein is a "non-whites" only beach. The only other beach that Coloureds can go to is Woodstock beach, which is covered with industrial waste, and is almost gone now because of the extension of the dock. Strandfontein is a big flat beach, good for walking on, with beautiful mountains to look at, but the currents are too dangerous for swimming. All that you can do with the water is to fish in it.

The beach is on False Bay, halfway between the Hottentots Holland Mountains and the side of Table Mountain. The sea is expansive, the towering waves crash onto the beach, the Cape Flats extend forever behind us, and the mountains in the distance are very high. Roy says, "When I see how small I am, I wonder what gives another person the idea that he is big enough to dictate to me what I can do and what I can't."

On the way back from Strandfontein Roy's brother dropped us in Maitland and we caught a "non-whites only" bus to the city. There we met up with Roy's friend Henri, and went to the Space Theatre. This new theatre has somehow avoided the law, and allows multiracial audiences. There were stacks of Coloureds there, but they were all with each other, and the Whites were all with each other, so the three of us got stared at.

The play was two plays put together, "Enemy" and "Botticelli", with the voices of Nixon, Queen Elizabeth, Bob Dylan, and the father of a Kent State victim coming from above. The message was the futility of war. Afterwards we walked up to the Gardens. St. Georges Cathedral was bathed in moonlight. Henri announced that he was tired and was going to go home. I said, "Hey, stay with us, then if we get arrested under the *Immorality Act,* they won't know which one of you two to accuse." He laughed, and went home.

Roy and I went back to St. George's Street and caught a bus to Kloof Nek. From there we had to walk down the path through the forest to the youth hostel. It was full moon and the Palatine pine trees stood out in black silhouette. We were afraid of being arrested under the *Immorality Act*. Suddenly Roy jumped out of his skin. But it was only the shadow of a tree. "Paranoia," we both said together, then laughed. Then I nearly jumped out of my skin at my shadow on a tree. Walking around together in the daytime attracts stares and gapes, but if we were found out together so late at night we would be in a lot of trouble.

Just as we were approaching the place where the path rejoins the road we heard voices and saw vague figures. "Just be quiet and listen," I said. When a clear sound drifted towards us the accent could be heard.

Great relief, they were Coloureds, and they would not call the police. Then they seemed to be coming closer and one had something long in his hand. His attitude was menacing.

"I, I hope they're not going to interfere," said Roy. The menacing one approached us, others hovering near and far. Roy took my arm and started to drag me away, but I resisted. I thought that running away would be asking for trouble. The one with the weapon leered closer, then stopped, bemused. In the bright moonlight we could see the confusion on his face as clearly as he could see the pigmentation on ours. I moved about to see if a glint came off the thing in his hand, but it was dull, probably just a branch he had picked up. He did not know what to make of us. His surprise at seeing us together put him off. Soon we were chatting about irrelevancies. I could sense that Roy was keen to leave, but I kept talking. When we left the one with the weapon said, "Sorry Merrem, sorry, hey?" He was apologising for his bad intentions.

The path leading from Kloof Nek to the Camps Bay youth hostel, still the same in 2015.

There was more paranoia as we approached the hostel because we could see figures moving about, and we did not know who they were. Roy's teeth were chattering, half from fright and half from cold. I took off my warm jumper and he put it on. He stayed in the shadows while I made it to the hostel. I waved goodbye, scurried to my room, and climbed into this warm, safe bed.

Sunday 24th September 1972

I went to say goodbye to Tam and Eileen Howie because I am leaving Cape Town on Wednesday. They said that I should phone once I got to Newlands station, but there are no telephones on Newlands station, so I walked a while and found a cricket club. I tried to open a closed glass door, and a man inside jumped up and down and gesticulated wildly. I thought that he meant that I should go in through a door to my left. I found myself walking across a big barren room with a counter at the far end, around which some men were standing drinking. They all stared. I was not accompanied by a male with dissimilar pigmentation, so I wondered what they were staring at. In the next room there was a phone, and while I waited to use it a flustered little man rushed up and said, "You've just broken a record. You are the first woman ever to go into that bar."

"Well I hope I'll be the first woman on the moon," I replied, then the phone became free and I could say no more. The man hung around, and when I had finished he guided me down a staircase and along a passageway to make sure that I did not go out the way I had come in. They get so excited just because a woman has been inside their sacred bar. And what a barren unatmospheric bar it is too. I bet I'm not the first woman to go into that room. Do they employ only male cleaners?[21]

Tam picked me up and I was treated to a grand lunch. Tam is a pilot and Eileen sells Tupperware and is a member of The Black Sash. She was holding forth about the panel that decides what race people are going to be classified. "They sit there like little gods deciding which person is going to be classified Coloured and which is going to be classified White." I thought that the Nats had finished classifying everybody, but apparently they are still at it.

Tuesday 26th September 1972

I am sitting under a pagoda shaped pergola which is covered with wisteria flowers. There are no leaves, just flowers. It looks like mauve heaven, and the perfume is overwhelming. A little squirrel came and buried an acorn just ten feet away from me. He held it in his mouth while he dug a hole with his pointed front feet, then he pushed the acorn into the earth at the bottom of the hole. His head vanished as far as his shoulders, all that could be seen was the little body rippling with effort. He filled in the hole, zap, zap, zap, with deft movements, put a stone and two sticks on it, gave me a cheeky look, then scampered away across the lawn, his nose embellished with mud. In Cape Town squirrels are classified as vermin, but they live happily here in the Gardens and all over Cape Town.

This morning Stephen fetched me from the hostel and took me to see District 6. Now I understand why the Nats are in such a hurry to move the Coloureds out. It is one of the best suburbs in Cape Town, with an unsurpassable view of Table Bay, the Cape Flats, Lion's Head and Table Mountain. You feel as if you are about to slip down into the sea, which is deep blue far below.

Slum clearance my foot. Some of the houses will not be changed before Whites move into them. They are solid, well-built houses. The Nats have quite some audacity saying that they are doing it for slum clearance when there are hundreds of real slums which are not being cleared. Whites have Tamboerskloof, Sea Point, Clifton, Camps Bay, Bishopscourt, Rondebosch, and lots of other scenic suburbs, but the Nats think they have to have District 6 as well. So much for "separate equalities".

Stephen also drove me to Wynberg Park, which is a favourite spot of his. This has to be the most beautiful city on earth. So much suffering and bitterness in the beautiful *Cape of Good Hope.*

Wednesday 27th September 1972

Stephen came to the hostel to fetch me and my luggage. The warden was out so he was able to sit and chat with the Australians and Americans. When it was time for Roy to arrive we went to the road to meet him, but he had missed the hostel and was well on his way to Camps Bay. From the edge of the road we saw him way below us, running down the pine log steps, with my red jumper over his shoulder. He heard us calling,

---

21 Newlands Cricket Ground thinks that it is the bee's knees.

and started up the hill again. While we waited a little Fiat went by with Barbara Barnard at the wheel. She is easy to recognise because there are so many pictures of her in the newspaper, as she is the wife of Chris Barnard, the heart surgeon who did the first heart transplant.

After Roy reached us we drove to a petrol station in Tamboerskloof. Next to us was the same little Fiat with Barbara Barnard in it, and boy, did she gape at the three of us sitting in the car together. In this country you do not have to do much to turn the tables on celebrities.

Stephen dropped Roy and me at the university, and after I had put my luggage in Lydia's room we went to the canteen for coffee. We were not stared at there. Henri came and sat with us. He and Roy talked about Black Consciousness. "The Afro has done more for Black Consciousness

Chris and Barbara Barnard on the front cover of Paris Match, 21 March 1970.

than anything else." That may be true, but most Blacks are struggling to keep body and soul together on a starvation wage and they don't have time to think about Black Consciousness.[22] Roy says he would rather be called Black than Coloured, but anything is preferable to "Non-white".

Henri is a member of the SRC, so I asked him if he could get me an interview with Steve Jooste. He did, and I asked Steve for the details of what had happened on the day that Geoff Budlender was arrested, which was the day before I arrived in Cape Town. Steve leaned back with a big smile, tapping his pen on his knee. "Well, first Geoff got arrested, so we told the policeman that although we weren't guilty of anything, we were just as guilty as Geoff, and demanded to be arrested too. The policeman said, 'Don't tell me my job, I'm the policeman around here,' Then we all sat in the office in Caledon Square ..."

Suddenly a thought struck him. "By the way," he said to Henri, pointing at me, "Who is she anyhow?"

Henri said, "She's writing a book."

I might have been a member of the Security Branch, or the Broederbond, or the latest agent from Odessa, but Steve was satisfied as to my integrity. The smile came back to his face, and he continued, "So we wrote a report, and asked to give it to Mr. Crous. They said, 'No you have to give it to Mr. Osborne.' So we asked if we could give it to Mr. Osborne, and they said Mr. Osborne was busy, and we could not go into his office to see him. We asked if Mr. Osborne could come out for a minute, and they said, 'No'. We milled around for a while, then Mr. Osborne, not knowing that he was busy, came out of his office, and we gave him the report. He did not want to take it,

---

22 I was wrong about this. The Black Consciousness Movement had a profound effect.

but we put it firmly in his hands. I don't know what Mr. Osborne did with the report, whether he filed it, tore it up, or read it. A fuzz came out and said, 'You are not going to be arrested, and if you don't get out of here, I'll knock the living daylights out of you.' So we went outside. Then this other fuzz came out and said, 'You had better move off, because you are contravening the act.' How do you like that?"

"They've invented a new crime," I said. "It's called 'contravening the act'".

Geoff was allowed out on R500 bail. A rapist or murderer can get lower bail. If the police were not trying to intimidate him as an individual, they would not have arrested only him. A week ago Geoff's house was petrol bombed and badly damaged. No doubt the police will be unable to find the culprits.

Roy and I took our leave and went and sat beneath the World War II Memorial, looking out over the Cape Flats to the Hottentots Holland Mountains. Away to the left with a similar view is the Rhodes Memorial. When Rhodes looked out this way he saw a dream of one country from the Cape to Cairo. It is not even one country from the Cape to the Limpopo.

Roy, Stephen, and Kevin larking about.

Kevin fetched us and we collected my luggage and went to Kevin's house. Stephen was there too, and Kevin's mother made us dinner. After dinner the three of them started reminiscing about their high school teachers. They mimicked the idiosyncrasies of the various teachers and fell about laughing.

On the way to the station we went to Stephen's house so that I could say goodbye to his parents. When we got to the station I suggested that the three of them should see me off at the train by going in at their entrance, then walking along the platform to my compartment. They refused. "It would be like calling a traffic cop 'boss' so that he wouldn't give you a speeding ticket," said Stephen. So I said goodbye under the "whites only" sign, and set off with my ton of luggage, the reels of copper wire half falling out of my haversack.

Thursday 28th September 1972

At one am I was woken by an excited babble of voices as the other occupants of my compartment, five Afrikaans schoolgirls, climbed on. When I awoke this morning they had calmed down, but were still full of vitality. They and the six schoolboys from the compartment next door spent the whole day in here.

Before eating their sandwiches they sang a grace thanking God for his generosity. If I were to tell them that yesterday evening I shared a meal with Coloured friends, they would freak out and rush into the next compartment to avoid being contaminated. They are so brainwashed by their culture and their schools that they not only believe that Coloureds are contaminated, they also believe that a white person who mixes with Coloureds is contaminated. And the irony is that most of them are not pure white.

They like me, although they do not know me. If my skin were darker they would not like me, although they would not know me. I feel for them. Their innocence makes me almost fear for them.

Most Whites never get to socialise with Coloureds. The Nats have been very successful at separating people. The only reason that I met Stephen and his friends is that I sailed away on a ship to England for a holiday. If I had not left the country I never would have met them.

Friday 29th September 1972

Usually the guardsman wakes me up when I have to get off a train in the middle of the night, so I was expecting to be woken when the train reached Bloemfontein, where I am stopping over so that I can spend a few days with my Bloemfontein relatives. Upon waking I was surprised to find that the train was not moving, that I was alone in the carriage, that the rest of the train had disappeared, and that my carriage was parked on the far rail opposite the entrance to Bloemfontein station. I dressed and packed and put my luggage on the platform. All was quiet and there was no one around. The sky was aglow with dawn and the air was fresh. I found one of those huge trailers that porters use, put my luggage on it, and pushed it along the platform, looking for a subway. The platform ended, so I turned around. There was a walkover bridge across the lines, but I could not take the trailer up the stairs. I could see that at the other end of the station there was a ramp leading down to line level, so I set off, enjoying the novelty of driving a huge trailer. Then I met with an immovable obstacle in the form of an even bigger trailer piled with magazines. I walked ahead and found two white men sitting in an engine. They came back with me and all three of us managed to push the magazine trailer out of the way. I said, "Thanks, I can get by now." But no, the one chap had not finished his display of strength. He kept at it, straining himself unnecessarily, until the magazine trailer crashed into a decorative Victorian pillar. Then he took my trailer and insisted on pushing it the rest of the way along the platform and across the railway lines for me.

On the other side he let me take over and I headed back towards the station entrance. Further along a white man standing next to some crates told a sullen black man sitting on the crates to help me. While the black man was driving the trailer I foraged for a tip to give him, but when we got to the station entrance a white man started yelling abuse at him and he slunk off without the tip and with an extra grudge in his heart.

Bloemfontein is the only city in the Orange Free State. It is a backward place, but it has the excuse that it is surrounded by hundreds of miles of semi-desert, and this has helped preserve it from the encroaching permissiveness of the twentieth century. In the Orange Free State it is illegal to lie within 12 inches of a person of the opposite sex at public swimming pools. I don't know if the police are armed with tape measures, but the law really exists. It is illegal for Indians to live in the Orange Free State, not that any of them would want to.

Last year seven farmers in the Orange Free State were charged under the *Immorality Act* because they were having sex with the black women who live on their farms. Mr. Vorster, our honourable prime minister, stepped in and made the police drop the

Eartha Kitt. Photo in public domain.

charges and close the case. He said that he did it because the case was not good for the reputation of the Free State farmer. The Free State farmer did not have a good reputation to start with. They are known to be the most narrow-minded, hypocritical, racist bunch in the country.

When Eartha Kitt came to South Africa she was given permission to perform in all centres. It is legal for an all-white audience to watch a black performer as long as there are no whites on the stage with the black performer. However, after the permits were issued, someone in Bloemfontein discovered that Eartha had brown skin, so her permit for performing in Bloemfontein was cancelled. I went to see her show in Johannesburg, and she made a dig at Bloemfontein in the song *An Englishman Needs Time*. With her famous long pauses she sang, "The Eskimo .... needs a whole lotta snow .... and so does .... Bloemfontein." The audience roared, while she reclined on a chaise longue with a wicked grin.

She did not react with humour to all of the rebuffs that she received in South Africa. She took a ride on the bumper cars at the funfair in Durban, and the attendant, not knowing that she was a celebrity, told her to get off, as the cars were for the use of Whites only. She said that at that moment she understood the South African Black better than at any other time. I don't understand why the Nats allowed Eartha Kitt to tour South Africa when they refused Arthur Ashe a visa to play tennis here two years ago.

Despite Bloemfontein's shortcomings it is great fun to be with my cousins, and the weather is always good. After we all had dinner I went with my cousin Johnny to see the movie *The Concert for Bangladesh*. I was surprised that such a movie could be showing in Bloemfontein. Apparently seeing people of different shades on celluloid is not as corrupting as seeing live actors of different shades on a stage. Before the movie they showed the trailer of *Skin Game*. At the point where James Garner and Lou Gossett throw their arms around each other in happy reunion, there came a gasp of horror from the audience.

When the movie started there were whistles and shouts. Beatlemania has just hit Bloemfontein. The audience was bored by Ravi Shankar's music, and showed it by lounging in their seats, with their feet on the backs of the chairs in front of them, talking through it all. But that all changed when George Harrison appeared on the screen. The girl in front of me sat bolt upright, sighed, and half screamed. The boy next to her stood up and went out. A minute later the volume of *My Sweet Lord* escalated by about seven decibels. The boy came in again and gave a grateful thumbs-up sign to the projectionist. I expected him to give the thumbs down sign when the heavier music started, but he just left his seat and chatted to the usherette. "Chaafed her," as the yokels would say.

Johnny says that he always feels embarrassed taking people out in Bloemfontein. I asked him if I had been imagining things when I heard that shocked gasp at Black embracing White. He said, "No".

Saturday 30th September 1972

My Uncle Leslie has a chemist shop in the town centre which has not been renovated since the Boer War. It could be used as a set in an old-time movie. He allowed me to serve a few customers, and he also allowed me to dispense. I made a blood purifier out of arsenic, vitamins, and some other liquids. He told me how he makes ointments by mixing wax and oil. "You have to have it at exactly the right temperature to make it smooth." He also told me that Karroo Freckle Cream, which the Blacks use to lighten their skin, contains mercury.

A thin old black woman with a baby on her back came up to the counter, pointed to a jar of yellow ointment and said, "Ek wil die pille daardie blink" ("I want pills that colour"). Aunt Mary opened every bottle of yellow pills she could think of, but none of them were what was required.

Bloemfontein means "flower fountain", and it is aptly named. All the gardens are beautiful, and flowers abound. Aunt Mary says that is because there is nothing to do in Bloemfontein other than gardening. She took me to see the state president's house, which is built in the beautiful Cape Dutch style, with acres of well-tended gardens. Then she took me to the station to buy my train ticket to Johannesburg. The grand old station building was adorned with masses of flowers, and a line of soldiers were standing stiffly at attention all the way from the road into the building. When we stepped into the station foyer we found ourselves surrounded by a magnificent abundance of flowers.

Aunt Mary said, "Oh, they must have known we were coming." I cracked up laughing, but rows of unamused faces glared at us from under soldier's caps. Aunt Mary says that she takes delight in ruffling the dignity of the sour-faced Free Staters because they have no sense of humour. The state president was going to leave Bloemfontein by train today, so all this adornment was done in expectation of his walking through the foyer to the platform. The state president has no political power, he is just a ceremonial figure, but a greatly revered ceremonial figure. What an unreal world the Nats live in. One guy gets a room full of flowers that he is going to see for less than a minute, while thousands of children die of starvation because of the policies of his government. And they think that they can keep it up forever.

Lydia and I witnessed a situation in which the state president was not treated with such adulation. It was the centenary of the birth of Jan Smuts, who had been prime minister of South

Aunt Mary, 1963.

Africa from the beginning of World War Two until the United Party was defeated by the Nats in 1948. Some people say that the United Party lost the election because Smuts refused to allow the sale of white bread. They say that voters were angry because the war was over and they felt that they should be allowed to have white bread. Despite the white bread debacle, Jan Smuts is still fondly remembered by the adults I know because he worked closely with Winston Churchill during the war.

There was a ceremony to commemorate the centenary of his birth at his old house near Pretoria, and Lydia and I went along with my mother and Mr. Vaughn. When we arrived there were rows of empty chairs on the veranda where the dignitaries were going to sit, and there were about a hundred old men in suits with medals pinned to their jackets sitting on chairs on the ground below the veranda. Smuts was an Allied commander in World War One, and the old men were veterans of World War One. We common folk were supposed to sit on the ground below the veranda on chairs that we had brought along, and as we had not brought enough chairs, Lydia and I had to sit on a big log.

While reading through the programme Lydia and I discovered that some Nat cabinet ministers were going to attend. We made a variety of uncomplimentary remarks about the cabinet ministers on the list. I noticed that a young man with blue eyes who was sitting on a picnic chair near us was listening to us with amusement. It turned out he was prime minister Vorster's nephew, and not a fan of Vorster.

The dignitaries arrived and settled themselves on the chairs on the veranda. When the state president, Mr. Fouché, was introduced, everyone clapped politely. But when the leader of the opposition, Sir De Villiers Graaf, was introduced, they clapped loud and long. It went on and on. It just did not stop. Lydia and I started grinning, then laughing with embarrassment. The clapping went on for many minutes. To the crowd this clapping was a serious business, they kept at it with determined faces, until Lydia and I were almost prostrate with laughter on our log. We felt sorry for Mr. Fouché.

The State President, Mr. Fouché, arriving at the ceremony for the centenary of the birth of Jan Smuts on 24 May 1970.

Sir De Villiers Graaf smiling for the camera as he arrives at the ceremony.

Sunday 1st October 1972

My cousins took me to see all the beauty spots of Bloemfontein. All two of them; Maselspoort and Naval Hill. There is a big white horse made of stones on the side of Naval Hill, which was laid out by the soldiers of a remount camp at the base of the hill. In 1904 it was falling into disrepair, so my grandfather asked the authorities to do something about it. His request was ignored, so one night he and two friends climbed the hill and painted the front of the horse red, the back blue, and the middle white. Next morning Bloemfontein awoke to a transformed horse memorial. The authorities soon had it painted white again, and they collected all the stones that had started rolling down the hill, and put them back in place. Since then it has been properly looked after. When you are ignored by the authorities you have to protest in a way that makes them pay attention.

When we drove past the Ritz Cinema we saw that all posters advertising *Skin Game* had been removed. Another film has been put in its place. Someone must have complained after seeing the trailer with the hug between James Garner and Lou Gossett. I do not understand why they can tolerate and even enjoy watching Billy Preston play the piano so brilliantly, but they can't bear the thought of a black man and a white man being friends. How can a place be so backward when it has an airport big enough to take jets, a railway station with gigantic shunting yards, and the biggest stained-glass window in the world?

Monday 2nd October 1972

I was quite getting to like Bloemfontein, but it displayed its nasty side as I was leaving. Johnny took me to the station, and my train did not leave on time, which is unusual because trains usually leave on time but arrive late. This is because the drivers and conductors get paid overtime rates if the train is late. Johnny and I chatted through my compartment window while we were waiting for my train to get going.

In Bloemfontein there is a curfew for Blacks at 9 pm. At 8.45 pm a long siren blew. I said to Johnny, "I suppose that means that all Blacks have to disappear from sight".

"Yes," he said, "And if they have not disappeared by the time the next one goes at nine, they are in trouble."

A train rattled in on another line. The loudspeakers announced that this was the train from Kimberley, and said, "Would all porters help those who are changing to the Johannesburg line." This explained why our train had not left. A minute later a stream of white passengers came down the walkover steps and went out of the station entrance. Straggling behind was a black man with a big suitcase, and behind him was a white man kicking him all the way and swearing and shouting abuse. I usually rush up to someone who is kaffirbashing and tell them to stop, and it works. But my train was about to leave so I yelled at him from my compartment window. The other people on the platform just stood and watched, either with approval or with acceptance. No one thought it was worthwhile saving this guy from his bruises and humiliation. Imagine being in a situation like that, and knowing that you can't turn to the law for help, because the law is against you too.

It is the government's fault that the train from Kimberley was late because the government owns the railways, and they employ white skinned loafers to run it. It was not yet 9 pm, but that was not going to spoil the kaffirbasher's opportunity to have some fun.

I felt sick as the train moved off, but I cheered up when I learned that the girl in my compartment attends the high school that I went to. This school is a trifle more insane than most because the headmistress is unhinged. It is known as "the peanut school" because peanuts and peanut butter are banned. This headmistress believes that peanuts are an aphrodisiac, so her first act after becoming headmistress was to ban the consumption and possession of peanuts and peanut butter. If it had happened in Bloemfontein no one would have been surprised, but it happened in Johannesburg. It was not long before people as far afield as Durban and Cape Town heard about it, and all sorts of peanut jokes were being created. Rumour spread that sales of peanuts and peanut butter were increasing daily, and people started calling peanuts "the sex pill". The peanut board made a poster showing two girls in school uniform devouring peanuts, with "They're good for you too", written above. The owner of the café up the road from our school put the poster on the corner door that faces the school. The funniest thing is that before the school became famous there was already a South African band called *The Peanut Butter Conspiracy*.

Lindy, the girl in my compartment, did not believe that it was true that peanuts were banned until her parents were sent a list of school rules. The mad woman only came to be our headmistress in my last year. Before that we had a lenient old dear who was always too busy to be bothered with issues like girls found bunking lessons in the locker rooms, but the peanut woman is rather different. She is a member of a cult that does not cut their hair nor eat in front of a non-cult member. She is puritanical, anti-Semitic, joyless, and makes life unpleasant for all around her. The old headmistress used to bang her fist on the lectern and say, "Beauty is truth and truth is beauty", but to the other one beauty is a sin of the flesh. Hair that is not tied in a plait causes hysteria, longish finger nails are a sign of "easy virtue", and even the singing of a descant by one girl in the choir who had a beautiful voice was not allowed because the mad woman considered it sinful.

She took us for "religious instruction", and at the beginning of the year the curriculum said that she must teach about the religion of Ancient Egypt. She told us that Memphis was a state in the south of Egypt, and Thebes is a city in the Nile Delta. As I had recently been to both places, (despite having a South African passport), I knew that it was the other way around. To avoid embarrassing her I went up to her after the classroom had emptied, and told her that I had been to Memphis and Thebes, and that Thebes was south of Memphis. Her face turned crimson, her voice went an octave higher, and she screamed at me that she was talking about four thousand years ago, and the Nile Delta has since moved, the way the Euphrates River has moved.

Lindy tells me that a new trial and tribulation has been introduced into their school life; *Youth Preparedness*. *Youth Preparedness* is based on the *Hitler Youth* movement. The Nats want to indoctrinate the children into believing in their ideology. I asked Lindy what it is like. "Ag, we just have to march up and down the hockey field. You know the lower hockey field? Well for an hour every Wednesday we have to march in lines. And it's so stupid 'cos you know how all the girls laugh. And they chew gum and their boyfriends come to the fence on motor bikes and look at us." I could see it in my mind's eye. Not what Mr. Vorster has in mind I am sure.

Chapter 4

Tuesday 3rd October 1972

My train arrived in Johannesburg at 7 am, and by 9 am I was at the Bryanston Country Club listening to Dr. Worrall talking about "South Africa's Position in the World Today". Dr. Worrall is a lecturer in political science. He spoke all very well and all very true, but never did he give away what he felt about apartheid. Even in question time he avoided giving an opinion. Then a woman stood up and announced that the way to do something about the situation is to make personal contact with Blacks, to invite Blacks into your home, which is quite legal, to start communicating, and just leave the government out of it.

This started some chatter among the audience, and the question arose about what to do when they invite you back into their home, as a permit has to be acquired to visit the home of a "Bantu". Dr. Worrall said, "It's quite easy to get a permit."

Being nice to a few natives is not going to prevent a violent revolution. They need to vote people into parliament who will get rid of the evil laws that are going to destroy this country. They drink their tea and eat their dainty sandwiches, and ignore the conditions in resettlement areas and the hunger in the townships right on our doorstep. They vote for the United Party so that they don't have a guilty conscience, meanwhile they know in their hearts that if the United Party won an election, very little would change.

Wednesday 4th October 1972

Although the Nats are a lot like the Nazis, they are not as ruthless, and they want to appear to be morally upright. The Nazis did not care that the rest of the world thought they were scoundrels, but the Nats are very sensitive about their reputation. That is why they get upset with people who report their evil deeds. They are also afraid of economic sanctions. They keep saying, "Sanctions have not brought us to our knees", but they know that the sanctions imposed so far are not serious. In an effort to appear respectable in the eyes of the outside world they not only try to silence people who talk the truth about South Africa, they also use euphemisms for apartheid. We keep hearing about "separate development" instead of apartheid, and another phrase that is subversively creeping into their vocabulary is "separate equalities". The S.A.B.C. heroically defends the "government's policy of separate equalities."

Another favourite phrase is "separate but equal". They know that they are lying because when they first brought in the *Separate Amenities Act* it said that the separate amenities had to be equal, but not long after that they changed the law to say that the separate amenities do not have to be equal.

"Harmonious co-existence" is another favourite of the S.A.B.C. They want to draw a picture of the "different sections of the community" living happily in their own areas. Anyone who criticises apartheid is accused of "upsetting harmonious race relations".

I hear continual bleating that people overseas do not know the truth about South Africa because the mass media of the world is biased against us. They whine that journalists throw coins into a dustbin, then take a photograph of black kids retrieving the coins, and then they print it with a caption saying that the kids are hungry and looking for food. Even if this does happen, it does not alter the fact that children are starving and that Blacks are underpaid.

Whites who love apartheid think that the attitude of the rest of the world is unjust, and that they are being persecuted. They think that the Blacks who are forced to work for low wages and to live away from their children are not persecuted, but the Whites who are disapproved of and threatened with sanctions are.

I know many Whites who are irate that the overseas press showed pictures of the bulldozers knocking down houses in Sophiatown, "But they never showed the pictures of the lovely houses that the natives were given." I never saw the photos of the houses in Sophiatown being demolished because they were banned, but I do know that the "lovely" houses to which the people were moved are not lovely.

The S.A.B.C. calls it, "blackening the name of South Africa abroad". The voices adopt a tone of extreme disapproval when they condemn people who "drag South Africa's name through the mud." Whether they are newsreaders or politicians they are so self-righteous that I could scream. The Nats have such warped logic that they think that anyone who has views different to their own is not just wrong, but is also immoral. In their view anyone who talks about the bad things that the Nats do is immoral, but the Nats who are doing these bad things are not immoral.

And the genteel ladies who vote for the United Party are the same. They say that I don't love my country if I don't love the government, and that I am unpatriotic because I don't believe in apartheid. Some call me sick because I don't think that Whites are superior. You can't have a rational conversation with these people. If you say there should be equal opportunity, they say you are a communist.

"Once you are mature you will realise that all your ideas are nonsense." The idea that I will start approving of apartheid when I grow up is a common theme of the ladies who sit and drink tea and complain about their servants. They think that when I grow older I will become selfish like them. The amount of time they spend complaining about their servants is incredible.

Thursday 5th October 1972

One day when I was six years old I was collected from school by someone I hardly knew and taken to her house for the rest of the afternoon. I could sense that something was up, and when my parents arrived to fetch me everybody talked at great length, but I was not told that Ester had been taken to hospital to have a baby. The next day Ester arrived home with a big bundle of blankets inside of which there was said to be a baby. The baby's was named Patricia, and she was kept indoors for six weeks, as was the Zulu custom. I was allowed to go into Ester's room to look at her, but all I could see was her cute little face.

Patricia, 1962.

Patricia lived with her mother despite it being illegal, because our property in Bryanston was big enough for her to not be seen by the neighbours. We could not get away with it once we moved to Parkview, so Patricia had to go and live in Soweto with Ester's sister Kessiah. Kessiah was living illegally in Soweto with her husband, George Zulu. When she had applied for permission to live in Soweto legally she had been told that if she married George the white way as well as the Zulu way, permission for her to live in Soweto would be granted. So she and George went to Natal and married the white way. When they came back Kessiah again applied for permission to live in Soweto, but she was told that she had to leave Johannesburg.

So she and George decided to go and live in Natal near Newcastle, as there was industrial development at Newcastle, and George would be able to find work there. My mother was pleased with this plan because Kessiah has asthma and the smog in Soweto was not good for her, and because "It will be better for Patricia to go to school in the country than in that ghastly Soweto, where she may be influenced by the wrong types."

So off went Kessiah and Patricia to live in a relative's hut near Dannhauser, while George continued to live in Soweto and work in Johannesburg. Kessiah went to the Bantu Affairs Commissioner to apply for a house near Newcastle, and was told to come back after a month. The next month she was told to come back next month, and the next month she was once again told to come back next month. This went on for two years before she appealed to my mother for help. So my mother drove the two hundred miles to plead her case with the Bantu Affairs Commissioner, and was also told to come back a month later. She had to keep on going back. On her fifth trip in January I went with her, and the Bantu Affairs Commissioner was very polite, and explained that there were people living in dreadful conditions who had to be dealt with before people like Kessiah, who already had a place to stay, and merely wanted to live with her husband. He suggested that the fastest way for her to get a house would be to buy a piece of land in the patch of Bantustan near Newcastle and build a house on it. My mother wanted to put down the money right away, but there was a problem. Black women are not allowed to own land, even in a Bantustan, so the land had to be put in George's name. George was registered in the Msinga area, and his pass says that he was born in Mbabane, which is a small town in the Transvaal. Before he could own land near Newcastle his pass would have to be reregistered in Newcastle. The capital of Swaziland is also called Mbabane, so when George tried to get his pass transferred to Newcastle, the ignoramus behind the counter saw that he was born in Mbabane, and said, "Go back to Swaziland." After many attempts at clearing this up he asked my mother to intervene, and finally the officials believed him that he was not born in Swaziland, and they transferred his pass to Newcastle.

Today an envelope arrived from Kessiah, containing letters from her and Patricia, and a note from the Bantu Affairs Commissioner which said;

>Bearer Kipu George Ndaba Zulu qualifies for
>a building site at Ozsweni.
>W de Kock
>Bantoesakeskommissaris
>Bantu Affairs Commissioner
>NEWCASTLE

This means that now it is only a matter of choosing the piece of land and building the house, and they will be able to live as man and wife with their foster daughter, after six years of struggling.

Kessiah wrote;

>Dear Madam,
>Thank you for your letter and money we were glad me and Patricia be couse in school they want R6 to beld the schol house they send them back at home to want money yes good madam be couse same time we came take the big money same time and lost oh madam the new castle commicher they not colling us we donow what is meter
>I Regards to you and wendy
>Kessiah Zulu.

My mother gave it to me to translate.

>Dear Madam,
>Thank you for your letter and money. Patricia and I were very glad because at school they want six rand to build a school house. They sent the children home to fetch the money. Yes,

dear Madam, isn't it good that they should make the demand at the same time as we receive a big sum of money? And last of all, oh Madam, the Newcastle commissioner has not asked us to come and see them, we don't know what is the matter.

I send regards to you and Wendy.
Kessiah Zulu.

Kessiah has not understood that the note from the Bantu affairs Commissioner means that her struggle to be able to live with her husband is nearly over.

Patricia wrote;

> Dear Wendy,
> How are you? we are all well at home and Mirriam is well now thank you for your letter that I received on July the sun is very hot hear in natal I was very glad to get the parcel that you gave to me that you wrote it my name P thank you very much in Jun and July it was very cold there was a snow at school I did pass in Jun Kessiah looks very well now and at school it is very nice.
> Mirriam Elsie and Gladys regards to Madam.
> Yours sincerely,
> Patricia.

Friday 6th October 1972

Katie and I went to school to say hi to our old teachers. When I told one teacher that I was writing a book about apartheid, she said, "Aren't you the girl that was always going overseas? That's what did the damage."

We were really privileged because we went to a project school, and most of our teachers encouraged us to think. I can't mention their names because if the government knew that they encouraged us to think they would be accused of trying to disrupt the South African way of life.

I asked my ex-form mistress[23] what the *Youth Preparedness* entails. "Oh it's ridiculous," she said, "They have to march up and down like soldiers. And we have to tell them about outside influences which are trying to destroy our national way of life, and subversive, communistic, permissive forces. Oh you know all the rubbish. And it's such a waste of time. Most schools don't do it. It's only because of our Miss Waterfield that we do it." (Miss Waterfield is the mad peanuts woman.)

The Nats call the education system *Christian National Education,* but it is better described as *Unchristian Nationalist Indoctrination.*

During June Week one Nat said in parliament, "It is a pity we could not have introduced *Youth Preparedness* ten years ago, then we would not have had the debacles

---

23 Miss Parker.

of Friday and today." He said that *Youth Preparedness* will bring an end to such demonstrations. "It is high time that our youth be subjected to *Youth Preparedness*." Subjected is his choice of word.

As I keep hearing people say, "The government knows what it is doing".

Monday 9th October 1972

At primary school I was taught that Shaka Zulu and the devious Dingaan are typical natives, but I was not taught that Hitler and Machiavelli are typical Europeans. I was also taught that South Africa is the best country on earth because we have cheap labour. In the long run cheap labour is going to backfire.

The pass laws do not stop people coming to the cities in the hopes of finding work. They have to choose between starving in a Bantustan or running the risk of being arrested in the city. When they are arrested their court case is less than a minute long, then they are sent out to work as prison labour. You often see gangs of prisoners in brown uniforms making the roads. When I was young I thought that they were criminals, but now I know that most of them are just pass offenders. I once saw two Blacks being taken out for prison labour. On the card of one it was written that he had been arrested for a pass offence; the other had something scribbled on it which had been crossed out. They were not quite sure why he had been arrested. When I queried this I was told, "He's only a bloody kaffir, and probably a useless bloody kaffir too." If a prisoner runs away from the place he has been sent to work he sinks deeper into entanglement with the law. He has no pass, cannot get work, so his only option is to turn to crime.

Meanwhile white-collar criminals have a fine time. The newspapers keep on reporting about financial corruption, but no charges get laid. The Nats are above the law.

Wednesday 11th October 1972

In today's newspaper there is an advertisement for Matson's 4-year-old Scotch. The picture shows a white male holding a crystal glass. He looks as though he has a stomach ache. I don't think that is intentional. The photographer probably told the model to look "determined", because he has thrust his bottom jaw forward and screwed up his eyes in a stern frown, which together with the weak handhold of the glass looks particularly idiotic. Printed across the top in big letters is, "To hell with woman's lib!" Beside the picture is written, "You're not saying that women shouldn't be allowed to vote. But you often wonder if they know what to do with even that simple little right. So why all the bra burning and the shouting? Next thing they'll start campaigning to drink your Matson's 4-year-old Scotch. And, sweet as some of them are, that's one liberty you'll never allow. Cheers! Matson's 4-year-old Scotch. Not for women."

I know lots of white males who have exactly this attitude. It's different when you go overseas. But I have to admit that the advertisement has a point; White women do have the right to vote in South Africa, and the fact that the Nats have been in power for 24 years suggests that they do not know what to do with that colossal right.

Thursday 12th October 1972

They are selling a poster on campus which has a drawing of a sinister pair of eyes at the top, and then below in big letters is printed;

> The streets of our community are in turmoil. The universities are filled with students rebelling and rioting. Communists are seeking to destroy our country. Russia is threatening us with her might, and the Republic is in danger. Yes, danger from within and without. WE NEED LAW AND ORDER. Without it our nation cannot survive.

This is the type of thing that Mr. Vorster says all the time. But in tiny letters on the bottom right of the poster it says "ADOLF HITLER, 1932."

The first time I read the poster I thought it was quoting Vorster, and I got quite a shock when I saw who had actually said that. That is the aim of the poster. It is a reminder that South Africa is in danger from this lot who are in power. I bought a poster and showed it to my classmate Shelley at lunch time. After reading it she said, "My God, it scares me. Thank heavens I'm going. Just thank heavens I'm leaving in time." She is going to London soon.

The Nats can rest assured that not all students care about their fellow human beings. One day I was sitting on the library lawn with my friend Chris James while he was arguing about education with a bunch of Engineering students. Chris said, "You don't want Blacks sitting in a lecture with you because you don't care whether they get an education or not."

One of the Engineering students said, "I don't want them sitting in the same lecture theatre as me because I don't want them to get an education."

Saturday 14th October 1972

I sold lots of jewellery in Hillbrow today. The only thing that gets in the way of my making millions is people's shyness. They walk past me as slowly as they can, looking at my wares, but they feel uncomfortable about stopping to examine.[24] Once one person is lifting specimens to take a closer look, others lose their embarrassment and crowd around too.

Blacks are less inhibited than Whites, they will change course from ten feet away to come and have a look. But they are scared to touch. Some ask if they may try a ring on, while others are too shy to ask, but do want to touch, so I have to suggest they try on the one that they fancy.

---

24 In those days informal stalls were not common in South Africa, whereas now there are stalls all over the streets.

Hippie necklace with stone beads and chokers with goulamine beads.

Necklaces with goulamine beads and bracelets with Greek and other beads.

    My price depends on the customer, so it becomes complicated when a crowd of different types surround the goods. Sometimes I have to sell something cheaply to a rich person because he heard me quote a low price to a poor person. But if I quote a low price directly to a rich person, he won't buy it. In this society it is easy to assess people by how they are dressed and by the way they move. However, today I met someone who did not fit in with any of the stereotypes. He was black, and suddenly words like "incongruous", and "the trend" and "limitations" met my ears. The explanation was that he was not South African. He was from Swaziland, and consequently was educated.

    A night watchman in a brown uniform came up and chatted. He was not educated. He carried a knobkerrie that was decorated with interesting burnt-on designs. He wore a gold wedding ring, and when I told him that the puzzle rings I had for sale are what the Arabs use for wedding rings, he was fascinated, but he did not know what Arabs were. I don't know the Zulu word for Arab, so I tried to describe Arabia and Arabian people. I would not like it if I were not educated.

I have to have a hawker's license to sell jewellery in public places. When I applied for the license I was given a piece of paper proving that I had applied, but I had to wait five months for the real thing. When I got the license I had to pay a fine because it had taken so long for the license to come through. The man who took the money for the fine said, "Don't worry, it's not your fault, it's because the municipality is slow."

The hippie jewellery is still stylish after fifty years. My daughter sent me the selfie below when she was about to head out one evening.

Sunday 15th October 1972

Jerry Lewis is touring South Africa, and for some reason his agent booked him to do a show in Soweto. This is legal as long as there are only Whites on the stage with him. It is illegal to have White and non-White people on the stage at the same time, and it is illegal to have White and non-White people in the audience at the same time, but it is not illegal to have a white audience watching people who are not white on the stage, nor to have people who are not white watching white people.

Jerry Lewis appeared in a stadium made for thousands, but only a handful of people turned up to watch. The organisers were embarrassed and Mr. Lewis was not amused. He lost his wit, lost his nerve, lost his temper, and snapped at newsmen. One journalist wrote, "Soweto took the humour out of Jerry Lewis." Another journalist suggested that his type of humour "does not appeal to Blacks." He has got to be kidding. The reason that no one went to the Jerry Lewis show in Soweto is that the Blacks have not heard of him. They have not even heard of really famous people like Frank Sinatra or Elizabeth Taylor, let alone Jerry Lewis. Most of them cannot read and there is no TV in South Africa, so they have no way of knowing about American celebrities.

In 1964 Dusty Springfield came here to sing, and she knew that the law required her to perform in front of all black or all white audiences. She only agreed to do the concert tour if people of any colour could buy tickets to her concerts. Her first and last show was in Cape Town, with a mixed audience. The Nats did not like it so they made her go back to England.

When I was young they allowed a Maori to get a visa to play the part of Joe in *Showboat,* even though everyone else in the cast was white. There was a big hoo-ha about it. Some people were outraged that a Maori was allowed to be on the stage, while others tried to make people see that the law was stupid, and that the producer should always be able to choose someone who is suitable for the role.

Recently the Nats allowed a Maori and a Samoan to play rugby against the Springboks, rather than face not being allowed to play against the All Blacks. They are such hypocrites.

Monday 16th October 1972

"Rock Opera Superstar Banned" says the billboard. Someone had been hoping to produce the show *Jesus Christ Superstar,* but it has been banned by the censorship board. The censorship board is called *The Publications Control Board*, and they censor films, theatre, music, books, and magazines. They are headed by Mr. Jimmy Kruger. Their professed aim is "to protect public morals", and their unprofessed aim is to protect the National Party.

Every book is submitted to the censorship board for review. A group of three men are allocated to each book. Number one reads it, and underlines any words or phrases that he finds objectionable. Number two then reads the underlined words, and if he agrees that any of them are objectionable, the book is banned without number three having a look at it. Sometimes they only read the title. In 1953 they banned the book *Black Beauty* by Anna Sewell. After a while they unbanned it because someone told them it was about a horse.

When a song is banned it is illegal to bring it into the country, but it is easy to get it past customs because the customs officials are stupid. It is also easy to find out the names of songs that are banned, because every week *The Star* publishes the top ten songs for New York, London, Lourenço Marques, and *Springbok Radio*. That way I could see that *Indian Reservation* by Don Fardon and *Melting Pot* by Blue Mink were banned here, so I bought them while I was overseas. "What we need is a great big melting pot, big enough to take the world and all it's got, keep it stirring for a hundred years or more, and turn out coffee coloured people by the score. What a beautiful dream." What a horrible nightmare for a Nat. They banned *Melting Pot* because it might give Whites the idea that white purity is not the answer, but the reason for their dislike of *Indian Reservation* is more complicated. The topic of colonised people being dispossessed is a touchy subject, even though in this case it happened in America. They do not want white teenagers in South Africa to be thinking about such things. *Young, Gifted and Black* is of course also not in line with their way of thinking, so the song is banned.

Records are not always banned outright from the country, some of them are merely banned from the S.A.B.C. so that people do not hear them and will not know that they exist. Tom Paxton is never played on the S.A.B.C., but you can buy his records if you know about them. The Beatles were banned from the S.A.B.C. after John Lennon said that the Beatles were more popular than Jesus. The only radio station on which you could hear the Beatles was LM Radio, but that was before LM Radio was taken over by the S.A.B.C. The Nats are such hypocrites that they played *Lady Madonna* on the S.A.B.C. in a programme that wanted to show how depraved pop music is.

A film can either be banned completely, or have pieces cut out of it. *Me Nathalie*, *The Graduate* and *The Music Lovers* had bits cut out of them, while *Bonnie and Clyde* was banned outright. Someone I know drove to Lourenço Marques to see *Bonnie and Clyde,* and was peeved that there was too little sex in the film to make the trip worthwhile.

Violence is not cut from films, but love scenes and sex scenes are, and so is anything that they feel is not in line with their racist ideology. It is odd that they allowed *Skin Game* to pass. Although the romance was between two Blacks, there was a friendship between a black man and a white man, which I would have thought would have made them ban it outright. They probably ban a lot of movies like that that I do not know about.

The censors lack artistic sensitivity, and they wield the scissors heavily. When you are watching a movie and the scene suddenly ends in the middle of a sentence, the audience groans.

An edition of a magazine can be banned if it contains an "objectionable" picture or article. The magazine can be distributed with the offending pages torn out, or the editors can go to court to appeal against the banning, and the courts usually overturn the ban.

Wednesday 18th October 1972

The phone just rang. When I lifted the receiver a female voice said, "Have you got any Swipe for the washing machine?"

"Um, I think you must have the wrong number."

"Oh dear. Isn't that Mrs. Green's house?"

At least her opening line was unusual. The usual course of the conversation goes like this, "Hello kin ah please spic to Joan."

"There's no Joan here. You must have the wrong number."

"Isn't that 412813?"

"No, I'm afraid not."

"Oh sorry." Click.

The telephone system is supplied by the government, and they do a very bad job of it. When you dial a number you are likely to get through to the wrong number, or not get through at all. When the phone rings it is likely to be someone who dialled someone else's number. Our record is thirteen calls in one day that were not intended for us. Sometimes there is method in the madness. One day all the numbers that came through to us had the first four digits the same as our last four. Other times the wires connect at wild random and not one digit is in its correct place. We continually get calls for a firm in Port Elizabeth that has a similar number to ours once the area code is included. As the system works on payment per call, not a monthly rental, every wrong number costs money.

On the other hand, you can't be sure that you are getting charged for actual calls. People go overseas for months leaving their houses locked up, but the phone accounts keep rolling in month by month, on an average the same as when they are at home. There is no point in refusing to pay because the phone just gets disconnected. Mr. Vaughn brags that his phone bill is always very low because someone has told someone in the telephone department that he votes Nat.

Sometimes you dial and strange bleeping noises occur. Other times there are musical clicks, or whining, or buzzing. Sometimes it rings at two different places at once, and if it is answered at both places you can actually converse with both parties at the same time. Other times there is nothing but infuriating silence. If there is no reply to your call you do not assume that your friends are not there. You dial the number again in case the first call was making the wrong number ring. Crossed lines happen every day, and can be quite entertaining. You can tell when someone has connected with your conversation because of clicking noises, but some people don't notice the clicks and you can listen in on their conversation.

The postal service and the telephone service are part of the same government department, and like everything else, they do not work properly because of job reservation. The security police listen in to telephone conversations "in the interests of state security", which is really in the interests of Nat security. Recently they passed a bill in parliament allowing for telephones to be tapped and for letters to be opened, but they were just legalising what they had been doing all along anyway. And our joke of an opposition party hailed the bill as a great step forward.

If their telephone tapping equipment is as inefficient as their telephone service, they won't be listening in to as many conversations as they would like to hear.

Saturday 22nd October

Last night I went to a movie with Johan, and then back to his house for coffee. His father was sitting in the kitchen looking tired. South African conversations can start on anything; sport, travel, the weather, but they will end up on one thing; politics, because that is everyone's hang up. Johan's father has very definite reasons for being a Nat. "I can trace my ancestors right back to the Trekkers' leaders." He listed them. "And I know that my ancestors fought and suffered for this country. So I am not going to give it away to the Blacks just because some United States official says I must."

I said that it is not a question of giving the country away, it is merely a question of giving all the people who live in the country a fair deal. So he told me a story to illustrate the saying, "Give them an inch and they will take a mile." There was this Bedouin in the desert with his camel. The camel said to him, 'Please won't you just let me put my head inside the tent?' But the Bedouin said 'No'. Eventually the camel persuaded the Bedouin to allow him to put his head in. The camel then asked if he could put his neck in. After pleading for a while he was allowed to do so. And so it progressed until in the end the whole camel was inside the tent, and the Bedouin was pushed out into the cold, windy night. "So what do you think is the moral of that?" said his father.

"He should have got a bigger tent," I replied. Both he and Johan roared with laughter, as if I had cracked the joke of the century. But it is so obvious. South Africa is a very big tent. There is lots of space, lots of gold, lots of food; more than enough to be shared by all. No one has to be deprived.

"Listen my dear, I would not pretend to any overseas person that the Black is a free man in this country, but they are going to have their Bantustans one day, and they can go over there and do what they like." His vision of the Bantustans does not include the departure of all domestic servants from white suburbia.

When I asked, "What about the Coloureds?" he replied, "I am not talking about that now." There is to be no Bantustan 'solution' for the Coloureds.

He knows that I am writing a book. "How many high schools for Whites are there in the Transvaal?" he asked me.

"I don't know."

"What is the total amount spent on Black education?"

"I don't know."

"If you don't know that you have no right to be writing a book about education." I never said that I was writing a book about education.

The topic of Black education led onto the topic of student demonstrations. "Do you know what these students do?" he asked.

"I have an idea," I replied, but my tone escaped him.

He started telling me that the Wits students had destroyed this, and smashed that, and attacked the other. "That is nonsense," I said, "I know because I was there."

He was taken aback, more shocked than chagrined. "Well, all I can say to that is, 'What is a nice girl like you doing in a place like that?'"

"I'm not a nice girl," I started to say, but he was regaling me with the wrongs of demonstrating.

"Every person has the right to vote. There's no need for people to walk around with placards. They can demonstrate their opinions at the polls."

"Every person does not have the right to vote."

"Tell me my dear, to whom are your loyalties?" This was a strange question. I had to think about it. There would be no need for loyalty if there were no enmity. "Well, to my friends and family I suppose."

"No, no, no. To whom are your loyalties when it comes down to basics."

"To my friends," I said assuredly, having decided that if it came down to basics, I would choose my friends.

"No, your loyalties are to your own kind."

I don't even know who my own kind are. Are they the Scots? Are they the French? Are they the people who think like me? And anyway I don't want to deprive people who are different to me of a decent life.

When I was leaving he said, "I also had some funny ideas when I was young." "Although they weren't like yours" he added quickly. He was probably a Nazi sympathiser during the war.

I replied, "And when I grow up I'll grow out of my childish ideas, won't I?"

"Yes", he said. "Well my dear, I admire your courage for writing a book, but I think you should make sure of your facts first."

As Johan walked me home he said, "I never argue with my father because he knows everything."

Johan's father is a news writer for the S.A.B.C., and he sometimes helps with the writing of *Current Affairs*. He is different to most of the pro-apartheid Whites that I argue with because he is honest, and he does not lose his temper and shout abuse at me.

Wednesday 25th October 1972

Yesterday evening I had my wisdom teeth out, and when I woke up from the anaesthetic, the first thing I saw was my swollen bottom lip. As I raised my eyes I looked into those of a very concerned mother. She handed me a cup of tea, and one sip tasted like nectar, but the heat made the blood flow again. The dentist said, "If I had known that your roots were like hockey sticks I would have put you in a nursing home for the night." It had not occurred to him to take an X-ray before putting me under anaesthetic in the chair. He complained that it was such a hard job getting the teeth out. "Those roots were terrible. Now you won't be getting any more of those headaches you have been getting." If I had been able to speak I would have told him that I have not been having any headaches, but boy, do I have a headache now.

"The poor man had such a struggle to get them out," said my mother. I felt no sympathy for him.

Back at home I could see, through the blur, Julie and Gail, two Australians who had arrived while I was at the dentist. We had met in the Camps Bay youth hostel, and I had invited them to come and stay with us once they had made their way to Johannesburg via Durban.

Julie and Gail on the veranda of the Camps Bay youth hostel.

I couldn't go to work today because I can hardly walk. My mother's friend Ruth came to visit and we all sat in the sun. Ruth told Julie that the university has put a lot of funny ideas into my head. I pointed out that I already had those ideas when I was in high school.

"Oh, so that's when you were corrupted." Then she launched into a long moan about how intolerable her servants are. Then, "Mind you, have you read that book *Cry the Beloved Country*?"

"Yes," I said.

"Well, I've just read it, and it opened my eyes a bit. You know, I've always been a very strong Nat, but that book made me think that perhaps people do commit crimes because of circumstances."

"No, they want food because they are bad, not because they are hungry," I said sarcastically, but she wasn't listening, she was already complaining about her servants again.

When Ruth asked Julie what she thinks of South Africa, Julie replied, "The scenery is beautiful."

During my school years I used to express my opinion loudly, and I was usually ignored or patronisingly smiled upon. As soon as I became a university student I got a heated reaction whenever I said exactly the same things. Mr. Vaughn would pounce with, "That university has been putting ideas into your head."

Johan came round after work, very despondent, and sat back with a big sigh. Of the six hundred and three students and journalists arrested in June, all except two journalists have been acquitted. Johan says that he does not mind that the students have been acquitted, he just minds that the police had so much of their time wasted in arresting them. One of the two journalists not acquitted is a woman who was charged with assaulting a police officer, the other is a chap who was fined fifty rand, and is now appealing the fine.

I feel rather silly for having been so scared of jail at the time, but not silly for being scared of getting injured. A lot of them did get badly injured while they were being arrested. If Johan thinks his time was wasted, what about the students who had their time wasted sitting in court every day when they should have been at lectures?[25]

Friday 27th October 1972

At last I can eat again. I had three squashed bananas and a cup of yoghurt. After three days of not eating, and after working all day yesterday and today, I did not feel like going out, but we already had the tickets, so I went. The play was *A Touch of Spring* with Leonard Whiting acting as the Italian. I have never before seen the Civic Theatre filled with young girls. The theatre is normally seen as "square" by my generation, but not so when Romeo turns up.

It is a relief to be home. It is surprising how you can put off collapsing until a convenient time. Too sore to ask for things, too weak to get them for myself. Too tired to eat and too hungry to sleep. I wonder how many people there are on earth who have not even had one banana to eat today.

Sunday 29th October 1972

We went on a Bird Club outing today and took along Gail and Julie and an Australian friend of theirs called Allan. It was on a farm in the Magaliesburg, and like most South African farms, very little of the land is used for production, so it is a bit like being in a game reserve without the lions. Allan said the scenery was very much like parts of Australia.

---

25 The main grounds for the acquittal was that the police had been trespassing when they arrested the students. Perhaps history will reveal what the security police were intending to do about the fact that Craig Williamson was one of those arrested, had the magistrate not acquitted the students. There may have been a plan in place before the event which made Craig feel confident about letting himself be arrested. The thugs who attacked the students did not know that he was one of them. The fact that he was arrested enhanced his credibility, and helped him achieve his later heinous crimes against humanity.

"But are the trees the same?"

"Nau".

"Are the rocks the same?"

"Nau."

There is something about Africa that gets you. The sky. Every minute that you are away from Africa there is something wrong with the sky. In Egypt the sky is right, in Jordan it is not.

We walked along a dirt track on the farm. The bird watchers went a different way, bird books and binoculars at the ready. I love the birds, but I don't love creeping through the bush, not seeing the aloes, bagworms, butterflies and stones because of a fixation on birds. We saw some Blacks ahead who were behaving strangely. Normally they would be laughing and talking loudly, but when we got closer we saw that they were digging a grave next to a fresh one, which explained their quietness. Only one of them could speak Zulu. He was surprised to hear that I come from Johannesburg as most Johburgers don't speak Zulu, and then he expected the Australians to speak Zulu too. He had not heard of Australia, but he had heard of the sea. The Australians wondered why there were Blacks living on a white farm, and even burying someone there.

We walked further then made ourselves comfortable on the flat rocks in a river under a large willow tree. Willow trees were brought here from China a long time ago, so they have had time to grow huge.

The Australians were talking about the South African mentality, and the restrictive censorship. Allan said, "What I can't understand is the way they cut out all sex but leave in all violence. Now I find that strange, because I like sex but I don't like violence." It is hard to make them understand that the censors really do think that violence is fine.

After a while I felt the need to explore. I climbed over a boulder about fifty feet wide, and suddenly came face to face with a leguaan. It stared at me for a minute, then scramble, scramble, plop it dropped off the ledge into the water. When I was little I was scared of leguaans because they look like small crocodiles.

When the bird club wound up we drove to where we thought we would find an archaeological dig, but lost ourselves and arrived at a beautiful house overlooking Hartebeespoort Dam. Allan can't stop raving about the standard of living of Whites. It is as impressive as the mentality, apparently. The owners of the house invited us to have lunch with them, but we declined and had our picnic lunch on the lawn near the house. They sent out a servant with a soup plate full of ice cubes for us.

That is another thing that foreigners find impressive; the hospitality. It is ingrained in our national character to offer food and accommodation to a stranger whose skin is white. After eating our sandwiches and chasing the butterflies we were led to the site of the dig by the son of the home owner. The archaeologists had already packed up and left, so we did not find out what they had discovered. At a dig a few miles away from this one Dr. Revil Mason has found a pot burial that contained the bones of a Bantu person carbon dated at 460 AD. The Nats teach children in school that the Whites and the Bantu arrived in South Africa at the same time, so the Bantu have no special claim on the land.

There is a huge site near Olifantsnek from 1400 AD where the Tswana used to live in a city with stone walls. The huts had sliding doors, and there was a road lined with stone walls leading to the cattle kraal in the middle of the city, so that the cattle would

Three generations at the Tswana city that was emptied of its occupants by Mzilikazi.

not wander off into the housing area on their way home. There was copper jewellery, and evidence that San had lived in the city as servants. Yet the Nats want us to believe that the land was occupied only by a few San up until 1830.

We drove past Pelindaba Nuclear Power Station on the way back to Hartebeespoort Dam. In high school our science teacher arranged for us to have a tour of Pelindaba, and among other things we were shown a slice of bread that had been zinged with gamma rays more than a year before. It was grey in colour, sealed in plastic, and it looked very unappetising. They said that by this method of preservation they were going to end world hunger. Meanwhile there are starving children right nearby who do not need food to be preserved, they just need to be able to buy it.

When we got to Hartebees we sat at a spot overlooking the valley, and ate watermelon sprinkled with salt. Some little boys dressed in ragged clothes came along and rummaged through the dustbins beside the car park. Gail grabbed her camera and photographed them. If South Africa does not want her image abroad besmirched by tales of black children foraging through dustbins, then they should pay the parents of the children a living wage. There are always children in rags on the side of the road. They are called picanins. Wherever you stop the car they will appear. Whites who look down on the thin little boys should remember that one day they will be grown men.[26]

Swollen knees and swollen bellies are a sign of kwashiorkor.

Two hungry boys in affluent Bryanston.

---

26 This was not correct as some of them would die of kwashiorkor before becoming men. Back then I thought that the big tummies and swollen knees were genetic.

Top: Children near Harrismith, 1973. Thin, dressed in threadbare clothes, and definitely not at school, like millions of others. The land on which they lived was owned by a white "farmer", who didn't necessarily do any farming.

Left: Four boys with homemade wire toys near Harrismith, 1973.

Bottom: Griqua boys in the Orange Free State, 1981. Thin, dressed in threadbare clothes, they have to make their own toys, with no possibility of attending school, looking hopelessly into the future; but you can see they got enough food as they did not have kwashiorkor.

Thursday 30th October 1972

Johan came rushing in this evening, his whole demeanour one of glee. "Did you hear about Timol and Essop?"

"No. I've just got home."

"Well, they've been found guilty and they're now in jail. So I want to hear what the students are going to say now."

I had to explain to Julie and Gail that about a year ago Ahmed Timol had either jumped from a tenth floor window in John Vorster Square, or been accidentally dropped while being held out of the window by his ankles, and Mohamed Essop had been detained and bashed at about the same time. Timol is not in jail because he is dead, and Essop has been in jail ever since he was detained, apart from the time that he spent in hospital being treated for injuries inflicted by the police. An autopsy on Ahmed Timol found that his nails had been pulled out, and there were bruises and torture marks on the side of his body that had not been smashed by the impact of the fall. Now a court has declared that both men were guilty of being communists and were planning to overthrow the government.

So far twenty one people have died in detention.[27] One of them was the popular Imam, Abdullah Haron. They said that he "fell down some steps" in jail. An autopsy showed that he had been bashed to death. When his widow was going to sue the government she was paid five thousand rand out of court. Rev. Father Bernie Wrankmore, an Anglican priest, spent sixty-seven days fasting on the side of Signal Hill in Cape Town to try to bring about a commission of inquiry into the death of Imam Haron. The Nats would not start a commission of inquiry because they know just as well as we do how he died.

Imam Haron was well known because he spoke out publicly each time a new apartheid law was brought in. He produced pamphlets criticising apartheid, and he organised speeches by other anti-apartheid activists. He also did charity work to help the poor in the Black townships.

The police do not have to inform the relatives when a person is detained, and if the relatives know that their family member is detained, the police do not have to give them a reason. The prisoner is not allowed to see a lawyer, and can be kept in solitary confinement indefinitely. Imam Haron had been in solitary confinement in Maitland for four months before he died. He was buried two days later, and on that day the Western Cape shook. Buildings swayed and houses collapsed. Earthquakes are not common in the Cape, and some Muslims believe that it was caused by the wrath of Allah.

Tuesday 31st October 1972

Whites are not allowed to enter Soweto unless they have been issued with a special permit, or if they are on the daily coach tour that takes tourists around. Foreign visitors are encouraged to go on the tour, "To see what we are doing for the Blacks". Gail and Julie wanted to go, so I went with them.

---

27 This does not include the uncounted numbers who had been murdered by police outside of detention facilities.

We had to go to a building in the city where we were given a lecture on Soweto before getting on the bus. The lecture was delivered by a woman with dyed red hair and huge false eyelashes. She arrived late, and when she came into the room she slammed the door loudly. Only some people in the room fell silent, so she flounced out and came back in again, slamming the door even harder. Gail and Julie were agog at her behaviour. She spoke in a whining tone, and added an aggrieved tone whenever she said, "And let me tell you" as she was about to refute the wicked critics of South Africa by describing some wonderful facility that the Blacks in Soweto enjoy.

We were each given a booklet that portrays life in Soweto as being one step away from Utopia. The reality is rather different. There are a million people living in Soweto, and most of them have to endure terrible living conditions. A few individuals have managed to make some money, even though they are not allowed to set up businesses outside of Soweto. The Johannesburg City Council does not spend nearly enough money on improving conditions in Soweto.[28]

It is a long drive from Johannesburg to Soweto. When we first entered the township we whizzed along a main road, and the dyed-haired lady pointed out a school, a library, a stadium, and a post office. She told us that there is a house to house delivery every day. If you go on a coach tour of Paris the tour guide does not tell you that there is a house to house postal delivery, it is taken for granted. But Soweto is such an abnormal place that anything normal has to be mentioned.

The front cover of the booklet they gave us.

The dyed-haired lady told us that there is not enough money to build and staff enough schools because 55% of the population of Soweto is under 20 years of age. "But," she ended with, "Four out of five do manage to attend school." She did not mention that they are forced to drop out of school after only a few years.

We were taken to a sheltered employment workshop where over a hundred handicapped Blacks are given work. As we entered they fell silent, but carried on with their work. The atmosphere was uncomfortable. They must feel like a zoo with a daily busload of Whites coming to look at them. When you smile at them they just stare back, but at least speaking to them in Zulu made them smile and reply.

Back in the bus again to another zoo, a happier one. A nursery school. The kids, dressed in the cutest uniform, were at playtime when we arrived. A Scandinavian woman took lots of photos of her toddler son with them. The children were fascinated by his blonde hair and pale skin. They patted his head and stroked his hair, and he

---

28 It was only in 1976 that I became aware that the only money that the Johannesburg City Council spent on services in Soweto was obtained by selling alcohol in Soweto.

began to wail. I said in Zulu that he was frightened because he was young, and they moved back. Then one little girl went on her knees and put her arms around him. The mother took a photo.

It was a beautiful nursery school, well equipped and happy. When I spoke to one of the teachers in Zulu she replied in English, and the look in her eyes said, "Drop dead." As we were leaving I heard a white woman say to her friend in a South African accent, "They have nothing to complain about, have they".

"No, no they don't," said her friend, in a tone that was both patronising and complacent. Now they can go back to their well-appointed homes and feel at ease about that dark place Soweto, because there is a nice nursery school there. They can forget about the one fifth of children who do not even get one year at school.

The dyed-haired lady kept on saying that what has been done for the Blacks is tremendously admirable because there is so little money. The reason why there is so little money is that the Johannesburg City Council does not give the Non-European Affairs Department enough money. That is not because they lack money, it is because they spend too much on making life luxurious for the Whites. The Argus Group of newspapers have started a charitable fund called TEACH, "Teach Every African Child." The money is pouring in, and schools are springing up all over Soweto. They are doing what the authorities should be doing.

The road went through the golf course, and as the bus was driving through it the dyed-haired lady said, "This golf course has some hazards that you don't find on most golf courses. Ha, ha, ha." Hazards like marshes, rivers, reeds, roads, and knee-deep grass. She said it with contempt, as though it were their childish black fault for having so primitive a golf course.

There is a grassy park with a strange tower in it called the Oppenheimer Tower. We were taken there for tea and scones. From the top of the tower you can see the familiar skyline of Johannesburg in the distance. The skyscrapers look strange behind a foreground of rows and rows of same-styled little houses.

The Johanesburg skyscrapers on the horizon are very faint in this photo that I took from the top of the tower. There are also three minedumps.

Sir Ernest Oppenheimer started the building of these little houses in 1956. Each little house is a rectangle and divided into four rooms. The early houses did not have floors or ceilings, but now they are built with floors and ceilings. There are 9.1 people living in each little house, and there is no sewage, running water, nor electrical connection. Their living conditions cannot improve because when they get jobs working in white Johannesburg they are paid a pittance of a wage, and it is hard to start a business when you have no money.

The few who have succeeded in starting businesses within Soweto live in Dube, a tiny section of Soweto, which has normal sized houses. The dyed-haired lady told us that there are three millionaires in Soweto, which is something that you hear about all the time because Whites think that it proves that there is nothing wrong with apartheid. There is one cinema in Soweto, owned by one of the three millionaires. When we drove through Dube our dyed-haired lady told us exactly what sort of car everybody owned. At one house she came out with, "And let me tell you," (in that injured, indignant tone), "That this man drives a Jaguar SJ6, a Mercedes 280, and his wife has a red Ford Capri."

There are thirty thousand people living in hostels in Soweto, but they did not show us any hostels.

She did not say much about Baragwaneth hospital, which I thought was strange because most Whites think that they are so generous for allowing Blacks to have a hospital. The hospital was built during the war for soldiers who had been injured in North Africa, and when the war ended it became a hospital for Blacks. Because of the poverty and crowding in Soweto there is a high crime rate, and on Friday and Saturday nights the trauma unit gets a constant flow of stabbings to operate on. It is a great place for surgeons to train. Some doctors work many hours of overtime for no pay. The hospital is underfunded because the Nats don't value black lives, but the way that the doctors and nurses cope with the situation is fantastic.

Before leaving Soweto the driver turned into Pimville, an area that is a terrible slum. The lady kept saying that this area will be gone in three months. She did not say it frequently enough for the American woman sitting behind me and Gail, who turned and asked her male companion, "What did she say about this place?"

He replied in a South African accent, "This is what the whole place was like once, and this will be gone in three months' time."

I turned around and said to the man, "Do you really believe that?" He did not answer and just stared in front of him.

The bus got stuck in the mud, and once we were moving again we passed a woman washing some clothes in a tub of muddy water. Our dyed-haired lady pulled a face of disgust and made a contemptuous remark. Like it is her fault, dirty native, washing her clothes in muddy water.

I turned to the man in the seat behind me and asked him, "Do you really believe all that she says?"

"I don't believe anything my girl," he shouted. "I know your type. I don't believe anything and I don't want to discuss anything with your type. I know your type, anti-establishment and, and, (he was lost for words about my type). That place will be gone in three months' time and if we had enough money it would have been gone earlier." He was shouting loudly. Usually it takes a bit more provocation to make such fury boil over, but I suppose he was feeling sensitive because he had brought the American tourist on the tour to impress her with how kind we are to the natives. He spluttered with rage, his face turned red, and he was agitated in his seat.

The American woman was greatly displeased with me. Her painted eyebrows went up, and with a look as if there were a dead rat in front of her she said to me, "You know nothing about the world, little girl. You should see how poor people live in other countries."

"Actually I have seen the back streets of Cairo, and the back streets of Palermo, and ...."

The painted eyebrows nearly hit the hairline. "You've bin to a lotta places for a little girl."

Suddenly she perked up. We had left the slum, and on the right was a row of tiny red brick houses. They were like English council houses, except single story and half the width. Some had bright flowers growing in front of them. "Oh," said the American, "There are some *lovely* little houses on the right."

"Would you like to live in one?" asked quick-thinking Gail. They glared at her.

The first white suburb we went through after leaving Soweto was Mondeor. The southern suburbs of Johannesburg are regarded as "poor" by the northern suburbs, as the houses and gardens are small, and not imaginatively designed. But after being in Soweto the houses of Mondeor looked like palaces. I said, "Oh look, there are some *lovely* little houses on the right." They glared.

Back in the city we caught the municipal bus back to Parkview. And who should be on the bus but Mr. Ermert. "Hey," I said, "Do you know that the last time that I met you was in June on the way to the university?"

"Yes, I remember". He replied. I told him what had happened on those two days, and that I was writing it all down and planning to publish a book about what goes on around here. "I'm very glad to hear that," he said. "Freedom is the most important thing a man can have. Freedom to read what he wants and to think what he wants, and most important of all, to work at what he wants." His words sound almost corny, but they are rare sentiments around here.

****

On the 12th April 1973, five and a half months later, I went on the Soweto tour again, to see whether Pimville was still a slum. This time the courier was blonde, and had no false eyelashes. While the previous one had had a disdainful, arrogant attitude, this one had a forthright, arrogant attitude.

During the pre-tour lecture she pointed at Pimville on the map and said, "This is still a slum area. We hope it will be cleared by the end of the year." This time the bus passed through Pimville at the beginning of the tour. The shacks were in exactly the same condition as before, and as there had been heavy rains, the roads were once again deep in mud. She did not say it would be gone in three months, just, "This will be cleared by October, we hope."

She pointed out the fire station with its two fire engines as we passed it, but she did not mention that there are few telephones in Soweto, so it cannot always be contacted in an emergency. She pointed out a beer garden, but did not mention that the Johannesburg City Council gets the money from the beer gardens and beer halls. We were told that there is running water, but she did not mention that very few houses have it, and when they have it, it is just a tap outside. We drove past the eighth and thirteenth TEACH schools that have been built with donations to *The Star's* education fund. We saw one of the nine hostels, with its close-together windows, and were told that it holds five thousand and seventy-two single men. "Single" men. Some rooms have sixteen men to a dormitory. She did not mention that there is only one dentist in Soweto.

When we passed through the rich area we heard again about the millionaire who owns the cinema. At the house of the man who owns three cars she said, "There stands the Ford Capri that his wife drives. He owns a Mercedes SJ6, oh, I mean, ha, ha, ha, a Jaguar SJ6, and a Mercedes 280." One can make mistakes when one has to recite it parrot fashion every day.

A young American asked what the infant mortality rate is, and she said, "It used to be forty per cent but now it is three per cent." He did not believe her.

This time on the bus tour I was surrounded by foreigners who were not at all conned by the way she tried to present the situation. They laughed at her and shook their heads. One asked me, "Do you think she really believes all that she says?" Another one remarked that she must have been through a thorough training course to be able to answer awkward questions so "smoothly, untruthfully, and unashamedly."

The way that the people of Soweto have to live, as part of the wealthiest city in the world, with no street lighting, below the breadline incomes, and being in constant fear for life and possessions, made me feel sick on the way back to the city centre. As I walked to the municipal bus stop I knew that it was inevitable that Mr. Ermert would be on the bus. His encouragement was almost enough to cheer me up.

Chapter 5

Saturday 4th November 1972.

Tonight I went with Gail and Julie to the house warming party of a British couple in a flat in Hillbrow. I was the only South African there, and was accidentally introduced as Australian, so nobody tried to be polite about my country in front of me. They talked about the wage gap, about how they can earn so much more here for doing half the amount of work they would have to do in England, and about the conservative attitude of South Africans. They also discussed how South Africa is different to what they had expected. They had known that it had an oppressive system, but they had not known about details like job reservation, the contract labour system, and the pass laws.

One woman said that before she came here she would have thought it impossible that she could pay someone twenty rand a month for looking after her children, but now that she is here she finds it very easy to pay that amount, and enjoys it.

Another woman said, "I thought that this was a police state, yet I've only seen two uniformed policemen in a week." It is not the uniformed policemen that go to making up a police state, it is the ones who are not in uniform. They are called the Security Branch. In the Wits University Rag parade this year one of the floats depicted the Security Branch. The float consisted of a little car with a huge branch on its roof. Beside the branch sat a man in a black suit with dark glasses. He had a note book and a pen in his hand, and was writing down the names of all the communists he could find. He would get off the roof of the car, pick on one of the spectators, and explain to them why he knew that they were a communist, then pretend to write their name in the file.

The Rag parade is lovely. I enjoy participating in it even more than I used to enjoy watching it because you can see the happy faces of the crowd as they watch the procession. There is no apartheid in the crowd, a variety of races stand cheek by jowl. Many servants are allowed to have the Saturday morning off so that they can watch the Rag parade. Even the police can be made to smile, or at least some of them. They line the streets to keep the crowds in order. Most students just ignore them, but I always ask them for money. They are usually too embarrassed to say anything, but they do smile. Only two were rude to me this year. One swore at me, and the other said, "If it wasn't for your Rag, I wouldn't have to work today."

The Wits University Rag is the biggest student fund raising effort in the world, bringing in over a hundred thousand rand a year for the chosen charities. The parade through town is only a part of it. There are debutant balls and many other events to raise money. I organised a raffle this year, and by law I had to ask people an easy question when they bought a ticket, to make it into a game of skill instead of gambling.

The Security Police are not really a joke, although we joke a lot about them. One joke is that they always sit in the fourth row from the front at political meetings. When there are student meetings in the Great Hall the speaker will usually extend a welcome to the security police sitting in the fourth row.

In the week following June Week, plain clothes police swarmed all over the campus. They were not good at disguising themselves, and were very obvious. But there are the clever ones, the ones that we do not know about.[29] The government quite proudly says that it knows everything that is going on inside the universities. There are spies who look and behave just like students, we cannot know who they are. It does not matter. Everything that the students do is done in the open. There is nothing to hide.

It bothers me that if a spy is paid for information, he or she is going to provide information, whether or not it is true, and it does not need to be proved in a court of law that the information is correct.

The Nats also spy on people by tapping their phones and opening their mail. They have been doing this since long before they passed a law making it legal. People whose phones are tapped can hear a whirring noise soon after they lift the receiver, and there are sounds that go boomp-click every few minutes.

I know many people who have had their mail opened. One is my friend Penny who received a phone call at work from someone who was pretending to be her friend Phil van der Merwe, who is banned. Although Phil has an Afrikaans name he does not have an Afrikaans accent. The caller's Afrikaans accent was Penny's first clue that the caller claiming to be Phil van de Merwe was not Phil van de Merwe. The caller asked questions which showed that he had read a business letter that Penny had sent to someone completely unrelated to Phil. This shows that the Nats have it on record that Penny is friends with Phil, and that they have opened and read at least one of her business letters.

Roy also had his mail opened over a period of a few months. They did not try to hide the fact that they had opened his letters, they just sealed them again with sticky tape. After a while they started opening his brother's letters too. Then they stopped opening both of their letters.

Sunday 5th November 1972

The Oppenheimer estate has its open day today, so we went to look at the flowers. When I spoke to the watchman at the gate in Zulu he said that I must have grown up on a farm. That is a common assumption because city Whites don't tend to speak black languages. I guess Bryanston was half way towards being a farm.

The Oppenheimer gardens are laid out in an interesting way, and there is an abundance of beautiful flowers. A large group of Indians was among the crowds

---

29 For instance, Craig Williamson.

wandering about, and the women were wearing the most exquisitely embroidered saris that I have ever seen. The flowers embroidered on the saris competed with the beauty of the real flowers. I get to see lots of saris because I take Lalli-dog for walks at the Zoo Lake every weekend, and there are always lots of Indians picnicking on the lawns. Indians are forced to live in an area that has no parks, but it is not illegal for them to come to the Zoo Lake. So the ones who are affluent enough to own cars can get away and enjoy the fresh air. I get to talk with them because Lalli-dog likes children, and always runs up to them. The conversation seldom moves beyond what a nice dog I have. It is as if they are afraid to be too forward. White South African culture expects me to treat an Indian as an equal, even though the government certainly does not. Most Indians live in Natal because their ancestors were brought there to work in the sugar cane fields.

In 1969 we were booked to go on a trip to India in which we were going to travel around for 14 days, then go to Nepal for a week, then back to India for 14 days. This trip had been organised by Claire Rheinallt Jones, who knows how to get things done. Normally white South Africans are not given visas to enter India, but we had each been given two fourteen-day visas. Unfortunately the Indian government cancelled our visas three days before we were due to leave, so we never went. Because some of us still wanted to go somewhere, the chairman of the Archaeological Society arranged a trip for us to Morocco and Egypt. These are also countries that are not keen on giving visas to white South Africans. *Marrakesh Express* by Crosby, Stills, and Nash had just hit the hit parade, and I was really looking forward to being in Marrakesh. When we arrived at the airport our travel agent told us that our visas for Morocco had been cancelled. It was the same travel agent who had broken the news to us that our visas for India had been cancelled, so at first I thought he was joking. He was not. The Organisation of African Unity was holding a summit in Rabat, so they thought it would be dangerous to have white South Africans in the vicinity. We spent the whole day at the airport while the travel agent found a way for all ten of us to go somewhere else. I took the opportunity to phone all of my friends, and I became an expert on the ticky boxes[30] at the airport. There was a row of twenty of them along an interior wall, and once I had found out which phones worked, I acted as a guide to the people who came along wanting to make a phone call. At the end of the day we set off for Spain via Munich. Generalissimo Franco does not object to white South Africans visiting his country.

We were supposed to get our visas for Egypt in Morocco as there is no Egyptian embassy in South Africa, so we were not sure they would let us into Egypt. After Spain we spent time in Italy and Greece, then flew to Cairo without visas. When we turned up at passport control the chairman said, "We are members of the South African Archaeological Society, and we don't have visas." The man behind the counter said, "That will be two dollars each." So we were able to use our bookings in Cairo, Luxor, Aswan, and Abu Simbel.

While we were still thinking that we were going to India, the Institute of Race Relations arranged for us to visit an Indian family in Lenasia. We had to get special permits to go to Lenasia, just like we would have to get special permits if we wanted to

---

30 Pay phones were called ticky boxes because a ticky coin (thruppence) was needed to make a call.

go to Soweto. In Lenasia the rich people's houses were in a row next to the main road. Behind them were the not-so-rich houses, and then the slum area. That was three years ago; I hope things have changed by now. The family that we visited were gracious and gave us violently hot triangular cookies to eat. They were wealthy but not happy. They had been forced to leave their home because it was near the city centre and was wanted by the Whites. Our hosts told us that being moved so far out of town had made transport impossible for the poorer people, and those who owned cars now had to spend so much on petrol. There are still Indians living close to town in Vrededorp, where I buy my sandals and other clothes, but the government says it is going to move them away.

14th Street in Vrededorp in 1981, after the demolition had started.

To justify what they are doing to Indians, the Nats have declared one white area as Indian. They chose Isipingo, which is south of Durban. Some of our relatives used to live there, and I loved visiting them because the houses were nestled in the jungle, and there were monkeys and pythons in the trees. I was not allowed to play outside alone because of the pythons. Our relatives were not happy about having to sell up and leave, but they had no choice.

Today the *Sunday Times* has eight articles about the Broederbond. The Broederbond is a secret organisation that has the professed aim of protecting Afrikaner culture. Members have to be invited before they can join, and only Afrikaners who are Nats get invited. All meetings are held in secret, and there is a secret telephone number which is known only to members. However, somewhere there is a leak. For a while the *Sunday Times* has been printing whatever facts it can uncover about the Broederbond. They even have lists of names of members. It is becoming apparent that all the people who hold important positions in government organisations are members of the Broederbond. For instance, the people who control the S.A.B.C., and those on the Publications Control Board, are members. The Cabinet Ministers are all members, and the junior politician Dawie de Villiers, one-time captain of the Springbok rugby team, is a member.

Despite all the revelations we still do not know exactly what the organisation does, nor what its real aims are. All that we know is that the people who have power are all meeting together to have secret talks. Organisations like NUSAS and the Institute of Race Relations do not hold their meetings in secret. They do not have secret telephone numbers, nor print secret documents. Any member of the public is free to join the Institute of Race Relations, and any student is free to join NUSAS. NUSAS and the Institute of Race Relations are two of the organisations that are at present being "investigated" by the government to see if there is anything in them that could threaten state security. We know that this means that they are being investigated to see if there is anything which could threaten National Party power.

The Broederbond is what should be investigated. Some people believe that the Broederbond is a continuation of the Ossewa Brandwag, the Nazi organisation that tried to undermine the Smuts government during the Second World War. A great many of its members are the same. If there were nothing sinister about the Broederbond, it would not be secret.

Tuesday 7th November 1972

The most classic thing has happened. There is this guy, Mr. Carlos Santos, who is a Nat. A "prominent Nationalist" is what the newspaper calls him. On September 25th he and his wife and some friends set off for a holiday in Lourenço Marques in Mozambique. Mozambique is a Portuguese colony, and a group called Frelimo is fighting for its independence. When the family got to the Mozambique border Mr. Santos handed over his passport to be stamped, and after waiting half an hour for it to be returned, he was told that he was under arrest. He knew that there was a mistake, so instead of bolting back into South Africa, he waited for the matter to be cleared up. He was taken in a police van to Lourenço Marques, where he was locked up in the Machava Prison. His wife tried to find out why he had been arrested, but the Mozambique security police would not tell her.

In prison he was not allowed to exercise, and the food was so dreadful that he could not eat it. He says that worst of all was that he had to share the "shocking toilet facilities" with black prisoners. There are more than a thousand prisoners in the Machava prison, and most of them are political prisoners. Mr. Santos was questioned twice a day for twelve days as to whether he was a communist and whether he supported Frelimo. He was told that he was suspected of blowing up a statue of Dr. Salazar, the dictator of Portugal, on the 16th of February 1962, but no one else was told why he had been detained. He had no way of getting in touch with his family to ask them to bring evidence of the fact that he was in Pretoria on February 16th 1962. He kept on telling the security police that he was a "staunch and active member of the Nationalist Party," but they did not believe him.

He says, "The fact that I was a South African citizen made no impression. The DGS are a law unto themselves. They are above the courts and have no respect for international rules. They would not even allow the South African consul to see me, or tell him why I was held." The DGS is the Direcção-Geral de Segurança, the Portuguese secret police.

At first his family were not allowed to contact him, but fortunately for Mr. Santos his father is a big wheel, with contacts, and after a long struggle, his father was allowed to see him. Mr. Santos was then able to tell his father why he was being held, and his father was then able to furnish proof that his son had been in Pretoria on February 16th 1962.

Mr. Santos says, "If I had not been allowed to see my father I would have been there for many years, like hundreds of others who have never been to court. This is what made me think of our own 180 day detention clause. I still agree with it, but there must be some provision to allow a person the opportunity to prove their innocence. How can he do so if he is not allowed to see someone like a lawyer?"

So being hoist by his own petard has made him think, which is a great step forward in the life of a Nat. The likelihood of his doing anything about making it possible for detainees in South Africa to prove their innocence is not great. Once he has settled down at home he will forget about all the innocent people in South African jails who have no access to a lawyer.

What Mr. Santos does not realise is that South African law allows indefinite detention, not just 180 days. Part of the Terrorism Act reads;

1. Notwithstanding anything to the contrary in any law contained, any commissioned officer as defined in Section 1 of the Police Act, 1958, of or above the rank of lieutenant colonel may, if he has reason to believe that any person who happens to be at any place in the Republic is a terrorist or is withholding from the South African Police any information relating to terrorists or to offences under this Act, arrest such person or cause him to be arrested, without warrant and detain or cause such person to be detained for interrogation at such place in the Republic and subject to such conditions as the Commissioner may, subject to the directions of the Minister, from time to time determine, until the Commissioner orders his release when satisfied that he has satisfactorily replied to all questions at the said interrogation or that no useful purpose will be served by his further detention, or until his release is ordered in terms of subsection 4.
4. The minister may at any time order the release of any detainee.
5. No court of law shall pronounce upon the validity of any action taken under this section, or order the release of any detainee.
6. No person, other than the Minister, or an officer in the service of the State acting in the performance of his official duties shall have access to any detainee, or shall be entitled to any official information relating to or obtained from any detainee.

White South Africans want to believe that the law is never abused, and only terrorists are detained. When I ask them how they would feel if it happened to them, they say it would never happen to them because they are not terrorists. "The government knows what it is doing."

Mr. Santos says, "The strain was tremendous, and the feeling of helplessness cannot be described. You reach the stage where you would sign or confess to anything just to get out." Mr. Santos had to spend three days in hospital for his nerves to recover after twenty-two days imprisonment. Can you imagine what they can do to a person in 180 days? Once they have a "confession" they can simply leave the prisoner in jail, or they can put him on trial and prosecute him with this "evidence".

My mother believes that detention without trial "protects" our society, so I asked her what she thought about Mr. Santos' experience. "But that's Portugal," she said. "It's completely different to here. That could never happen here." Oh wow. There is a law allowing it here, but she thinks it could never happen here.

Friday 10th November 1972

The lawn is covered with fallen jacaranda flowers and the plaintive cry of the Diederik Cuckoo is wafting through the air. Jacaranda trees were in fashion when Parkview was established sixty years ago, so they were planted on every property and along all the streets. Now the whole place turns mauve in November. The streets get covered in a layer of mauve, and when you drive over the fallen flowers they burst pop, pop, pop softly.

In springtime we first have the fruit trees in blossom, then the jasmine and wisteria burst into fragrant bloom. After them comes the yesterday, today and tomorrow, with it white flowers that turn mauve the next day and purple the next. When all of its flowers have turned brown the jacarandas burst into mauve, and the Diederik Cuckoo starts calling "dee, dee, deederick". I sat many hours in school with my mind outside with the Diederik Cuckoo. After New Year summer settles down to heavy heat and heavy greenness, broken only by quick thunderstorms, heralded by the Piet my Vrou, the cuckoo that sings "Piet my Vrou" nonstop.

I am lying in the sun drying my hair, watching the zizzy bees squiggle into pollenous flowers and leave with blobs of orange pollen on their legs. I cannot see the Diederik Cuckoo because they are elusive birds, flitting from tree to tree, so that the sound comes from a different direction every minute. Two sparrows are quarrelling in the plum tree, and I can hear peacocks calling from the zoo. When a dove flies down to the bird table there is a whirr, whirr, whirr of wings, then snack, snack, snack when it flies up. The roof next door is being painted, and the Blacks climbing all over it are talking loudly in a language that I don't understand. The masked weaver is tearing strips off the palm leaves and flying away with pieces five times as long as himself trailing behind him. A wagtail is strutting across the mauve lawn, and the bees that concentrate on the fallen jacaranda flowers fly off with bright yellow, not orange, pollen on their legs.

The sound of distant traffic hardly reaches me through the heat. I can feel the sun's rays penetrating my skin, doing me a dose of vitamin D. Tiny blue Lycaenidae butterflies are inspecting the geraniums, the Barberton daisies are looking droopy from the sun. The mauve jacaranda cuts a line against the blue, blue sky. No wonder people find it easy to forget the real situation. Every winter we knit and collect clothes for the poor, comes summer and our consciences are eased away by the warmth. And apartheid goes on; the security police go on, people sit in jail with no hope of a trial; husbands and wives are forced to live apart, children leave school at nine years to keep up the supply of cheap labour, people die of hunger in the Bantustans, and the sun shines and the bees buzz and the sparrows squabble and my hair is dry and sparkling like the sea in Table Bay.

Sunday 12th November 1972

On the way to the shops I passed a friend's house and his mother was standing in the front garden watching her "garden boy" work. She started telling me that Britain had gone to the dogs because of the strikes and the way that the authorities kowtow to the young people. "I am not proud to be British anymore. I still have a British passport, and I do not intend giving it up, but I am not proud to be British anymore." It was not long before she got onto the topic of June Week. When I told her that I had taken part in it, she said, "Well I'm sorry, but we have to have discipline. Look at the countries overseas, what's happened to them, just because of the way young people are allowed to behave."

An old black man came to the gate and started opening it. She grabbed the collar of her Alsatian[31] and shouted, "Go away. He'll bite you." She turned to me and said, "I don't give them anything when they come, which you would probably also say is wrong of me." I had hardly said anything at all, let alone that she had done something wrong, so it is strange that she used the word "also". She just knows that her attitude is wrong, so she expects me to tell her so. The old man had not come to beg, he had come to visit the "garden boy", who was sweeping the driveway, and was obviously expecting him. The "garden boy" will be "off" in a few hours' time because it is Sunday. It would have been better if the frail old man had been able to rest in the gardener's room while waiting for him to be off. Blacks don't come to beg in the white suburbs because they would be arrested. In England a thin man wearing worn out clothes would be a beggar, but here it is normal for Blacks to be thin and poorly dressed.

"I think the students are wrong," she continued, "They have no right to riot and cause an upset."

"They didn't riot. They just stood there holding placards. It was the police that rioted."

"Well I don't know. I wasn't there. But I think the students are wrong."

"Wrong to want another person to be given an education?"

"But they *are* being given an education. It has to take years. It can't be done in a few months."

"They are not being given an education."

"We Whites built up this country. We can't just give it away to the Blacks."

---

31 German Shepherd.

"We Whites built it up with exploited black labour."

"Nonsense. They get paid for what they do."

She carried on with a twenty-minute lecture about why apartheid is right. Her opinions are typical of most of the white housewives in Parkview. "Yes, I know that a lot of black people become doctors in other countries, but Blacks in other countries are different to our Blacks."

"Only because they get an education."

"Our Blacks don't want an education. That's why they leave school so young."

"That's not why they leave school so young."

"We can't hand over power to the Blacks. They'll abuse it. If they get into power they won't allow the Whites any privileges."

"I'm writing a book about people like you."

She must have heard that comment because later as I was leaving she said with a warning look, "You needn't tell anyone what I have said." Why not? Is she ashamed of her attitude? She keeps her British passport while enjoying life in Johannesburg's luxury. If she got South African citizenship she would be able to vote and help keep her beloved Nats in power. Perhaps she is aware that her vote is not necessary because the Nats are not going to let themselves be voted out of power.

Monday 13th November 1972

We went to Pretoria to make a reservation for the Kruger National Park. Visitors who are not white are allowed to stay in the park, but in a separate camp, which I am told is not as nice as the camps for Whites. The Parks Board building is on the top of a hill with a sweeping driveway leading up to it. There are wide steps leading up to the entrance, and above the huge glass doors is the "Whites only" sign. To the right of the steps is a little door leading into a little room, and on the door is a sign that says, "Non-white reservations". I went in through that door and asked the white woman behind the counter, "Is this where we have to book if we want to visit the non-white reservations?" The sour expression on her face got sourer.

Sunday 19th November 1972

Cheryl and I went to Bryanston to say goodbye to our classmate Shelley. She leaves for London tomorrow. Escape. The patronising adults are pleased that she is going to Europe for a year because it will "broaden her horizons." A few of them have told her that it will be good for her because it will make her realise that South Africa is the best country on earth. They are hoping that she will come back believing in apartheid, but she won't.

This week there was an article in *The Star* by Professor Arthur Keppel-Jones, the author of "When Smuts Goes," who has returned to South Africa for three months after being away for thirteen years. He says that he has met with some surprises during his time here, one of them being that a Dutch Reformed minister, Rev. D. F. Malan, was kicked out of the Dutch Reformed Church because he preached a sermon in which he said that it was both evil and dangerous that white wages are ten times greater than black wages. Professor Keppel-Jones says,

> It is strange enough that the wage gap should be a topic for a voice crying in the wilderness. Even if the two groups belonged to the same race, a gap like that would be a classic recipe for revolution, and when the two groups are also two races you have something like a social nuclear bomb. It happens that I myself mentioned this point in a lecture, but to a more receptive audience than Mr. Malan's. His audience was more than unreceptive. It was shaken by the enormity of the scandal; the scandal not of the wage gap, but of his speaking of it.
>
> To one accustomed to breathing a fresher air there was an eeriness about this event. Mr. Malan was pressed to resign his pulpit. One had to rub one's eyes and read again to make sure that it was not a dream. The crushing weight of public disapproval had fallen upon a man whose offence was to warn his people of a danger threatening both their souls and their bodies. Apparently there was no better way of meeting this danger than shutting one's eyes and pretending that it didn't exist.
>
> The reporting of the case was the occasion for bringing some related matters to light. The press quoted from an Afrikaans paper, on the subject of sermons in the Dutch Reformed Church, the statement that, about the love of God and one's fellow men, 'there simply is not preached because it gives ammunition to our enemies and because it would make the person suspected of being a liberal'. Again there was a sense of unreality. What is Christianity supposed to be about?

We who live here are not surprised by this perverted way of thinking because this kind of thing happens all the time. When I say to Whites that the cruel laws of apartheid are going to lead to a violent revolution, I am given warning looks and then told to shut up. When I continue I get shouted at for "being irritating" and told to wait until I am mature and have more experience before criticizing things that I don't understand. I don't mind being shouted at, but I do mind that they are leading my country towards a violent revolution.

Professor Keppel Jones also said that the government's refusal to have a judicial enquiry into the "grim confrontation between police and students" in June indicated that they knew that such an enquiry would bring discredit to the government and to the police.

His attitude when he discusses this and other aspects of apartheid suggests that South Africa was not like this 13 years ago. What will it be like in ten years' time?

Professor Keppel-Jones says that as usual friends and strangers treated him with warmth and hospitality. He says,

> It is the magnificence of the country and the charm of the people that make the political conditions so poignant. If South Africa were like a piece of the Sahara it would be easy simply to write it off. But it is not.

Maybe Shelley does not realise how much she is going to miss it. You rush off joyfully to breathe freer air, then after a while things like the Kalahari start subverting their way into your mind. Every time you look upwards and remember the African sky, the longing grows stronger, until the main thought in your head is how many days till you see home. Flying home is an exhilarating experience. If it is daylight you can watch the land change. In 1969 I flew home from Athens via Nairobi, and I could see Khartoum where the White Nile meets the Blue Nile as if I were looking at a coloured-in map.

If you are on South African Airways you don't see much land because you fly mostly over the sea. Their planes heading for Europe have to go around the bulge of Africa to avoid being shot down. Those flights come in over miles and miles of deserted South West Africa, and as the earth grows greener and more inhabited, the joy increases. The cumulous clouds over the Transvaal are beautiful from above as well as from below. The northern suburbs of Johannesburg are a mosaic of blue swimming pools, then the plane goes further east over fields of green and brown that are speckled with black townships. You can tell the difference between where Whites live and where Blacks live from a few thousand feet in the air. As you drive from the airport towards the skyline of Johannesburg your heart sings, and then Lalli-dog goes wild with excitement, and all is joy and comfort. Then you hear your first *Current Affairs* telling you what you must think, and you hear your first moan about black servants, and you feel like catching the next plane out again.

The S.A.B.C. often accuses critics of apartheid of "trying to disrupt the South African way of life". The theory of the *South Africa Way of Life* is quaint and charming. We eat boerewors at a braaivleis, we laze about on a Sunday or go for a drive in the car. We play sport and we enjoy the sunshine. The dishes wash themselves, the beds make themselves, and dirty clothes pick themselves up off the floor and appear clean and ironed in the cupboard 3 days later. The family unit binds the *South African Way of Life* together.

The reality of the South African way of life is unreality. It thinks that by making a person who speaks about the wage gap stop speaking, the wage gap will not be a problem. It thinks that by hitting students on the head, the lack of education for Blacks will not be noticed. It believes that by suppressing and embittering four fifths of the population, it will stop a revolution. It ignores the fact that the Whites have the highest divorce rate in the world, and millions of Blacks are not allowed to live with their spouses.

At social gatherings of Whites there is discussion of servants and the United Nations, and what has gone wrong with England. The stock exchange and motor cars also feature. Even if they all agree that Blacks are inferior and that the government knows what it is doing, they still talk about it. There is no discussion of how awful it must be to live in Soweto, nor how stressful it must be to look for work when you don't have the right stamp in your pass.

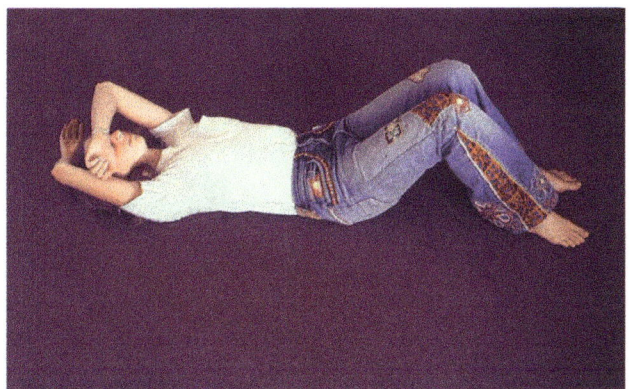

Shelley the day before she left for London.

On the way back from Shelley's house Cheryl and I reminisced about the wonderful time we had in Greece. We are so privileged to have the freedom and the money to travel, but lots of other people could have that freedom too if our society was not designed to be so unjust.

Monday 20th November 1972

Prime Minister Vorster held a press conference this afternoon and some of it was replayed on the radio this evening. It was rather boring. He is not exactly a charismatic speaker. He was talking about the future of South West Africa, or Namibia, as the United Nations calls it. It is unusual for him to hold a press conference, so he must think that what he has to say is going to help the Nats achieve their aims.

South West is a dry land that is eight hundred miles long. The Namib Desert, with its handsome sand dunes, runs along the Atlantic coast. It is also called the Skeleton Coast because people who were shipwrecked on it seldom survived. The rest of the country is semi-desert, except for the Etosha Pan in the north, which is a huge salt pan. The salt glistens in the African sun, creating a mirage that blanks out the ground below

The southern border of what is now called Namibia, in July 1969.

Sand dunes in the Namib desert, and the road made of salt next to the sea.

The wall of a bank building embedded with tigers eye.

Welwitchia trees have their trunks underground.

the horizon, so that a distant herd of wildebeest looks like a black line suspended above the horizon. When I was there I knew that I was looking at a few thousand animals, but it was hard to be sure that they were really there, as the black stripe danced above what appeared to be nothing.

Although South West is dry it is not boring. The terrain changes all the time with fascinating rock formations. When you take a stroll away from the road you can come back with huge chunks of semi-precious stones like rose quartz, lace agate, and tiger's eye.

The land of plenty is filled with diamonds too. Large parts of the country are sealed off by the government to prevent people from taking them away. In the 1930s Ernest Oppenheimer told my mom that he had arranged for a patch of earth in South West to be sealed under six feet of concrete. He said that he did it because there were so many diamonds in the ground that if they were ever mined they would cause the price of diamonds to fall.

The plants are also intriguing. There are prehistoric trees called welwitschias whose trunks grow underground. Their big leaves splay out over the sand, and funny looking insects take refuge under them. There is a forest of kokerbooms, which are yellow trees that look like overgrown succulents. In some areas there are fat little succulents that look like stones, and it is hard to spot them interspersed between the real stones. Hard baked anthills grow taller than men, and when you come to an oasis in the desert area there are palm trees just like in the Sahara.

There are millions of flamingos in the shallow water at Walvis Bay. You can watch for hours while thousands of them land or take off, swirling in the sky, making the sky pink. The road from Walvis Bay to Swakopmund is made of salt, yet it looks like ordinary tar. Where the desert ends the waves begin, and the guano islands just off the beach are jam-packed with fat herons.

Rivers can be seen from the distance even though there is no water in them, because trees grow along their course. If you want water you have to dig a few feet down into the sand of the river bed. The Fish River Canyon is easy to see because it is two thousand feet deep. It looks like a small version of the Grand Canyon in Arizona.

Herero names like Otjiwarongo and Omaruru alternate with German names like Steinhausen and Luderitz. The Herero women wear old fashioned dresses with bulky sleeves and skirts right down to the ground. They dress like that because it was the fashion in Germany when German missionaries first came.

After World War One South Africa took over control of the colony from Germany, and they introduced apartheid so that the original inhabitants have to carry passes. There are quite a few different tribes in South West, and the Nats are setting up Bantustans for them. The United Nations says that South West Africa should be independent, but the Nats don't want to let go of it because of all those diamonds.

Today Mr. Vorster talked about the proposed Advisory Council for South West Africa. He said, "There are those who believe there are [sic] no freedom of political expression in South West Africa. The facts are that there are [sic] freedom of political expression in South West Africa, and that will remain." As if the outside world is going to believe him just because he says it.

The Ovambos live in the north, but to get jobs they have to go further south. They work on contract only, so that when their time is up they have to go back to their homes

When we visited the Fish River Canyon on a coach tour in 1969 we were told we had an hour and a half at this stop. So I ran down the path for 45 minutes, then turned and started up again. It was a lot harder running up, but I made it in time, and then the bus didn't leave for another hour.

I wrote that the kokerbooms are "yellow trees that look like overgrown succulents". They actually are succulents.

The little plants that masquerade as stones are called lithops.

for a month at least. The contract system applies to domestic workers as well as farm labourers and other workers. The minimum wage was set down by the South West Africa Native Labour Association last year. For house servants and general workers it was set at R8.25 per month for an A class experienced worker returning to his former employer on a twelve month contract. "A" class means that he is completely fit. If the worker agrees to an eighteen month contract he gets R9.00 per month. A "B" class worker, who is not so fit, working under the same conditions, gets a minimum wage of R7.50. For an inexperienced B class worker it is R6.00. A "C" class worker, who is under sixteen years of age, gets R3.75 per month. Employers can pay more than the minimum wage, but they don't, even though they could easily afford to pay decent wages. Workers are not allowed to visit their home during their contract, not for any reason, and if they get injured they just get sent home.

Around New Year the Ovambos went on strike. There were thirteen thousand on strike, with five thousand of them being in Windhoek. The S.A.B.C. kept on saying that agitators had caused the strike. All the strikers were sent home on special trains with the help of the police, and white schoolboys who took over some of the jobs were paid R100 per month. *Current Affairs* explained in its smooth, sanctimonious voice that R8 a month is all that an Ovambo needs. It accused the Ovambos of being unreasonable for wanting to be able to choose what type of work they do and for wanting their wives and children to be able to live with them.

Herero women dressed in 19th Century German fashion.

When I visited this precarious rock in 1969 I felt that it was about to fall down. It fell down 19 years later, which is less than a second in geological time.

The anthills in Namibia, which are really termite mounds, house about a million termites. The tops tilt towards the north.

Some of the white people around here were shocked when they heard how low the wages for Ovambos were, but they don't realise that the wages are the same on most farms in South Africa, and in some city jobs. For instance, farm labourers brought by contract to the western Transvaal are paid R8 per month, and male cleaners and "tea girls" in hotels and offices in Johannesburg are paid R8 per month. American and British firms pay their black employees just as badly as the South African firms. You don't have to go to the Bantustans to see hungry people. There are plenty of very thin people walking around Johannesburg. Blacks employed as domestic servants have a bit of flesh on them. Some have too much flesh on them because they are fed mainly sugar and mieliepap (maizemeal). They get very little protein. Gardeners get meat because they do physical work, and their strength is needed. At the butcher you ask for "boy's meat", and they give you the cheapest cut of meat for your servants.

In the countryside the Blacks are very thin. They are desperate, so it is no wonder many of them come to the city illegally to try to get work. The migrant labour system produces farm workers that do not get paid anything at all. When someone who is looking for work in a city is found by police, they get arrested for being a pass offender, and after a very short trial are sent out to a farm to work off their sentence. This is great for the farmers, most of whom are Nats, because they get free labour.

Tuesday 21st November 1972

One of the buildings that I went into today has four lifts. Three are whites only, and one is for Blacks. This building has delusions of grandeur because not only do they have a black elevator operator wearing white gloves to operate each lift, they also have a white man in a white coat who stands in the foyer in front of the lifts and points out which lift is available, as if you can't see for yourself.

One day last year when I visited this building I walked into a lift that was waiting, and a black man came in too. The white man in the white coat dived after him and dragged him out by the arm yelling, "No, no, no, you don't go in there." As the lift doors shut I saw him being directed to the "non-whites only" lift. I was then alone in the lift with the white-gloved elevator operator. I expressed my opinion about the incident, partly to let off steam and partly to let him know how I felt. He turned and looked at me, shook his head, and said, "Do you know that that Baas was going to the same floor as you?" It is the only time in my life that I have heard a black man referred to as "Baas". Some white men demand to be addressed as "Baas" or "Boss" by any black man they speak to.

In blocks of flats they usually have one lift which is padded for the moving of furniture, and that lift is the one that Blacks are allowed to use. In a building where there is only one lift, and in department stores, Blacks and Whites are allowed to use the same lift. But when Blacks get into a lift that has a white person in it they usually stand in the corner with their eyes downcast. Sometimes when I speak to them they don't even realise that they are being spoken to, because they are not expecting it.

One time I deliberately got into a non-whites only lift, and every time it stopped and the doors opened, the black people who were waiting to get in saw me, and stepped back, and didn't get into the lift. I have not done that again.

Friday 24th November 1972

Last night the telephone rang an hour after I had fallen asleep. I staggered in the direction of the noise. The pale moonlight seeping through the glass doors almost blinded me. I banged my head on the receiver when I put it to my ear. Then I heard Stephen's voice asking me to collect Temba and her friend from the train station in the morning.

I set the alarm for an hour too early by mistake, and after I got to the station I found that the train was arriving half an hour later than Stephen had said. Although the station has different entrances for different coloured people, cars can drive down onto the platform and go to any part of the platform. I drove past where the whites only carriages come to a stop, and parked at the other end. First I took Lalli-dog for a walk along the cold, deserted platform, then there was nothing else to do but curl up with her on the back seat of the car and go to sleep. When I awoke I opened my eyes to see a flood of black faces moving past the window. The trains from Soweto had begun to pour in.

The people streaming past the car were dressed in colourful, individualistic ways. Some of them were draped in blankets decorated with African designs. Even at this time of year it is cold at the early hour that they have to rise in order to be at work at 8 am. There were wild colours and shapes of clothing that would make Mary Quant cringe. Some women were wearing pleated skirts; hand-me-downs from the 40s and 50s. The hats were incredible. One unusual chapeau went past on a tall young man. It was basically of Davy Crocket design, only the tail was too short and thin, while the crown was too deep, at least six inches too deep. It was made of that scarlet fluff out of which they make cuddly toys. To set the whole thing off he had stitched a strip of Zulu beading to the front, a band only five inches long and an inch wide. The brilliant colours rode above the heads of the crowd as he strode along the platform.

I have lived in this town for 19 years, yet until today I have never watched the trains roll in from Soweto and discharge their contents. These flamboyant people vanish into the factories and firms of the Golden City, don overalls and become to someone "the boy" or "the girl" for the rest of the working day, then they catch the train back home, back to the dismal world of Soweto, and out of the minds of Johannesburg Whites.

A whites only bench at Johannesburg station.

When the train from Cape Town arrived I took Temba and her friend Nafiza to our house for lunch, and Nafiza's aunt fetched them later. They are leaving for Germany tomorrow night.

Nafiza is an Indian word for "the precious one", Temba is the Xhosa word for hope, and Wendy is Teutonic for traveller. They were interested in my identity card.

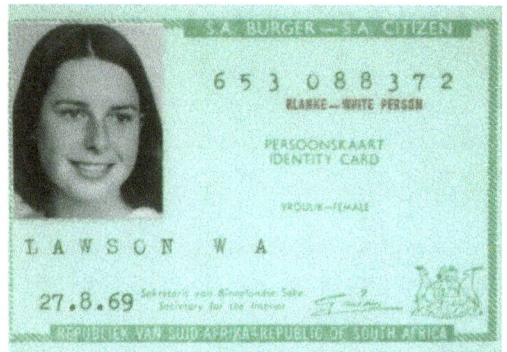 

My and my father's identity cards. His from 1960 has a W to indicate "race".

Nafiza said, "Do you know that Temba is classified "Other Coloured?""

"Yes, I know" I said, and I felt like adding, "I'm sorry". They put on a brave face, but the hurt shows through. Nafiza is classified Malay, although she is pure Indian. I am classified white, although when you are classified white you don't think of yourself as classified.

Saturday 25th November 1972 AM

Last night I had the new experience of attending an SRC party. An American student who is staying with Dave Gurney and his mother is on the Wits SRC, so I went with him. At first there were not many people, and I was the only non-male. They are all going on a convention soon, so they were reminiscing about past conventions. After a while I asked, "Do you do anything other than booze-up at these conventions?"

"No, not much," said one, laughing, "Not much."

I was spared the subject of motor cars, but the stock exchange did feature. Although not usually discussed by people of our age, the stock exchange has become a topic worthy of discussion since the demise of Mr. Chweiden. This has to be the most novel swindle in the history of the Johannesburg Stock Exchange. A few days ago there was talk of "possible irregularities," now the most common phrase is "international repercussions". Another topic was how Jenny Cunningham had spoken at such great length about the lack of black housing at a meeting they had been at earlier in the day.

The conversation became more lively once Adam Klein and Franco Frescuro and his wife arrived. The party ended up being very jovial, with lots of laughter, and singing and dancing. I really enjoyed it. Ralph Judah got a ribbing in one of the songs, and he took it with good humour. I was highly entertained by the arrival of a bevy of girls in long trendy dresses who flowed in through the door and arranged themselves decoratively on the steps leading down from the entrance hall to the living room. I suppose that with the dearth of rock 'n roll stars there is around here, the next best thing is to be an SRC groupie. They talked indignantly about a rival who had most brazenly tried to impress the guys by wearing only one earring.

The two maids in the kitchen stayed on duty until 9 pm. They had nothing to do except wash glasses. I was the only one who spoke to them, and soon gave up because of their unresponsive attitude. I don't blame them, I was just as much a cause of their having to work so late as the others.

Adam told me that on the day we arrived home from Greece, when that row of security police lined the route to passport control, he was taken aside for questioning, and after they let him go he discovered that they had taken his address book from the breast pocket of his jacket. They seem to be more talented at pickpocketing than they are at phone tapping.

Craig Williamson was one of the people arrested during June Week, and he told us some of the incidents from the trial. He said the highlight was the policeman who asked the judge if he could have the picture of himself pulling a student along by the hair. The cop said that he wanted to frame it because he liked the expression of pain on the student's face. This cop walked into the witness stand, took out a pocket book and shouted that he had arrested him and her and her, and they had all been released and he wanted to know why. Someone told him that he was there to answer questions, not to ask them, but he shouted his question again.

The newspaper had reported about this policeman. He had picked out the student before the charge because he had a full beard. "It was my intention to drag him away by his beard," said our duty-bound young friend. The student was running away when, "I dive-tackled him and we both fell to the ground. A fight developed and I had no choice but to grab him by his hair. I put my knee in his back and forced him to the ground. After overpowering him I dragged him along the ground for about five metres. He then managed to get to his feet and I pulled him by the hair to a police van. I love fighting and enjoy a good fight." Craig reckons that they had discharged all those whom he had arrested because they wanted this cop to feature as little as possible in their prosecution.

Jenny Cunningham being dragged to the police van.

Then there was the plain clothes cop who had been sworn at by Jenny Cunningham. His feelings had been hurt. In the police van he asked her who she was and she refused to give her name until he identified himself. He banged her head on the floor of the police van four times. When asked by the lawyer about this he said that he had slipped. She had already been viciously beaten by four men before this, and had been picked up by her hair from where she had been sitting on the lawn.

Many of the plain clothes police told the magistrate that they did not have batons with them at the demonstration, even though there are photos of them using batons to bash students.

Craig told us more amusing stories about the trial and the stupid behaviour of the police, mimicking the voices and expressions. Someone asked him if he would like to live through it all again. "No, never. You can't imagine what it's like to have to sit there and listen to these people telling the most incredible lies about you, and not being able to speak for yourself. It makes you sick."[32]

After the trial had ended Helen had told me that the whole procedure was like being in a sensory deprivation experiment. Despite the fact that they could see that the prosecution was crumbling and that they were not going to be landed with a serious sentence, their studies suffered, and it was generally an unpleasant experience. It could have been much worse.

Saturday 25th November 1972 PM

I picked up Temba and Nafiza in town, and we went to the Hillbrow flea market so that I could collect money from jewellery sales. On the way back to the car we were in Claim Street, so I suggested we go up the Hillbrow Tower to have a look at Johannesburg. I love the mine dumps. It fascinates me that they are not all the same shade of yellow. Perhaps the colour depends on how much gold is left in them. As we approached the entrance to the tower I suddenly remembered "whites only".

We strolled past a very surprised door keeper. At the ticket machine I told the man behind the change counter how refreshing it was to find a slot machine that actually worked. He smiled in a bemused way. And then we were safely in the elevator before they had decided what to do. On the observation platform the woman behind the souvenir counter watched us silently.

Temba and Nafiza were impressed by the size of the city, but not by much else, not even by the drive-in cinema on top of a mine dump. I took them back to Nafiza's aunt's house, which they said was in Benoni. I could not think where in Benoni they could possibly live. They directed me to Actonville, one of those slyly hidden townships that one cannot see from the road. Once we had entered Actonville there were children playing football in the streets, like they do in Europe, and teenagers milling about. It is Saturday afternoon and the teenagers have nowhere else to go.

All the houses are exactly the same, built of dark brown brick, small and rectangular with shallow barrel-vaulted roofs, so that they look like rows and rows of dark and diminished aeroplane hangars. Temba says that the residents spend their money on big cars because they are not allowed to build their own houses.

Nafiza's aunt told Temba and Nafiza that the Hillbrow Tower is for Whites only, except for Thursdays, which is Non-whites only day. They were shocked and amused to learn that they had been up the tower on a whites-only day, but they soon forgot about it because they had to get ready to leave for Germany.

---

32 You have got to hand it to Craig Williamson that most of the time he did an excellent job of pretending that he was on our side.

I examined Temba's passport. Like mine it mentions height, eye colour, and hair colour, with no mention of skin colour. However, there is a C written in fountain pen in front of her passport number. In front of mine there is a J written in fountain pen, which I think stands for junior as I was 12 when the passport was issued. Nafiza also has a C squashed in in front of her passport number.

Laughing, panicking about the time, faffing over their packing, arming themselves for Germany's cold winter, they are just like any girls who are excited about their trip overseas, yet I am supposed to think that they are in some way different to me. I followed Nafiza's aunt's Mercedes out of Actonville. They carried on to the airport, and I turned off towards Johannesburg. The beautiful skyline of the city perched between green mountains stood out against a storm-threatening grey sky. I felt grey in my soul. I thought of Temba and Nafiza in Europe, with no "Whites only" signs on theatres, buses, toilets, taxis, benches, post offices, telephone booths, cinemas, restaurants, beaches, shop counters and trains, and then coming back here after three months of freedom, and I felt ashamed.

Monday 27th November

I went to visit Lydia's mother. She is such an amazing person. She says, "We South Africans are always talking about what we should do, yet we never do anything." Meanwhile she drives for meals on wheels, translates for Greeks at the hospital, visits the sick and elderly to cheer them up, raises funds for food for poor black people, and spends every evening organising and typing applications for bursaries for black children.

She told me that last week she had a "girl" phoning her in tears because the little boy of the household had been abusing her. Lydia's mother went to the house, gave the little boy a telling off, then went and told the boy's mother what he had been doing. The mother was not interested. She also told me that a while back she was speaking to a woman who is thinking of leaving the Anglican Church. When asked why, the woman said, "Because I'm sick of having kaffirs rammed down my throat." The Anglican Church is one of the churches that fearlessly speaks out against apartheid.

The Nats accuse churchmen who criticise apartheid of trying to subvert the state "under the cloak of religion." You hear that phrase "under the cloak of religion" very often on the S.A.B.C. Some churchmen speak out about the possibility of a blood bath being at the end of the road for apartheid. When someone warns of impending violence, the Nats accuse them of calling for violence. The Nats have such a perverted way of thinking that they accuse the churches of trying to stir up racial hatred. Meanwhile their church does not allow Blacks to attend services, it only allows them in as cleaners.

Two years ago at a campsite near Groblersdal I found myself walking behind four little boys. The two white ones had long sticks in their hands, and were prodding the black ones who walked in front of them. As the black ones sped up the prods became harder and the abuse more daring. The black kids were much bigger, but they knew better than to fight back. When I caught up to them I grabbed both sticks. The black kids must have thought that they were in for it because they turned into a cloud of dust at the camp site gate.

On the way back from that camping trip we stopped at a general store in Bronkhorstspruit. A young black man went up to the wrong counter. Instead of just telling him to go away, the man behind the counter dived out at him and removed him from the shop, kick, punch, kick, shove. The shopkeeper was shocked when I protested. He was not angry with me, just taken aback. The other white people in the shop looked the other way, or passively watched the scene.

The shop at which this incident occurred.

Kaffir-bashing is a popular sport. Last year Mr. Vaughn was walking along the pavement when he noticed that every time the white man in front of him passed a black man, the black man would swing around and swear at him. Then he saw that the white man was concealing an iron bar with which he lashed out at the legs of the Blacks as they passed. Mr. Vaughn grabbed the bar and the white man fled.

This kind of thing happens all the time. Every time I go out I either see someone being physically assaulted or being abused with nasty words. For writing this down I will be accused of trying to create racial hatred. The Nats want us to think that the people who do the bad actions are not the ones who create racial hatred. They want us to think that it is the people who talk about the bad actions that create racial hatred. They just want an excuse to silence those who draw attention to the consequences of their evil political system.

When a newspaper prints photos of a cop bashing a black man, the Nats accuse the newspaper, not the cop, of causing racial hatred. The newspapers also report that Blacks have to live with the fact that at any time there could be police at the door in the small hours of the night, and a family member could be taken away and never seen again. When a white person kills a Black for fun they don't get punished by the courts, and the newspapers criticize this. The Nats keep on threatening that they are going to "curb the irresponsibility of the press."

Thursday 30th November 1972

Ishmail came back. He has been at home for four months building another room onto his new house. He will not see his wife again until the Easter weekend. In the past she has spent time living here, illegally. Employers who allow spouses or children of servants to live on the property are sometimes arrested and charged, and some of them choose to go to jail rather than to pay a fine.

Ishmail's shining white false teeth festoon his smile as we discuss the past four months. He is amused that I went to that place "Kep Town" again. He cannot see the purpose in all this running around when one has a good home in which to stay. He whistles *Silent Night* as he works in the garden. The number of carols in his repertoire is a barometer of how close Christmas is. He goes to the Lutheran church in Parkview on Sunday afternoons. The Lutherans don't exclude Blacks on Sunday mornings, but the servants around here have to work in the morning, so the church has a service for Blacks in the afternoon. Now that Ishmail is back, the kitchen floor is so clean that Lalli-dog skids when she tries to walk on it. Ishmail is going to look after Lalli-dog and the garden while we are overseas.

Some people have said that they are pleased that he is back so that we no longer have to wash dishes and water the garden ourselves. "I just don't know how you have managed without him," said one. No one seems to care about how his wife and children cope without him when he is away from them.

Three years ago he was at home for nine months because the government had moved them, and he had to build an entirely new house. He wasn't moved because of the Bantustan policy, it was something to do with soil erosion. The government told him and all the others who had to move that they would be paid compensation for the houses they had to leave. I never saw his old house, but I remember the plans that Mr. Vaughn drew up for it. Ishmail had four years of schooling, so he can read a plan. My mother likes going to remote places, so she saw the old house after it was built. She says it was well tended and had three huge trees in the garden; a jacaranda, a mulberry tree, and an acacia, as well as three peach trees and a pawpaw tree. Mr. Vaughn drew up new plans for the new house that Ishmail had to build after being moved.

Ishmail and family at the front door of the part of the house that had been designed by Mr. Vaughn. July 1980.

Ishmail made bricks for the new house in a press, and baked them in the sun. He used beams and windows that he has retrieved from the old house. He planned to use the compensation money to buy a stove for the new house. He had to collect the money personally, on an appointed day. His train fare cost him R6. He left with a big smile and the intention of buying a stove. He was paid R33.60, not nearly enough to buy a stove. He came back very dejected and disappointed. The smile took three days to return.

When people are moved because of the Bantustan policy they don't get paid any compensation, and they are not allowed to take possessions or animals with them. They just get dumped in a place where there is no work and no crops, and a lot of them die.

Friday 1st December 1972

King Solomon's Mines is being serialised on the radio. There are quite a few black characters in the story, but the S.A.B.C. does not use black actors to speak their parts. The white actors who are trying to speak with black accents fail atrociously. They wander off into a variety of European accents. Usually the serials and plays on *The English* are quite good, and so are the musical, cultural, and scientific programmes. *Springbok Radio* is another matter. Last year I listened to *Springbok Radio* for a whole day while painting the garage doors. The serials have not changed since I was in primary school. Back then I used to listen to them when I was sick in bed.

Current Affairs has changed its name to *Editorial Comment*, which is an admission that it is an expression of opinion. Otherwise it is still the same old *Current Affairs*, presented regularly after the 6 pm news, with the same sanctimonious voice telling us what we must think. It is relayed again on *Springbok Radio* in the morning to make sure that no one misses it.

The S.A.B.C. tries to present itself as a free organisation and many Whites believe that it is. Meanwhile it churns out Nat propaganda in the "news", in actuality programmes, and in "interviews". In a few years' time they will be introducing television. I wonder how they will present *Current Affairs*. Perhaps we will get to see the face that goes with the voice. Or perhaps they will show attractive scenery to soothe our eyes while *The Voice* drones on. Will they pan over mountains and valleys as *The Voice* tells us that students are inspired by communist agitators? Will they show the Karoo at sunset, with a few sheep in the foreground, as *The Voice* tells us that the churches must set their house in order? Will they show lovely beaches with mountainous backdrops while *The Voice* tells us that every racial group wants separate development?

When TV did arrive it consisted mainly of a face telling us what to think.

Tuesday 5th December 1972

We are suffering the worst heat wave in twenty years. There is no wind and no one feels like doing anything. At least it gets a bit better when the sun goes down. I'm now back from Carols by Candlelight. They put it on every year at the Zoo Lake. We used to drive all the way from Bryanston for it, but now we just stroll there because we live one block away. The audience of thousands sits on a large sloping lawn, and the performance takes place on a raised embankment at the bottom of the slope. There is no "right of admission reserved", so lots of servants come to watch it. "Nanny girls" sit with white families to look after the children, while the other blacks sit at the back. It is actually illegal to have a mixed audience, but fortunately the Nats don't interfere.

The pageant is always magnificent, with a cleverly designed stage set, and real animals. In the weeks leading up to the event we can hear a donkey braying during rehearsals. The pageant starts with Zachariah's meeting with Gabriel, and the sound system is so clear that you can hear every word. Kids are wide-eyed at the angels that appear to the shepherds, and the Magi arrive on real camels. The Salvation Army Band plays phoom, phoom, phoom, and we sing carols in between scenes. Mothers and fathers hold hands, children gaze softly at their candle flame, and grandmothers smile. Lydia says it is the closest South Africa will ever come to Woodstock. The programmes get covered with candle wax, and I get nervous about the carelessness of candles so close to blankets and heads of hair. A minister gives a sermon, and Father Christmas arrives to collect all the presents that children are giving away to poor children. It makes me feel hope that this country could do better.

Thursday 7th December 1972

The news tonight reported that Mr. Whitlam, the new Australian prime minister, has had the temerity to say that he will issue no visas to racially selected sports teams.[33] After the news *Current Affairs* told us what we have to think about this. *Current Affairs* calls Mr. Whitlam "obstructionist and provocative", and says that he has made the move "for tortuous reasons". It says that the only "effective response" to "the sports busters" would be to ignore them, and offer them "no reprisals". In other countries "sport is hampered by intrigue, protest, demonstrations, and violence," while here in South Africa it continues "freely, unmolested, in the spirit of the game." It says that having our own sports meetings here, which are attended by foreign players, is a "notable achievement". "We have expended too much effort in the past fighting these protesters in enemy territory." Now we must see to it that, "South Africa remains a great and growing centre of sport," and this will be "a right royal response to the Whitlams of the world."

The Nats obstruct millions of South Africans from playing sport because they have dark skins, then they call Mr. Whitlam "obstructionist". They provoke the whole world with their evil racist policies, then they call Mr. Whitlam "provocative". They are the ones with tortuous reasoning, not Mr. Whitlam. Sport cannot proceed freely and unmolested when most of the population are excluded. Since when does "the spirit of the game" mean "whites only"? They say that preventing Blacks from participating in sport is not at all political, whereas it is "political" to want sporting opportunities to be available to everyone.

Current Affairs says that to ignore the "sports busters" will be the only effective response. In what way will it be effective? And what else can they do anyway? He says that we must offer "no reprisals". The only possible reprisal would be to refuse Australian players entry into South Africa. That would hurt white South African sports

---

33 Gough Whitlam made this announcement two days after becoming prime minister.

fanatics even more. The only option is for them to do nothing, but *Current Affairs* drapes our non-action in folds of glory.

When did they expend any effort fighting the protestors on "enemy territory", and where is that enemy territory? Australia? New Zealand? Britain? Are they now our enemies?

This edition of *Current Affairs* starts off in a tone of hurt indignation, then moves on to a tone of childish petulance, but recovers itself when it starts talking in a tone of glorious victory about The South African Games, and ends off with a tone of contempt for "the Whitlams of the world".

Despite the pique, hitting at apartheid through sport has certainly had results. Although Mr. Vorster stated categorically that there would be no mixed sport, outside pressure has brought about a change of strategy. Next year multiracial games are to be held in Pretoria. They are being called "multinational", because they don't want to use that word "multiracial". There are also occasional tournaments popping up, organised privately or sponsored by big firms, that are open to people of all races, and Mr. Vorster is turning a blind eye. Perhaps he realises that if the outside world sees Blacks and Whites playing golf together, they might let us back into the Olympics.

Saturday 9th December 1972

Last night I went to the midnight show of *Sizwe Banzi is Dead*, which is a new play that has been put together by John Kani, Winston Ntshona, and Athol Fugard. Roy phoned me last week and told me that that I "absolutely must" go and see it, and he was right. It is being presented by Phoenix Players, and they have made it possible to have a multiracial audience by pretending that it is a private event. You have to be "invited" to be part of the audience, but it is easy to be invited because the number you need to phone to get an invitation is advertised in the newspaper. One of the girls in the audience was a white girl who had come with some Indian guys, and she was politely not stared at.

The show was not in a theatre, it was in a big room, and the stage was just a platform in the middle of the floor. The audience sat on two sports stands which were on either side of the stage, facing each other. There was a small table and two chairs on the stage. We sat there looking at the other half of the audience for quite a while, then a black chap in a white coat wandered onto the stage with a newspaper under his arm. He sat down at the table and began reading the newspaper. Because of the drought, the headline on the front page of yesterday's *Star* was "Total ban on garden sprinklers."

He read it out to us, then said, "This country! What are they going to ban next?" A corny joke, but the way he said it made the audience roar with laughter. He went from reading actual articles to reading fictitious ones. He pretended to read an article about the enlargement of the Ford Motor Company in Port Elizabeth, then remarked that none of the benefits would reach the pockets of the workers. He knew, he said, because he had once worked there. He put down the newspaper, and acted out a day's work in the factory, making us laugh all the way through.

Then he described a day on which things were different because Mr. Ford himself was coming to visit the factory. The boss made the "boys" scrub down the floor and walls, paint lines on the floor indicating danger zones, and told them to shower and fetch new overalls. They were given safety glasses to wear, and the assembly line was slowed down so that they could work with ease. They were told that they had to sing, and they were allowed to sing any song they liked, even Nkosi Sikeleli. This was all told and acted out with great humour, by the one actor, who played the parts of the factory director, the translator, and the worker. The American boss glances in, then is whisked off again in a big car. The assembly line is sped up again to its normal pace, the singing ends, and the shouting at the "kaffirs" to hurry up starts again.

Having observed the confident poise of the American, the worker decides that he wants to become like that man. So he leaves his job and rents a room in which he starts a photographic studio. The actor does a brilliant skit on our bureaucracy as he relates and acts out the obtaining of a business license. A knock at the door heralds the entrance of Sizwe Banzi, arriving to have his photograph taken. Now there are two people on stage. More laughs are to be had from the posing for the photograph. As the camera clicks, the scene freezes, and from it emerges the story of Sizwe Banzi.

A pitiful, uneducated individual, lost in the world of white man's apartheid, Sizwe Banzi does not understand why he is not allowed to work in Port Elizabeth when there is no work in King Williamstown, where his wife and four children live. He cannot read his own pass, which has been stamped "endorsed out." The original actor becomes the nephew of a friend, who gives Banzi accommodation in his house in the township, and tries to explain that it is useless banging one's head against a brick wall.

On their way home from drowning their sorrows at a beer hall they find a murdered man lying in the street. The worldly-wise nephew wants to run away, but Sizwe Banzi feels they must find his address to inform the deceased's relatives. "Are you mad? The police will come, they find the two of us drunk, taking something off a dead man. Case closed. We did it." However Banzi insists, so they take the dead man's pass, then skidaddle.

Once at home the nephew has a bright idea. If they put Banzi's photo in this man's passbook, Banzi will be able to find work under a false name. Banzi objects to the prospect of losing his identity, and so starts the decision about whether to be a person or to be employable. The nephew speaks bitingly and cynically; Sizwe Banzi speaks plaintively and pathetically. The nephew tries to convince Banzi to take the opportunity, as Sizwe Banzi does not really exist anyway. He might as well be the ghost of that murdered man because he is a ghost under the pass system.

Cleverly constructed to cover every aspect of pass-law life, the play moves from one everyday incident in the townships to another. Winston Ntshona and John Kani are brilliant actors; they switch from one role to another instantly and convincingly. As the policeman demanding the passbook, the actor's whole demeanour changes to one of arrogance, then he jumps to face the policeman and answers himself, becoming the "yes baas" obsequious, nervous "native boy". The reality for Banzi is that if he does not behave like a "boy" to white officials, "My children will starve, my wife will weep, we'll have no place to live."

It was basic but effective psychology to make us laugh through the first half of the play, because we were nicely relaxed and more vulnerable to being shocked by the second half. While pretending to be a hurried clerk in the pass office demanding Banzi's name and address and NI number, the actor shouts at the confused Banzi, "Your number is more important than your name." Then, notebook in hand, he marches up to the front row of the audience, and surprised white people find themselves stammering out their names and addresses. "And your NI number?" Blank look. "Oh, so you don't have an NI number!" I could see the reaction of the people on the other side of the stage. One girl was so humiliated that she kept her eyes downcast for the rest of the play. Imagine how humiliated a black person feels when it happens to them in actual circumstances.

I feel an intellectual anger all the time. The knowledge that people in my own country are forced to live like this when it is not necessary is with me all the time. But to see it enacted before your own eyes, to be taken visually and emotionally into that world and to have to suffer captive in it for an hour was torture. The quiet anger spread from my mind all through me, down the side of my arms, melting, enveloping, and exterminating every bit of fear.

I had spent the whole afternoon worrying about the consequences that I might have brought on my head by writing this book. But that play made me realise that no matter what they do to me, my mind will still always be free. I will always be me and know that I am me. They can never do to me what they have done to seventeen and a half million people; taken away not only their material welfare and security, but their identity too.

Afterwards I went backstage to ask where I could buy a copy of the play. I found Winston Ntshona and John Kani in a makeshift dressing room, but before I could ask my question a white man with a beard came striding into the dressing room and blurted out, "Are you going to get heavier boots to kick their balls in?" Then he put his hand on Winston's shoulder, and said, "I can't find words to describe it. Courage to you." They have to have courage to do what they do, but I doubt they intend ever kicking anybody. I asked if the play had been published yet and Winston replied, "Oh, no. It hasn't been written down yet."

Tuesday 12th December 1972

I told my mother what the latest newspaper report has exposed about the Broederbond. They investigated the "Jewish Problem". This includes investigating how to stop Jewish immigration, and how to stop the influence that Jews have on the economy. She laughed and said that they are fools because Jews have contributed so much to the prosperity of the country. She objects to anti-Semitism at a personal level, but apparently when it reaches government level it becomes a laughing matter.

The government says that it is "opposed to anti-Semitism in any form", but the executive committee of the Broederbond that started the investigation into the "Jewish Problem" consisted of what are now two cabinet ministers, one member of parliament and a Nat MEC. There is also the usual sprinkling of Dutch Reformed Church leaders, S.A.B.C. leaders and Afrikaans university leaders. And Dr. Koornhof, who was Minister of Immigration at the time, assured the Broederbond that great care was being taken not to admit Jewish immigrants. The Broederbond is run on the fuhrer, gauleiter, and cell system. It makes me shudder. Do the Nats think they are going to go on for ever, or is a thousand years the length of time they have in mind?

I know lots of Jewish people here in Johannesburg who lost relatives in the holocaust, and now happily support apartheid. It is just like the way the Boers suffered so badly under the British invasion, and now they are doing even worse things to the Blacks. Human selfishness knows no bounds.

Thursday 14th December 1972

We had dinner at the airport before leaving. At 12.30 am the engines drew up. As we started to move forward I said to my mother, "This is where my book ends." She smiled, curious, still wondering what all this book writing has been about. I had thought it would end when I had run out of things to say, but you can never run out of things to say about the land of apartheid. A few days ago a posh lady asked me, "But do you say any of the good things about South Africa?"

"Oh yes, I've said how be-yoo-tiful the jacarandas are." I know that apartheiders will say that what I have written is biased, but I have just described what I see.

The posh lady also asked me, "And what do you give as the answer to the problem?"

I replied, "That you should vote for the Progressive Party". She did not like that. In her opinion the "problem" is that there are so many Blacks and that they want a fair share in the wealth of the country. She thinks that if the Blacks have less poverty, she will have less wealth. Most of all, she does not want to have to pay her servants a living wage.

You can never change greed, but you can change the effect of that greed. The people in power need to lose their paranoia and allow the rest of us to advance in a natural way. I believe that it is not too late to save South Africa from the violent end to which she is being led by this system. This country has so much potential that it could become one of the greatest in the world, but it cannot do so while it is the disgrace of the world.

As the aircraft moved forward the raindrops on the window-pane began to skim back across the surface of the glass until the speed smattered them so small that they were invisible. Up we lifted. In the towns below the house lights were out, and the street lights formed a delicate tracery on the black. One town was on a circular plan, with threads radiating like a spider's web. Each joint of the threads glowed like a Japanese pearl. Hong Kong, Tokyo, and Bangkok sound like very exciting places. Our pilot announced that we were passing over the Limpopo, heading directly over Beira to the Seychelles. My country was left behind us. I pray that change for the better of all will come to the beloved land between the Limpopo River and the Fairest Cape in all the World.

Kwapitela and Compensation

On 23 August 1900 Mr. Pitela Hlope purchased 323 hectares (798 acres) of land at Kwapitela in the British colony of Natal. It was arable land with good grazing grass and a river running through it. In 1910 Natal became a province of South Africa. In 1969, while the land was still owned by the grandchildren of Mr. Hlope, it was declared a "black spot" under the apartheid regime's maniacal Bantustan policy, because it was in a "white area".

In 1979 apartheid officials visited Kwapitela, painted numbers on the buildings, and told the residents that they were going to be removed from their homes. The place to which they were going to be moved was 70 kilometres away, and had been given the cynical name of "Compensation" by the Nats. Compensation was in one of the 29 patches of land that formed the "Zulu Bantustan".

In 1981 there were 630 people living in 76 households at Kwapitela. Most of them were tenants of the Hlopes. Tenant households had on average about a quarter of a hectare of land to live on, plus one hectare for growing crops. They also had access to common grazing grounds for their animals. Most households had erected fencing, chicken runs, toilets, and cattle kraals. They kept cattle, sheep, goats, pigs and chickens, and they grew maize, sorghum, cabbages, turnips, onions, beans, taro, melons and gourds. The households averaged eight fruit trees each. Six of the households managed to sell produce outside of Kwapitela. The white-owned land surrounding Kwapitela was affected by soil erosion, but the land in Kwapitela was in good condition because the Zulus used sustainable farming methods. There was fresh water from the river, and plenty of firewood. Some men had jobs within walking distance. Wages were low of course, but at least they could live with their families. A few residents owned a car or a horse. Kwapitela was without telephones or electricity.

The houses were made of concrete blocks with tin roofs and plastered walls. Some of the houses had wallpaper on the interior walls. Traditional huts were made of wattle and daub with straw roofs. There was a communal stone church building which doubled as a school during the week. The school had three teachers and 120 pupils. Because Kwapitela was freehold land the residents had greater independence and control over their lives than they would have had in a township.

My husband and I visited Kwapitela on 1 July 1981, the day before the people were due to be forcibly removed to Compensation. First we went to an Anglican church in Pietermaritzburg where Peter Kerchoff showed us on a map where to find Kwapitela, and also where to get a good view of Compensation. We drove to a spot on the dirt road that Peter had indicated, parked, and then climbed over the rise next to the road. We found ourselves at the domestic establishment pictured below.

Two women outside their hut at Kwapitela, 1 July 1981.

Maize and sorghum were cultivated together. It was midwinter, and the crop had already been harvested. The square hut with the flat roof was for storing produce.

One of the many fruit trees at this homestead.

There would be no melons at Compensation.

This hen had nine chicks.

The women in the photos gave me permission to take photographs inside the hut with the open door.

Sleeping mat, enamel bowl, and three-legged cooking pot.

The kitchen area.

Fireplace in the middle.

The sound system.

Looking away from this group of huts I took the next three photos of other homesteads.

The women were frightened because they knew that they were going to be removed, and our presence made them nervous. I doubt that they foresaw what a catastrophic effect the removal was going to have on their lives. After taking photos of this one household, and the view looking away from it, we decided to leave, rather than venturing further onto the huge property and taking more photos.

The sheep on the left was not aware that its owners were going to be forcibly removed the next day. It was midwinter so the maize crop had been harvested, and the land was not yet prepared for spring planting. When the photo is enlarged, cattle can be seen in the two fallow fields in the distance.

Further along the road I took these two photos of scattered households at Kwapitela and the river that runs through the property.

The telephone pole on the left carried phone lines to the nearby white farms.

The Zulus ploughed on the contour, unlike the white farmers.

Then we drove to the spot from which we could see Compensation. It was on a remote dirt road, and we had seen no other traffic. I put my camera with a long telephoto lens on a monopod and pointed it at Compensation, and along came an unmarked police car containing plain clothes police. While they were hassling my husband, I put the big camera back into the combi and picked up a dinky little camera, and wandered down to where they were accusing my husband of nefarious activities. After many claims by us that we were just taking photos of the view, and me waving the little camera about, they seemed to forget that they had seen a telephoto lens, and told us to leave, which we did.

The next day and the day after 80 trucks and hundreds of men turned up at Kwapitela, smashed the houses, and transported the people to Compensation. Cherryl Walker, author of *Landmarked: Land Claims and Land Restitution in South Africa*, and co-author of *The Surplus People: Forced Removals in South Africa*, was witness to the atrocity.

The residents were allowed to take bits of their houses with them to Compensation. Families who owned dogs were allowed to take them, but there was no food for dogs at Compensation.

15 *'GG' trucks removing households from Kwapitela, a black spot near Himeville in Natal, to Compensation.*

Photo: John Aitchison, *The Surplus People: Forced Removals in South Africa*, 1985.

Compensation was on a steep slope and the ground was not arable. Some of the families who were dumped there were provided with a 12 foot by 12 foot tin shed with no floor, and a separate latrine. Other families were just provided with a small patch of veld.

25 *Kwapitela women after the move to Compensation.*

Photo: Cherryl Walker, *The Surplus People: Forced Removals in South Africa*, 1985.

There was a bus stop three kilometres from Compensation, with a bus going daily to Pietermaritzburg 73 kilometres away. The bus fare was more than a wage would have been if someone had actually been able to get a job in Pietermaritzburg. A white-owned shop four kilometres from Compensation sold food at very high prices. There were no trees for firewood.

17 *The view remains, the people have gone: after the demolition in Kwapitela.*

Photo: Cherryl Walker, *The Surplus People: Forced Removals in South Africa*, 1985.

People were also removed from hundreds of other "black spots" during apartheid. By definition "black spots" were freehold land that was owned by Blacks, and the owners had title deeds that predated the union of 1910. The first purchase of land in Natal by a black South African had occurred in 1861.

Millions of subsistence farmers who did not have title deeds were also removed from their homes and dumped in unviable resettlement areas. In Natal, many of the ancestors of the subsistence farmers had run successful businesses, transporting their produce by cart to the diamond fields at Kimberley, until the British invaded Zululand, took most of their land, and prevented them from running businesses. One of the consequences of the land theft is that the cattle that are indigenous to South Africa ended up being owned by the European colonists. The theft of land continued progressively until the end of apartheid.

Deuteronomy 27:17.

District 6

District 6 was established in 1867 as the sixth borough of Cape Town. It is next to the city centre and the old Dutch fort, and is just above the docks. The land slopes gently upwards towards the foot of Table Mountain. In 1966 District 6 was declared a white area under the Group Areas Act. So began the relentless destruction of a vibrant and successful community. Sixty thousand people were removed from their homes and forced to live on the Cape Flats, and their solid homes, which had been built in Victorian times, were demolished.

The proximity of District 6 to the centre of Cape Town city was one reason for its destruction, but the fact that it was a successfully cohesive multiracial community also motivated the Nats to destroy it.

In May 1981 I visited Cape Town for a weekend, and after arriving at the train station on the airport shuttle I walked up the hill to take photos of what remained of District 6. This was the first photo that I took.

Then I walked a few steps further and turned the camera a bit to the left and took this photo. The main mountain in this photo is called Devil's Peak, and the one to the right is part of Table Mountain.

Again I turned the camera more to the left and took this photo. The church building is St. Mark's Anglican church. The new road coming from the left replaced Hanover Street, which before the demolitions was lined with double-storey Victorian homes.

By 1981 much of District 6 had become a wasteland.

When I posted the following photo on Facebook the Cape Town attorney Rafeek Hendricks commented, "That was our house in Chapel Street being demolished. We were forcefully removed to Hanover Park. I can still remember and feel those painful memories as if it was yesterday." When I contacted him he said that his parents had had a longing to return to District 6, but unfortunately it never happened. They died in 2015 and 2016. "My two sisters, my brother and I are the last generation who can lay claim that we were born in District 6, and each one with our unique emotional scars."

When I posted the following photo on Facebook, people told me that the homes that were being demolished were numbers 5 and 7 Muir Street, and that Dr. Ebrahim's parents had lived at number 3, which is the one on the left that had not yet been demolished. They also said that Chiba, who had a fruit and veg shop, had lived at number 5, and the lady who had lived opposite sold the best samoosas ever.

Closer up I could see there were still posters on the wall.

Life was normal life in District 6 in 1977, before the demolition. People lived in good accommodation, had jobs, and owned cars.

Photo courtesy of Rudolf Ryser. More of his photos of District 6 can be seen at https://www.facebook.com/rudolfryserphotographer.

By 1981 a palm tree remained, but the houses were gone. The mountain endures.

Before the demolition there had been twenty-one churches, three mosques, three major synagogues and two smaller synagogues in District 6.

The Salvation Army, at the corner of Muir Street and Roger Street, was no longer able to do its work.

Around the corner in Roger Street some people were still living in houses that had not yet been demolished.

Some comments prompted by my photos on Facebook were;
"Many of our parents died of a broken heart. The pain will always be there."
"The only positive thing is our glorious, beautiful, ever present Table Mountain. The mountain has seen our joy, songs and heartache. I simply love that mountain. As a child growing up in D6 we played on the slopes of the mountain."
"I was very young at that time and understood the old houses were demolished but was not understanding why very nice and solid houses were also being demolished."
Bernice Carter commented, "I was born in D6 and spent a happy childhood there. It was truly a multicultural and interesting place to live in. I remember the Jewish, Indian, Christian and Muslim community all living and trading side by side, with no problem. It was an experience that I'm proud to have been a part of."

My photos prompted the poet Alvie January to write;
When the South Easter blows we will remember,
Remember the sound of beloved voices
The sight of a busy house or busy street
The taste of a Sunday morning koesieste
Or the feeling of happiness when you hear the church bells
from all corners of the District
The sound of Kamalies drum as he commands the Atchars
The sight of the Majestic mountain behind us and the Bay ahead of us.
They have taken our homes but our souls and memories are not for sale.

A lady commented about the next photo, "The majestic Lions Head tearfully overlooking the 'aftermath', which looks like a war, yet there was no war, only the result of 60,000 men, women and children forcibly removed from District 6 by a greedy government who did not want to share anything with anyone who was not white."

This is the last photo I took before leaving District 6 that day. It shows how close District 6 is to the business district of Cape Town. The long wall that can be seen on the right is part of a Dutch fort built in 1679.

Some of the people who were removed from District 6 were wealthy enough to buy houses in the suburbs that were designated as "Coloured" under the Group Areas Act, while others were moved to purpose-built ghettos on the Cape Flats. In 1975, while I was on holiday in Cape Town, Roy took me to an area where foundations for some of the instant ghettos were being built, and I took this photo. The instant ghettos were not being built for the people living in the shacks in the background of the picture, but for the people in District 6 who were going to be removed from solid, well-built houses.

This photo shows Reverend Stanley Gray walking towards St. Marks Anglican Church, 27 October 1983. The pastor and the church building remained, but the congregation had been forcibly removed.

© Independent Newspapers 1983.

Vrededorp (Pageview)

We always referred to it as Vrededorp, but officially it was called Pageview. Pageview was a suburb very close to the centre of Johannesburg. It had been established as a "non-white" living area by the government of the Transvaal Republic in 1893, and by the 1970s most of the people living there were of Indian ethnicity. Like any normal community there were shops such as bakeries, green grocers, butchers, cafés, shebeens (unlicensed bars) and dry cleaners, but it was also famous as a haven for white shoppers who were looking for something exotic. The shop owners had contacts in India, so there was always an abundance of silk and cotton clothing to choose from. There were silk saris, silk scarves, brocades, upholstery fabrics, and a wide variety of cotton and linen fabrics. I was most interested in the hippie-type clothing that was in fashion at the time, but there was every other type of clothing as well. Most of the clothing and fabric shops were on 14th Street, which was always bustling with customers. Sometimes it was hard to walk along the pavement because the crowd was so thick. I never paid attention to what proportion of the customers were white; I was too busy looking at the wares. There were tailors who would make anything to measure. Some of the locals called the suburb Fietas, the name being derived from the "fitters" (tailors) who worked there. Furniture, ornaments, freshly ground spices, and Indian sweets were also sold on 14th Street.

The Nats declared Pageview "white" in 1956, and began evicting people and demolishing homes and shops in 1964. In 1981 I went to take photos of what remained of Pageview. I parked on Krause Street and took this photo as I walked towards the beginning of 14th Street.

The two buildings at the junction of Krause Street and 14th Street.

When I reached the beginning of 14th Street I was shocked to see what they had done to it. To add to my heartache the aroma of spices still hung in the air. The shop on the right that had not yet been demolished was Docrat Bros.

14th Street.

Docrat Bros was where I always bought my Indian sandals. When one pair wore out I would tootle off to 14th Street to buy the next pair. I went to Greece soon after taking part in the June week protests of 1972, and wore the same pair of sandals that I had worn when I ran away from the police. One sandal had a nail working loose that had bothered me when running, but was no problem when walking.

Docrat Bros.

Wearing my sandals in Greece in July 1972.

An advert for Docrat Bros in the *Wits Student* newspaper, 28 April 1972.

A man who saw me taking photos came running up to me and said, "Are you from the press?"

I replied, "No, I just want to have proof to show my grandchildren, or they might not believe that this actually happened."

He told me that he owned the apartment building that was still standing at the beginning of 14th Street, and he and his daughter invited me to come onto the roof to get more pictures. He was extremely frustrated that his building was going to be demolished because of the colour of his skin. He told me that all the buildings in Pageview were made of such high quality bricks that it was costing the government much more to demolish them than they had expected.

Looking down into a home that had not yet been demolished.

A bit of 13th Street is visible.

Looking south along Krause Street to a mine dump.

14th Street with the city behind.

Some houses were gone, some still there.

Mr. Rashid Jada and his daughter.

The skyscrapers in the city are less than two kilometres from Pageview. Proximity to the city is the reason why the Nats stole the land from its owners. Although Pageview was predominantly Indian in nature, there were also Malays, Coloureds and Blacks living there. The Indians were moved to Lenasia, thirty kilometres away, while the Malays and Coloureds were moved to Eldorado Park, twenty seven kilometres away, and Blacks to Soweto, twenty five kilometres away. Owners were paid token compensation for their properties, and tenants were faced with trying to find accomodation in their new localities.

When we came down from the building I took this photo of the man and his daughter. When I posted it on Facebook someone told me that he was Mr. Rashid Jada.

I then walked around what remained of Pageview and took more photos.

Looking down 13th Street towards Krause Street.

Dreams destroyed.

Waiting to be demolished.

Some families had not yet been removed.

A few moments after I took the photo on the left, along came the ubiquitous police van looking for pass offenders to bash. It was illegal to take photos of police vehicles, so I quickly snapped it.

Before the destruction there were four churches, two mosques, ten small schools, a community hall, some social clubs, a bank, and two cinemas in Pageview. Lawyers, activists, and Helen Suzman tried to stop the destruction of Pageview. The government agency that carried out the demolitions was called "The Department of Community Development". The apartheid regime had a predilection for giving Orwellian names to government agencies. The Department of Community Development was really the Department of Community Destruction.

The wealthy Indian family that we visited in Lenasia in 1969 had told us that many people had been driven into poverty by being forcibly removed from Pageview, and in 1972 I wrote that I hoped the situation had changed. Well, it had changed, but for the worse. More people had been removed from Pageview, and there was nowhere for them to live in Lenasia. In 1979 there were 3,700 families on the "waiting list", and by 1981 that had risen to 5,294 families. The Nats relentlessly kept on removing people from solid, well-built houses and apartment buildings, without providing housing for them to move into. In South Africa a cubby house for children to play in is called a Wendy house. Some well-off residents in Lenasia placed Wendy houses on their properties for relatives or tenants to live in. A family of six lived in a Wendy house because they could not find other accommodation. Some Pageview residents moved into flats in "white" areas, and if they got caught they were found guilty of a crime and fined.

Some countries were threatening economic sanctions against South Africa, so the Nats did things that they thought would make them look respectable. They thought that they could make the world approve of the destruction of Pageview by building a small mall with slightly oriental architecture in a suburb that was closer to Johannesburg city than Pageview itself. The shop owners who had been evicted from Pageview were allowed to rent space in it. This was some sort of compensation for the purveyors of exotic goods, but it was of no use to the owners of Pageview community businesses like butchers and dry cleaners. The "general dealer" in Pageview was one type of shop that was not suitable for the touristy mall. In South Africa the "general dealer" (algemene handelaar) sold every basic necessity, and there was one in every small town in the country. The general dealer in Pageview had been owned by the same man for 32 years, and by his father and grandfather before him. He was paid a pittance in compensation.

The following adverts are from the student newspaper *Wits Student* 28 April 1972.

Piru's Bazaar
22, 14th St.,

PIRU'S FASHION CENTRE
16, 14th St.,

for
Curtains & curtain making dress materials & saries haberdashery

A.H. Omar (Pty) Ltd.

51(a) Delaray St.,
Cr 14th St.

Stockist of high grade juvenile clothing 25 per cent discount to students

Leslie's
15, 14th St.,
VREDEDORP

Specializing in men's casual & mod gear 25 per cent discount & more for students.

WITH COMPLIMENTS
Habib's
sari boutique
28A, 14th Street

Gary's Bazaar (Pty) Ltd.
20, 14th St.,
VREDEDORP

Slacks, ¾ teenage coats, slack suits, suede coats

Bhamjee Brothers
3, 14th St,
VREDEDORP

Shoes specialists very special discounts for students

Ismails
7A, 14th St.,

Ladies & Childrens wear special prices for students

Mayet Store
4B, 14th St,

Quality stainless steel ware & cutlery at very special prices

Also household appliances

Angamia's Wholesale Bazaar
13, 14th St.,
VREDEDORP

Cutlery & Crockery at Special prices to students

Asvat's Store

Importers
The specialists in fine furnishings

Household linen & napery,

Let us furnish your flat at wholesale prices to suit your pocket satisfaction guaranteed finest make-up service

Clothes for that man at
Baby Centre
27(a), 14th St.,
VREDEDORP

Fantastic student discounts

SURTEE'S
23, 14th street
Vrededorp

THE LATEST & GREATEST IN MEN'S MOD GEAR CASUAL WEAR & EVERYTHING FOR THAT MAN

PHENOMENAL DISCOUNTS

'WE HAVE GOT IT'

L.H. Wholesalers

19, 14th St.,
VREDEDORP

*Complete stockists,
all types of bedding*

SPECIALS FOR STUDENTS

Gary's Shirt Bar

20, 14th Street,
VREDEDORP

*House of a million shirts
for R2-50*

The cheap store

Cr. 14th St & Delarey

Specialists in hats & ladies underwear, Lister's knitting wools — special discounts for students.

HANS STORE

Direct Importers & Wholesalers
Phones:
35-1217 & 35-6825

Specialising in:
- Greeting Cards
- Baby Goods
- Children's Wear
- Artificial Flowers
- Dress Patterns
- Imitation Jewellery
- Plastic Foam
- Nylon String and Bag Handles
- Buttons & Buckles Expertly Covered

P.O. Box 54013
P.O. Vrededorp
Johannesburg

11-14th Street
Vrededorp
Johannesburg

S.A. Docrat

General merchants and
Direct importers

*Specialising in Sarrie Material
and
Swiss Embroidery*

12b 14th Street
Vrededorp Johannesburg
Phone 35-5161

Abie's

13A and 8A, 14th St.,

Stockists of the latest fashion footwear at low prices — special discounts for students as arranged.

Orient Jewellers & Music saloon

8, 14th St.,
VREDEDORP

Rings, watches, & Gifts, very special discounts for students.

Record prices cut to H.L.

Green House

18, 14th St.,
VREDEDORP

The house of crimplene & material of all description

SPECIAL DISCOUNTS FOR STUDENTS

False Bay Station

False Bay Station is on the Cape Town to Simonstown railway line, with Muizenberg Station to the south of it and Lakeside Station to the north of it. Under apartheid False Bay Station was one of the amenities that was divided in an absurd way to try to keep the "races" apart. The path next to the station and the bridge going across the line were divided longitudinally, with signs indicating where those classified "non-white" and those classified "white" were allowed to walk. This was not the only outdoor space that was divided in this ridiculous fashion during apartheid, and the intention of the Nats was to install these divisions all over the country. Apartheid ended, however, before they achieved this aim.

In 1975, when I was on a short holiday in Cape Town, Roy took me to False Bay Station to show me the bizarre arrangement. We walked northwards from Muizenberg along the path next to the railway line. Next to False Bay Station we were confronted with a fence dividing the path we had been walking along. There was a sign on the left that said "NON-WHITES ONLY/NET NIE-BLANKES", and a sign on the right that said "NET BLANKES/WHITES ONLY".

The signs and the fence as we approached False Bay Station. Devil's Peak and a bit of the back of Table Mountain can be seen in the distance.

We walked along our designated sides, and after I had gone a little way I took this photo of Roy heading up the stairs to his side of the bridge. The bridge itself was divided down the middle by a solid metal fence.

The sign to the left of where Roy is walking says NON-WHITES ONLY/NET NIE-BLANKES, and was on the southbound station platform.

I then walked further and went up the first flight of stairs, from which I took the photo below. The path was divided all the way to Lakeside Station, two kilometres away. We then went onto the bridge. Roy was able to peer over the top of the barrier to see me on the "other" side.

All the barriers are gone now, and the floor of the bridge is completely smooth. The path that led to Lakeside still has evidence of damage where the fence posts in the middle used to be.

Throughout the country the trains had a sign on each carriage which could be flipped over, with one side of the sign saying "WHITES ONLY" and the other side saying "NON-WHITES ONLY". So the different "races" could travel in the same carriage, just not at the same time.

Epilogue

Adam Klein stayed one step ahead of the security police, and in 1976 he relocated to the United States just before his banning order was delivered. Documents released by wikileaks suggest that Henry Kissinger facilitated the relocation. Adam first taught at Harvard University and then at Columbia University, as well as working as a business executive in the world of media and digital media. One of his current roles is as executive advisor to the CEO of the S.A.B.C. (South African Broadcasting Corporation).

Adam Klein chairing a meeting in the Great Hall at Wits on 9 March 1973, at which two United Party members of the Schlebusch Commission sought to justify the banning of the NUSAS 8 and SASO 8. On the left is Marais Steyn, and the collaborator on the right is Lionel Murray.

The wise **Louisa** is now a psychologist.

David Gurney is an architect and town planner. He created Gurney Planning & Design in 1991, and has designed and overseen the construction of schools, churches, office spaces and office buildings, luxury lodges and many homes. He has also lectured at Wits.

Mr. Vaughn went to London for eight months in 1981 where he rode on buses, and sometimes found himself sitting next to a black person. After he returned to South Africa he said to me, "You know, I think that the reason why our Blacks can't talk about architecture and archaeology is that they are not educated."

John Vorster, who was prime minister of South Africa in 1972, had been imprisoned during WWII because he was a Nazi. His political career ended in disgrace in 1979 when the ambitions of other monsters prevented him from being protected from revelations of corruption.

Ishmail Moabelo retired in 1980. My husband and I had to obtain a permit to enter one of the patches of the Lebowa Bantustan to take a combi load of his possessions to him. Some of the conditions listed on the permit were; that we could not accept accommodation from a Bantu, that we must behave in a worthy manner and not criticise the government in our dealings with the Bantu, and that we must not get involved with any household or other issues of the Bantu.

The turn off to the Bantustan. The sign says Podile School.

The courtyard. There is maize growing in the background and the foreground.

The part of the house designed by Mr. Vaughn.

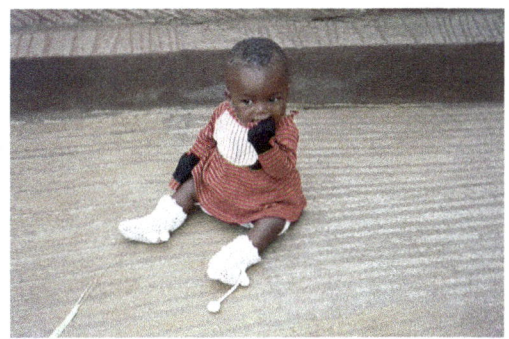

Enoch.

A grandaughter who was brilliant at maths.

The gogo and the cat.

The form.

In 1982 **James Mpendu Zondi** was offered a job at Crown Mines in Melville, but he felt so sorry for his frail old employer that he didn't take it. A year later he was once again offered the job at Crown Mines, and he took it.

James Mpendu Zondi and friends, 1982.

Helen Suzman retired in 1989 after spending 36 years in parliament. After retirement she became president of the South African Institute of Race Relations, was one the officials who oversaw the first democratic election, and was present when Nelson Mandela signed the new constitution in 1996. She received twenty seven honorary doctorates from universities around the world, was nominated for the Nobel Peace Prize twice, was awarded an OBE, and received numerous other awards from religious and human rights organizations around the world. While still fighting the good fight in parliament she had said, "I'm not interested in politics, I just hate injustice." Because she was in parliament she was not subjected to the censorship that everyone else was subjected to, and she was able to chronicle the social and economic effects of the vicious apartheid laws and the vicious behaviour of those who administered them in her parliamentary speeches. Her presence in parliament meant that the Nats were not able to carry out even worse atrocities than they did. As a parliamentarian she was able to visit some political prisoners, which led to better conditions in political jails. She also visited communities who had been "removed", or had had their shacks demolished, and she was able to bring international attention to the situation in South Africa without being deported, banned, or killed.

Abraham Tiro was killed by a parcel bomb on 1 February 1974. No individual confessed to his murder during the Truth and Reconciliation Hearings. The parcel bomb came from Switzerland. Craig Williamson was not yet stationed in Switzerland.

Before WWII **Professor Bozzoli** had lectured in light current electrical engineering at Wits, and during the war he was seconded to build radar equipment and to train people to use it. After the war his academic brilliance and genial personality led to his eventually becoming Vice Chancellor of Wits. In that role he had a profoundly beneficial impact on the development of new courses, and on the building of new and appropriate infrastructure. After retiring in 1977 he devoted his energy to improving educational and employment opportunities for the disenfranchised. In his memoir, Prof. Bozzoli mentions that while student protests were occurring all over the world, the protests in South Africa were unique because the students and the university administrations were on the same side. He also mentions the hatred in the eyes of the plain clothes police who attacked us.

Professor Ellison Kahn, Dean of the Faculty of Law, continued to use his towering intellect to work for justice until two years before his death at the age of 86. One of his post-apartheid projects was to chair a committee that investigated the secret government activities that had propped up apartheid, had murdered a lot of people, and had cost the taxpayer billions in secret funding.

I was able to quote verbatim from the speeches of Prof. Bozzoli and Prof. Ellison Kahn because I had timidly approached them and asked to borrow the originals, taken them home, written out the parts that I wanted to quote, then returned the speeches to them. I did not have access to a photocopier, although photocopiers had already been invented.

The chairman of the University Council, **Dr. F. G. Hill**, was a brilliant engineer and scientist. Much of his career was devoted to improving safety and the quality of air in the mines in South Africa. He published more than a hundred scientific papers on rock stability, dust control, and pneumoconiosis.

Even as a child **Peter Hain** was harassed by the security police because his parents were anti-apartheid activists. He was very obviously followed on his way to school, and his bedroom was invaded while he was sleeping. His mother was banned in 1964, and his father in 1965. As his father was unable to continue working as an architect the family moved to Britain in 1966.

Knowing that the white supremacists in South Africa desperately wanted to play tennis, cricket and rugby against the British, Peter campaigned against racially selected teams being allowed to play in Britain. The South African security police tried to kill him in 1972, but the bomb failed to go off. They also unsuccessfully tried to frame him for bank fraud. Peter became a Member of Parliament in Britain in 1991, and Leader of the House of Commons in 2003.

It was **Professor Phillip Tobias** who initially inspired me to write this book. When apartheid was created in 1948 Prof. Tobias was a medical student and was president of NUSAS. He worked tirelessly against apartheid from that time on because of his deep hatred of injustice. Prof. Tobias graduated as a doctor in 1950, and throughout his life he continued researching and lecturing at Wits and at overseas universities. He held professorships in three disciplines at Wits University, and received 17 honorary degrees from other universities, three nominations for a Nobel Prize, and numerous medals and awards. President Nelson Mandela awarded Prof. Tobias the Order of the Southern Cross in 1999. In 1972 he was Professor and Head of the Department of Anatomy and Human Biology at Wits University.

His interest in anatomy extended to palaeontology, and he has a doctorate in palaeoanthropology. In addition to being brilliant, he was also approachable and friendly. I was blessed with meeting him often through the Archaeological Society. Mary and Louis Leakey invited him to work with them in Olduvai Gorge, and while working there, one of his achievements was the identification, description and naming of Homo Habilis. He was successful in getting UNESCO to list the Sterkfontein Caves north-west of Johannesburg as a World Heritage Site in 2000.

In 1977 three medical doctors facilitated the murder of Steve Biko by the security police. Both the South African Medical and Dental Council and the Medical

Association of South Africa protected the three doctors from accountability. Prof. Tobias and four other doctors took the matter to the Supreme Court, which ruled that the Medical and Dental Council must re-open the case against the Biko doctors.

The fire hydrant continued to serve as a platform for protests.

I took this photo of the fire hydrant on the night of 29 February 1973, during a protest against the banning of eight NUSAS officials on 27 February. The next day eight SASO officials were banned. One was Steve Biko, who was murdered by the security police in 1977.

A security policeman who was taking photos of the participants in the protest on 29 February 1973. He was on the traffic island in the middle of Jan Smuts Avenue, so I crossed to the island to take his picture. He smiled for the camera, and when my flash went off the protestors cheered. He made a witty comment, which surprised me.

Helen passed her exams despite all the time spent sitting in court, and went on to graduate as a teacher. She says, "1972 was a memorable year."

Zorba says, "I remember the helicopters."

"The hut" was the last remaining wooden building of those that had been hastily erected after World War II, when student enrolments at Wits had rapidly increased. It is no longer there.

The leader of the black dancing group who could speak Zulu so fluently was **Johnny Clegg.** Johnny had started jamming with Zulu musicians at the age of 14, and by 1972 he and his friend Sipho Mchunu were already playing together in what became the band *Juluka*. They played in cleaner's rooms on the top of apartment buildings in Johannesburg, or at mine worker hostels. There was the problem that it was illegal for them to perform together, and they were often arrested and sometimes beaten up by police. *Juluka* produced their first seven single in 1976, and later went on to produce eight LPs. The fusion of Zulu music with international youth music embodied the spirit of unity felt by those South Africans who loved their country and wanted to be rid of the barriers.

Johnny sometimes brought his dance troupe onto the Wits University campus to dance. They wore "flat cleaner sandals", those amazingly decorative black and white sandals that the "flat cleaners" in Braamfontein used to make out of discarded car tyres. Braamfontein is a suburb next to the university which consists entirely of apartment buildings. The Black men who serviced these apartments lived in small rooms on the roofs of the buildings. As "flat cleaners" they were permitted to live there, and they did not have to commute from Soweto or Alexandra, so they could be seen out and about during their leisure time. White students sometimes purchased "flat cleaner sandals" from the flat cleaners, and I was told that they were very comfortable to walk in. The band *Juluka* had great success in Europe and North America, where it was not illegal for people of different skin colours to appear on stage together.

In France Johnny was called "Le Zoulou Blanc". When *Juluka* disbanded, Johnny formed the band *Savuka*, which continued the tradition of combining African and European/American music, and produced four LPs, one of which was nominated for a Grammy award. The live performances of *Juluka* and *Savuka* were always dynamic and dramatic, with thrilling Zulu dances. Johnny would share information about the background to the songs, which was often heartrending, but always uplifting. After graduating Johnny lectured in Social Anthropology at Wits, and has published academic papers on African history and African music.

The music played an integral part in ending apartheid, but Johnny also actively worked towards social justice in other ways. For instance, he worked for the United Democratic Front, the Free the Children in Detention campaign, and the End Conscription Campaign, and he worked against forced removals. Trade union activists were able to provide the workers with printed information about their rights in Zulu because of Johnny's fluency in the language. Johnny has been awarded four honorary doctorates, the *Chevalier des Arts et Letters* by the French government, and an OBE.

According to Professor Bozzoli's memoir, **Brigadier Schroeder** was punished for trying to stop the police violence against Wits students by being transferred out of Johannesburg soon after June Week. The career of **Colonel Crous** in Cape Town was also damaged by his efforts at trying to stop the police violence against protesting students and random members of the public.

Dr. Marius Barnard was one of the surgeons who took part in the world's first human-to-human heart transplant, with his brother Chris Barnard heading the team. As well as being a brilliant surgeon, Marius was concerned about patient welfare. One of his achievements was to successfully persuade medical insurance companies in South Africa and around the world to provide critical illness insurance. He was motivated to campaign for this because of seeing the financial hardship his patients suffered while receiving treatment for heart conditions. His fame spread even beyond the iron curtain, and he was able to establish a cardiac surgery unit in Romania. He was opposed to racial discrimination from an early age, and spent nine years in parliament opposing apartheid. In his autobiography, *Defining Moments*, he says, "The injustices and pure wickedness of apartheid motivated my service as a member of parliament during one of the country's bleakest periods."

Advocate Maisels, better known as Izzie Maisels, continued to work for justice until his retirement at age 87. After his death in 1994 Nelson Mandela said, "We fondly remember Advocate Maisels as an energetic and brilliant lawyer between 1958 and 1961 in the so-called treason trial, and as a person of profound knowledge, with whom we consulted on a variety of issues, especially after our release from prison in 1990."

This photo of Advocate Maisels was taken in 1961 at the end of the "Treason Trial" during which the Nats had tried to end the lives of 156 people, including the life of Nelson Mandela. All 156 prisoners were found not guilty instead of being executed, thanks to the effort of the legal team led by Advocate Maisels.

Reverend E. L. King was the Anglican Dean of Cape Town from 1958 to 1988 and was based at St. George's Cathedral, the church into which protesting students had fled and been followed when attacked by police on 2nd June 1972. Reverend King had been speaking out against apartheid since long before that incident. One of his classic comments was that when the government claimed that all of its opponents were communists, they were confusing Karl Marx with Almighty God. His memoir is called *A good place to be: Dean E.L. King on thirty years at Cape Town Cathedral*.

Sonny Leon entered parliament after P. W. Botha created the Tricameral system, which existed for the last ten years of apartheid.

Paul Pretorius says that being banned gave him "time to firm up on my political education." He was able to graduate in law by correspondence while under his banning order, and then worked for the trade union movement, which was still in its infancy. After four years he was invited to work as an advocate for the Legal Resources Centre in Johannesburg. Lawyers like Paul Pretorius used the law as an instrument of justice, and their activities contributed to the end of apartheid. Later he worked in Cape Town on many cases involving injustice, the most high-profile of which was the KTC trial in which the police were charged with a reign of terror that had involved the destruction of the homes of sixty thousand people and the murders of more than sixty people. This was dangerous work, and some attempts on his life were made during that period. Even before apartheid ended Paul established dispute resolution centres in black residential areas, partly to promote confidence in the rule of law. He still works as an advocate on behalf of "the poor and the penniless."

Paul Pretorius in 1972.

Reverend Peter Storey was a Methodist pastor in District 6 for five years while the Nats were destroying the community. He led protests against the forced removals, and brought White members into the District 6 church. He also created entertainment events for Christian and Muslim youth, launched various community centres for recreation, education, poverty relief and leadership training, and he established Life Line in South Africa during this time. After being transferred to Johannesburg he continued to work for social improvement and against apartheid. One of the times he was detained he was with Bishop Tutu, and they were taken into the bush and told they were going to be shot, but they were not shot. In 1984 he and other South Africans spoke at the United Nations, the US Congress, and six European parliaments about the need for international action against the forced removals policy of the apartheid regime. Reverend Storey had been chaplain to Nelson Mandela and other prisoners on Robben Island until the Nats had banned him from the island in 1964. After his release, Mandela appointed Reverend Storey to help select the members of the Truth and Reconciliation Commission. He has been awarded three honorary doctorates. His memoir, *I beg to differ: Ministry among the teargas*, is an engrossing read.

After being a rabid Neo-Nazi, forced removalist, and high ranking Broederbond official, **Piet Koornhof** joined the A.N.C. in 2001. At age 68 he left his wife and moved in with a woman who was not classified white, and had five more children.

Lydia graduated as a social worker and later on became an Anglican minister.

The banning order against **Cosmos Desmond** was lifted after four years and he was no longer subject to house arrest. He received many death threats which made him feel unsafe. After his activist friend Rick Turner was murdered by the security police on 8 January 1978, he moved back to Britain, only returning to South Africa after apartheid ended. His book *The Discarded People* had been banned for possession under the apartheid regime. This discouraged South Africans from reading it as there were lengthy jail terms for being found in possession of a banned book or magazine. However, the book had an enormous impact overseas, raising awareness of how the apartheid government was moving millions of people from their homes onto patches of land on which subsistence farming was not viable. When people were forcibly moved they lost their possessions as well as their homes; they lost their dogs, cats, sewing machines, porcelain tea sets, kitchen equipment and farming equipment.

The Group Areas Act, **Bantustan policy**, **black spot removals**, betterment policies, influx control, and other policies caused more than four million people to be uprooted from their homes and forced to live (or die) elsewhere. Forced removals were still occurring in 1987 while secret negotiations with Nelson Mandela for a peaceful settlement were already underway. The top Nats had realised that they were going to be murdered in their beds if they did not make concessions, so they started secret negotiations with Mandela in 1982.

An informal settlement at Noordhoek, south of Cape Town, just days before the forced removal of 2 December 1987. The shacks had been built in the invasive Australian bush that flourishes in the area, and the thick vegetation meant that they could not be seen from the road. When the bush that hid the shacks was removed by the government it became obvious what was going to happen, but nothing could be done to prevent it. Four hundred police arrived to take 600 people and their possessions on 40 lorries to the Cape Flats, 50 kms away, and dump them on the sand. The police were supposed to transport the possessions of the squatters, but they became impatient and smashed many of the possessions with bulldozers instead of transporting them. Back in Noordhoek the squatters had been supported by breadwinners who had jobs in the area. There were no jobs on the Cape Flats. One of the white landowners at Noordhoek had installed taps so that the squatters had access to clean water. He had been charged with a crime because there was a law making it illegal to give a homeless person a drink of water.

Hugh Tracey founded the International Library of African Music, which is now in Grahamstown, and his collection of indigenous African instruments is preserved there. His recordings can be downloaded from Smithsonian Folkways.

LM Radio has recovered from being taken over by the Broederbond and then later closed down by Frelimo, and can now be heard online.

Peter James became a metallurgist, and after some years returned to Wits to study law. He became a partner in one of South Africa's big law firms. He has now retired to a farm in the Magaliesberg where he builds cottages and grows organic food.

Ralph Judah graduated with a law degree as well as a bachelor degree in economics at Wits and then did an MBA at Stanford University in the United States. He was adviser to the Mandela Cabinet on post-apartheid restructuring of government and the post-apartheid economy of South Africa. His main area of expertise is in health policy and health insurance. He has advised business leaders, industry associations, and governments throughout the world on these issues.

Ralph Judah speaking at the meeting in the Great Hall at Wits on 9 March 1973, at which two United Party members of the Schlebusch Commission sought to justify the banning of the NUSAS 8 and the SASO 8.

On 11 February 1990 Nelson Mandela was released from prison, and on that day he paid tribute to many individuals and organizations who had been strong opponents of apartheid, including **The Black Sash** and **NUSAS**. "I also salute The Black Sash and the National Union of South African Students. We note with pride that you have acted as the conscience of white South Africa. Even during the darkest days in the history of our struggle you held the flag of liberty high". The Black Sash is still working for human rights in South Africa.

Sheena Duncan worked tirelessly for The Black Sash until the end of apartheid, both in the arena of political activism and in the daily grind of helping individuals who were victims of vicious officialdom. After apartheid ended she worked in various human rights organisations, including helping exiles who had returned, and was awarded honorary law doctorates by three universities.

Stephen married **Temba** and they moved to Germany to raise their family.

Geoff Budlender grew up in a home that believed in social justice, and during his years at university he worked tirelessly against the apartheid regime, undaunted by repeated attacks on himself and his property. In 1972 he was president of the SRC at the University of Cape Town, so he had the responsibility for organising marches, demonstrations and public meetings after the police attacked white students in the Cathedral and on campus. When Paul Pretorius was banned in February 1973, Geoff became president of NUSAS for the remainder of the electoral year. Geoff graduated in law in 1975 and joined a law firm that specialised in social justice work. Despite the apartheid regime's continual erosion of the rule of law, principled lawyers could use the law to undo some of the harm done by apartheid. In 1979 Geoff and colleagues founded the Legal Resources Centre, which used the law as an instrument of justice for the vulnerable and marginalised. Their work led to the pass laws being repealed in 1986, three years before it was apparent that apartheid itself was going to crumble. They were also successful at preventing the forced removal of some communities. While apartheid was being dismantled, Geoff was involved in formulating the new constitution and new land legislation, which included the re-incorporation of the Bantustans. From 1996 to 2000 he was director general of the Department of Land Affairs in the administration of President Nelson Mandela. He then returned to fighting for human rights in the courts, and is still working as an advocate.

Steve Jooste graduated as a doctor at the University of Cape Town in 1976, and then worked in remote areas in the Cape and Natal. After returning to Cape Town in the mid 1980s he worked in the political arena of health care, aiming to bring health care to the poor and the disenfranchised.

The Australian called **Tim** travelled around Europe and then got a job as a petrol attendant in Britain. After that I lost touch with him.

The famous **red jumper** that Tim had given me went on to lead an interesting life, including accompanying me when I hiked into the Grand Canyon in 1974. I gave it to a beggar who came to my door for food in the 1980s.

The Russian Empire, which called itself the Soviet Union, lost some of its colonies in 1991 and quit trying to get its hands on South Africa's mineral wealth.

Robben Island is now a museum and tourist attraction.

Tourists arriving at the former prison on Robben Island, 2015.

Sparks Mlilwana, a former political prisoner, who is now a tourist guide on Robben Island.

The **"dop system"** of paying workers in the Cape vineyards with wine instead of money is now illegal, but some vineyards still illegally use wine as part payment. Wages are still below the minimum wage, hours are still long, and some employers are still as brutal and violent as they were under apartheid. Activists say that boycotting South African wine would make matters worse for the workers, but pressure should be put on distributors to influence the way that the vineyard owners behave.

The **pamphlet** about "Sunny South Africa" that caused amusement in the hostel was printed by the Department of Information. Although there was corruption in every government department, exposure of massive corruption in the Department of Information resulted in the resignation of Vorster. The whole amazing story is told in *Muldergate: The Story of the Info Scandal*, by Mervyn Rees and Chris Day.

The Dutch Reformed Church in South Africa was split along racial lines, and in 1982 the World Alliance of Reformed Churches expelled the white branch of the church. The DRC has since repented and become re-integrated with the world alliance.

Roy pursued his love of the theatre, first becoming a drama teacher, then a successful actor, director, producer, playwright, radio presenter, composer and artistic director of the Cape Performing Arts Council. He has performed in over fifty theatre productions, including as Polonius in *Hamlet* and as Alonso in *The Tempest* for the Royal Shakespeare Company at Stratford-upon-Avon. Some of his film appearances are as Fingers Fortuin in *Felix*, as Rafiq Kaif in *Material*, and as Othello in Eubulus Timothy's *Othello*. The many roles he has played in TV productions include Goolam Padayachee in *Let Heaven Wait,* Pa September in *Erfsondes*, Grandpa Simon in *Vaselinetjie,* and Ahmad Abrahams in *Shooting Stars.* He co-authored the stage adaptation of *Echoes of Slavery* and the New Africa Arts & Culture Text books for grades four to seven.

Henri in 1976.

In 1974, supported by the Christian Institute of Southern Africa, an ecumenical progressive organisation founded by English and Afrikaans clergy in December 1963 to unite South African Christians against apartheid, **Henri** was awarded a scholarship by the Otto Benecke Stiftung to study electrical engineering in West Germany. He already had a passport that was valid for countries in Southern Africa, but had to extend its validity to Europe. But despite his application for this extension being approved by the Security Branch of the police, it was refused by the Minister of the Interior, Connie Mulder, who had close links with Hendrick van den Berg, head of BOSS (Bureau of State Security). The same happened when Henri made another attempt to take up the scholarship in 1976. It's a mystery that Henri wasn't known to the Security Branch (or at least the officer who questioned him), despite him writing a number of letters that were critical of apartheid to newspapers, speaking at student meetings critical of Government policies, and being a member of the UCT SRC on an election ticket that espoused black consciousness. He was also on the regional committees of both the multi-racial NUSAS and black SASO student movements. Henri was spared the detention without trial and torture that activities like this resulted in for so many people, even though he moved in the same student and social circles as undercover police spy Karl Edwards and BOSS agent Arthur McGiven. Henri's passport expired in December 1974, and after the final refusal to issue one that was valid for Europe, Henri was faced with a choice: should he remain, or leave the country. Should he leave legally, on an exit permit which would render him stateless, or cross the border illegally into Botswana where there would be a UN travel document? What then? Because he was a pacifist, joining one of the "liberation" guerrilla detachments was not an option. His experiences with student activists who merely "talk the talk" but didn't "walk the walk" had left him disillusioned with political movements, so the alternative of becoming a political refugee wasn't a palatable option. In the end, he resolved to stay in the country, support his family (his father had died in 1975), and make a difference at the individual level - in the workplace, sports, school, church, and civic associations, which is where he has focused over the last 40 years.

The state president's house in Bloemfontein is now Oliewenhuis Art Gallery.

Eartha Kitt's daughter wrongly remembers the bumper car incident as taking place in 1974. She and her mother toured South Africa in April 1972, not 1974. The New York Times says Eartha's tour of South Africa happened in 1984, and many websites parrot that.

The **white horse** on the side of Naval Hill in Bloemfontein is still there, and a huge bronze statue of Nelson Mandela has been placed on top of the hill.

Dr. Worrall entered parliament as a Nat in 1974, but he was packed off to Australia as ambassador in 1982. In 1987 he returned to South Africa and tried to enter politics again as a non-Nat. He is an international businessman who promotes investment in Africa.

The forced removal of 65,000 people from **Sophiatown** started in 1955. The people were dumped in various places that had inadequate housing. All but two of the houses in Sophiatown were demolished and replaced with houses that were of an architectural style that lacked charm. The new "white" suburb was called "Triomf" (Triumph). The suburb was renamed Sophiatown in 2006, and has become a tourist attraction with guided walking tours.

The property that my mother bought for **Patricia** in a Bantustan was stolen from her by corrupt apartheid officials.

Shelley spent a year in Europe then returned to South Africa. After marrying, she and her husband, motivated both by fear of a violent revolution and a strong desire to not be part of the SADF killing machine, moved to the United States.

South West Africa is now independent and is called the Republic of Namibia.

Chris James is a professor in the School of Civil and Environmental Engineering at Wits University.

Jimmy Kruger went on to become Minister of Justice, Police and Prisons in 1974. His comment about the 1977 murder of Steve Biko by security police was, "It leaves me cold".

Gail and **Julie** found jobs in Johannesburg, then continued their OE in Britain.

Professor Revil Mason was an archaeologist who conducted numerous excavations around Southern Africa during his long and productive life. He lectured at Wits University, where the Archaeological Research Unit was created to study and preserve his findings. Revil published numerous scientific articles and books about his discoveries. He was strongly motivated to reveal the truth about the history of Southern Africa as a way of bringing about justice. The Nats had created the narrative that there were no Bantu in South Africa before Europeans arrived. They said that the Bantu were moving southwards towards South Africa at the same time as Europeans were moving northwards, and that therefore the Bantu had no right to the land. Revil's excavations proved that the Bantu had been settled and thriving in South Africa as early as 350 AD.

Revil Mason at one of his digs in the Western Transvaal, 1973.

Iron hoes found at Melville Koppies by Revil Mason. The ground is red because it contains so much iron.

Revil Mason laid strips of paper to indicate the position of the walls at the Tswana settlement at Bruma, and then took aerial photos.

The jaw of a Tswana bovine unearthed at Bruma.

One of Revil's great achievements was ensuring that aerial photographs were taken of archaeological sites so that a wide view of the context of each excavation could be captured. Using aerial photography he found thousands of abandoned Tswana settlements in the Transvaal. He also found and preserved a number of early colonial sites. Revil's work was often under time pressure because he was up against developers and civil authorities who were not interested in preserving any heritage sites, including any colonial sites. In the 1980s, for example, he was able to excavate enough of the Tswana settlement at Bruma in Johannesburg to gain an understanding of the lifestyle of the occupants, and was able to use arial photography to capture the extent of the settlement before the developers moved in. Also in the 1980s Revil campaigned to have Northcliff Hill and its archaeological sites declared national monuments, but the Johannesburg City Council failed to take action. The remains of settlements on the hill ranged from the early stone age to the iron age, and consisted of kraals, stone walls, smelting furnaces and a large number of iron tools, like spears and hoes.

On 29 October 1972 I wrote that we were trying to find our way to an archaeological dig, but lost our way and got there too late to see what had been found. The dig I referred to as "a few miles away" was the Broederstroom site. We had previously been there many times. Revil succeeded in getting Broederstroom declared a National Monument in 1980. The people who settled at Broederstroom in 350 AD kept cattle, sheep and goats, and hunted wild animals for food. They built raised granaries, and smelted and forged iron and copper ore. The teeth found in burials reveal that the people were Bantu. Their pottery was similar to that of Malawi and Zambia from the same era. From 600 AD the inhabitants of Broederstroom also grew sorghum, millet, beans, and cowpeas.

During our school visit to **Pelindaba** our high school science was enough for my friends and me to see that the power station had the capacity to make atomic bombs. Suggesting that they might be making atomic bombs was a punishable offence, but after the visit we mentioned it to as many people as would listen. When apartheid ended it was revealed that they had six atomic bombs ready to go, and one under construction. The bombs were all dismantled.

A documentary called *Indians Can't Fly,* made in 2015, tells the story of the life and death of **Ahmed Timol.** The title comes from the mocking phrase bandied about by the security police after Timol died falling from a tenth story window at police headquarters on 27 October 1971. The Nats had conducted a fake inquest into the death of Timol in 1972 with a corrupt magistrate, corrupt prosecutors, corrupt police, and corrupt doctors. The evidence presented by Izzie Maisels and George Bizos, who were the lawyers representing the Timol family, was simply ignored by the magistrate. In 2017, George Bizos, aged 90, managed to get the inquest reopened with the aim of determining the circumstances surrounding Timol's death. This time evidence was not ignored, and on 12 October 2017 the South African courts ruled that Timol was murdered by the security police. The book *Timol: Quest for Justice*, by Timol's nephew, Imtiaz Ahmed Cajee, was published in 2005, and his 2020 book, *The Murder of Ahmed Timol: My Search for the Truth*, tells the story of Cajee's 20-year journey to find his uncle's killer and bring him to justice.

Mohamed Salim Essop was a third year medical student at the time that he was detained and tortured by the security police. The torture started immediately after he was detained. Fifteen security police tortured him relentlessly in shifts. They were not much interested in obtaining information from him, it was mainly done for sport. At one time he was held by the ankles over the stairwell on the tenth-floor landing. He was imprisoned on Robben Island for five years, where he studied by correspondence. After his release he moved to Britain where he studied politics and law at the University of Leeds, going on to became an academic.

During his lifetime, before he was tortured and murdered by the security police, **Imam Haron** found time outside of his busy work life to care for the financial needs of families of anti-apartheid activists who had been incarcerated or driven into exile. The funds for this relief work were obtained largely from the Defence and Aid Fund, which was supported by Christian churches overseas. He also provided food and money to the desperately poor in Langa, Nyanga, and Gugulethu. These activities led the security police to believe that he was a communist, and when torturing him did not produce information about a communist plot, they tortured him harder.

The Imam Abdullah Haron Education Trust (IAHET) was founded in 2005 to continue the good work of Imam Haron. The trust provides bursaries to disadvantaged students of all races, genders and religious beliefs, across the entire spectrum of education, ranging from pre-primary to postgraduate. The Imam Haron Memorial Lecture, which highlights issues regarding education in South Africa, is held annually. The Haron family had been forcibly removed from their home in Claremont in 1965 because the suburb had been reclassified as "white" under the Group Areas Act. A major road through Claremont and Lansdowne has now been renamed Imam Haron Road.

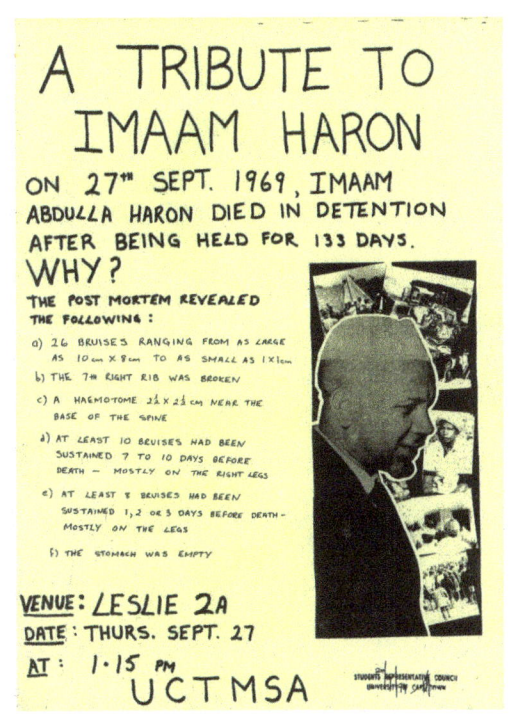

Above: Imam Haron and his son, 1964.
Right: Poster advertising a protest meeting ten years after Imam Haron's death.

The gruesome details of how Imam Haron was slowly tortured to death have been described in the 1978 book, *The Killing of the Imam,* by Barney Desai and Cardiff Marney. In 2010 Haron's grandson, Khalid Shamis, made a 10 minute film, also called *The Killing of the Imam,* which can be viewed on the internet. Imam Haron's son, Muhammed Haron, is an academic who is currently Professor of Theology and Religious Studies at the University of Botswana. Imam Haron's daughter, Fatiema Haron-Masoet runs the family business and is a trustee of the IAHET education trust. She and her brother have reopened the inquest into the murder of Imam Haron.

Rev. Bernie Wrankmore had joined the army at age seventeen and fought in North Africa against Rommel, then in Italy, where he was injured. After the war he had a variety of jobs before feeling the call to Christian ministry. After being ordained as an Anglican priest in 1963 he lived at the Cape Town docks where he ran the local Missions to Seafarers. This international organisation provides practical help, recreational activities, and chaplaincy services to communities of sailors who are sometimes very badly treated by ship owners.

Rev. Wrankmore's 67 day fast on Signal Hill in 1971, which aimed to persuade the government to hold an inquest into the death of Imam Haron, raised awareness within South Africa about the circumstances of the death, and it drew international attention to deaths in detention under apartheid. He was visited by thousands of supporters during his fast on the mountainside.

Two weeks after Rev. Wrankmore's death in 2011 a memorial service was held at the site of his fast. The service was hosted by the Muslim Judicial Council, the Cape Mazaar Society, St. George's Cathedral, and the Black Sash. One of his daughters says of him, "My dad, Bernie Wrankmore, built a bridge between people of different races and creeds at a time when the government was intent on building walls. I am so grateful for that bridge and for the incredible example of courage, determination, and perseverance he set for us all. I remember him so many times each day, with love."

Due to a population explosion **Isipingo** is no longer a jungle with monkeys and pythons.

The **Broederbond** has lost its control over every aspect of life in South Africa. The article about "The Jewish Problem" that I mentioned on 12 December 1972 was just one in a long series of revelations about the Broederbond that were published in the Sunday Times from 1963 to 1975. They were written by J.H.P. Serfontein, who was receiving information from a mole within the Broederbond. Joel Mervis was the editor of the Sunday Times, and was willing to publish the information. When Joel Mervis retired in 1975 the new editor of the Sunday Times refused to publish any further information. Serfontein then made a career change and provided information about apartheid to overseas news outlets. In 1978 he published the book *Brotherhood of power: An expose of the secret Afrikaner Broederbond.* He also published three other books about apartheid.

Frelimo became the government of Mozambique, and members of the **Direcção Geral de Segurança,** the Portuguese secret police, who had taken part in the murder, torture, and starvation of political prisoners, were locked up in Machava Prison. Some escaped to Rhodesia (now called Zimbabwe) or South Africa.

Cheryl graduated as a teacher, becoming a school principal in 1993. In 2005, after their children had flown the nest, she and her husband took teaching jobs in the UK to be better positioned to travel in the Northern hemisphere. In 2012 they took up teaching positions in Malawi.

Jenny Cunningham sustained severe injuries from the police assault on 9 June 1972, including a cracked skull, but she recovered. After graduating as a doctor she worked at Baragwaneth hospital until she was forced to leave South Africa in the 1980s. While overseas she continued to work for the end of apartheid.

Jenny Cunningham in 1972.

Craig Williamson. I knew he was a lout, but I did not think he was a significant lout. It turned out he was a very significant lout. He was a security police spy, and in 1982 he murdered Ruth First, and in 1984 he murdered Jeannette Curtis Schoon and Katryn Schoon. Williamson was granted amnesty for these murders at the Truth and Reconciliation Commission in 2000, which dismayed the families of the victims because the perpetrators were only supposed to be granted amnesty if they provided full disclosure, which Williamson did not.

Williamson played a significant role in a 1982 bombing in London that severely injured the caretaker of the building. In June 1995, while **Peter Hain** was a member of parliament in Britain, he tried to get Williamson extradited to Britain to face justice for the bombing, but the British government refused. The reluctance of the Brits may have stemmed from fear that cross-examination of Williamson could have led to revelations about murders committed in South Africa by the British Secret Service. There have been revelations of some murders committed in South Africa by the British Secret Service with the aim of propping up apartheid. In 1996 the commander of an apartheid-era police hit squad filed an affidavit and testified in the Pretoria Supreme Court that Williamson had been involved in the 1986 murder of the Swedish Prime Minister, Olof Palme. It is quite plausible because Sweden supported the ANC during apartheid. Williamson, however, denies that there was South African involvement in that murder. If he had admitted to it he would not have gotten off scot free like he did with the murders he committed in Africa.

The first time I encountered Craig Williamson was in 1971 on registration day at uni. He tried to bully me into joining NUSAS when I had gone up to the NUSAS table with the intention of joining. That was certainly not my last unpleasant experience of him. There is discussion on the net about why he was able to dupe so many of us, even though he was loud, rude, and a misogynist. When I told my daughter that the other young men were embarrassed by how he treated women, but did not do anything about it because they felt that the cause of ending apartheid was more urgent, she commented that the culture is shifting, and that some people who work for social justice nowadays would be more inclined to recognise that bad behaviour like bullying and misogyny could be a sign of something bigger. In the case of Craig Williamson, the "something bigger" turned out to be that he was a white supremacist and a murderer.

In 1973 **Franco Frescura** raised the ire of the establishment with his brilliant cartoons, and for punishment he was temporarily suspended from the university, made stateless, fined R500, given a suspended sentence of nine months, and forbidden to publish any more cartoons in the Wits student newspaper. None of these punishments diminished his commitment to social justice, nor was he deterred from contributing unsigned graphics to the student newspaper. While studying architecture at Wits, Franco included archaeology, anthropology, history, social anthropology and economics in his curriculum. Soon after graduating as an architect he was invited to become a lecturer in the School of Architecture at the university.

Most of his work as an architect has been linked to community advocacy. This has included the provision of housing for people who are homeless, the preservation of historical built environments, and the documentation of endangered knowledge systems and indigenous habitats. He also developed a methodology that has formed the basis for current national heritage policies. Franco's first book, *Rural Shelter in Southern Africa*, published in 1981, went beyond the bounds of conventional architecture.

In 1983 Franco joined the ANC, and in 1985 he relocated to the University of Port Elizabeth where he was ineptly spied upon by the security police. His wife and young daughter were harassed. After the ANC was unbanned in 1990 he served on a number of its national and regional structures, as well as on municipal services committees.

After the end of apartheid his interest in philately led him to work as a senior manager for the South African Post Office. He unionised the work force, designed stamps, and introduced self-adhesive stamps and standard postage rates. Over the years Franco has volunteered his many talents, including his artistic ability, to organisations like the South African Council of Churches, The Study Project on Christianity in Apartheid Society (SPROCAS), and the Pageview Residents Association. The latter tried to stop the forced removal of the residents of Pageview (Vrededorp), and to stop the physical destruction of the buildings in Pageview. Currently Franco is Professor and Senior Research Associate at the University of KwaZulu-Natal.

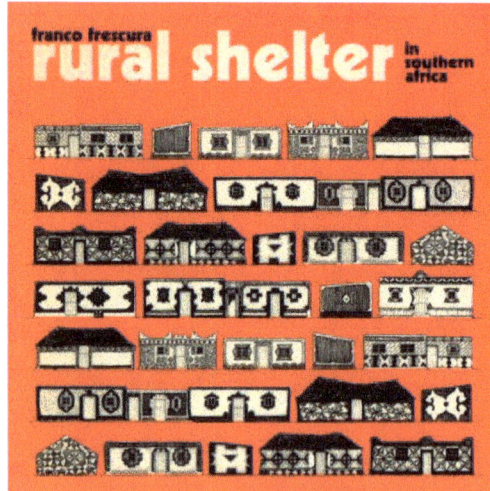

The front cover of Franco's first book, *Rural Shelter in Southern Africa*.

One of Franco's cartoons that was printed in the student newspaper, *Wits Student*. For readers unfamiliar with the face of Vorster, his is the one on the left. Vorster was locked up in an internment camp during World War II because he was a Nazi, as were all of the apartheid prime ministers.

Gough Whitlam was prime minister of Australia from 5 December 1972 until 11 November 1975 when the CIA arranged for him to be dismissed by the Australian governor general, John Kerr. John Kerr worked for the CIA as well as for the British government. Whitlam's commitment to social justice was what upset the CIA. Whitlam brought about far reaching improvements in Australian society during his time as prime minister, improvements that are still having an effect today, like universal health care, fairer funding of schools, Aboriginal land rights, environmental protection legislation, and so on. Subsequent politicians have tried to undo the good that he did, but they have not entirely succeeded.

The brilliant play *Sizwe Banzi is Dead* opened at the Royal Court Theatre in London in January 1974, and as I was in London but about to leave for Canada, I rushed to buy a ticket. There was only one seat available and the ticket lady warned me that it was not in a good position. When I got to the theatre I found that the upper seating curled around the back and sides of the auditorium, and that my seat was at the front on the right. This meant that I had a side-on, bird's-eye view of the stage, and an excellent view of the audience. Some might call it the worst seat in the house, but it suited me perfectly because I could watch the reaction of the audience to the confronting elements of the play. I observed that the London audience did not have a guilty conscience about apartheid, and that John Kani and Winston Ntshona worked on other emotions to provoke a reaction from them. The two seats next to me were the second worst seats in the house, and amazingly they were occupied by Buffy and Di, two London girls who had stayed in the Camps Bay youth hostel while I was there in 1972. It was a joyful reunion.

After the show I went backstage to ask how I could obtain a written copy of the play. John Kani told me that W.H. Smith & Son were selling copies. The W. H. Smith & Son branch that I went to the next morning did not have a copy. At some universities *Sizwe Banzi is Dead* is now a set-work for English literature, along with plays by Arthur Miller and William Shakespeare. *Sizwe Banzi is Dead* was originally created by John Kani, Winston Ntshona, and Athol Fugard without being written down.

Two Australian girls, Di, me, Buffy, Tim, and George on the veranda of the Camp's Bay youth hostel.

John Kani has won many awards, both as an actor and as a playwright, including a Tony Award for *Sizwe Banzi is Dead*. A theatre in Johannesburg has been named after him. He has appeared in more than 25 films, and his theatre work has included Shakespearean plays at Stratford Upon Avon.

Winston Ntshona also won a Tony Award for *Sizwe Banzi is Dead*. He has had a stellar career on the stage, on TV, and in many films, including *The Power of One* (1992) and *Blood Diamond* (2006).

Athol Fugard has written 33 plays and co-authored four, all of them imbued with a cry for social justice. Among his many acting credits he played Jan Smuts in the movie *Ghandi* (1982). He has been awarded six honorary degrees and multiple theatre and writing awards.

Sizwe Banzi poster from 2007.

Peter Kerchhoff was detained for three and a half months in 1986. He was held in solitary confinement and subjected to interrogation, but he was not tortured. The security police did not believe that he was a Christian because he helped the poor.

www.ingramcontent.com/pod-product-compliance
Lightning Source LLC
Chambersburg PA
CBHW061133010526
44107CB00068B/2918